PN
1996
P67
2001

Screen Language

'Invaluable and enjoyable reading for all who are interested in the theory and practice of film' Shane Connaughton, novelist, screenwriter and Oscar nominee (*My Left Foot, The Playboys, The Run of the Country*)

'Cherry Potter teaches us that screenwriting is a fusion of craft and emotion, of structure and passion, and in this book are lessons that I learnt as her student and continue to use every day of my working life' Ashley Pharoah, screen and television writer (*Where the Heart Is, Down to Earth, Life Support, Anchor Me*)

Cherry Potter graduated from the Royal College of Art in 1973. She has written for film, television and theatre. She was Head of Screenwriting at the National Film and Television School, Beaconsfield, for five years, and has taught at the Canadian Centre for Advanced Film Studies and for the EU Media Programme for Training European Screenwriters. She has also run courses on film in many European countries. Currently she is writing *Happily Ever After*, a book about romantic comedies, and has recently completed a novel. She is married to the playwright Brian Clark and lives in Brighton.

D1044411

SCREEN

FROM FILM WRITING TO FILM-MAKING

LANGUAGE

CHERRY POTTER

NSCC, WATERFRONT CAMPUS LIBRARY
80 MAWIO'MI PLACE
DARTMOUTH, NS B2Y 0A5 CANADA

Methuen

Methuen 2001

1 3 5 7 9 10 8 6 4 2

First published in Great Britain in 1990
by Martin Secker & Warburg Limited

This paperback edition published in 2001 by
Methuen Publishing Limited,
215 Vauxhall Bridge Road, London SW1V 1EJ

Copyright © 1990, 2001 Cherry Potter

Cherry Potter has asserted her rights under the Copyright, Designs
and Patents Act, 1988, to be identified as the author of this work

Methuen Publishing Limited Reg. No. 3543167

A CIP catalogue record for this book
is available from the British Library

ISBN 0 413 75290 9

Typeset in Palatino by MATS, Southend-on-Sea, Essex

Printed and bound in Great Britain by
Creative Print and Design (Wales), Ebbw Vale

This book is sold subject to the condition that it shall not, by way
of trade or otherwise, be lent, resold, hired out, or otherwise
circulated in any form of binding or cover other than that in
which it is published and without a similar condition, including
this condition, being imposed on the subsequent purchaser.

For Mary and Percy

Contents

Contents

Preface

How do we tell stories on film? How can we use images and sound to communicate meaning? How can we maximize our creative potential as film writers, producers and directors? These are some of the major questions I address in this book – a new revised edition of *Image Sound and Story*, first published in 1990. Fashions change but these major underlying questions facing film-makers remain the same.

Whilst continuing to celebrate classic works, I have included in this edition some recent films that will go on to influence film-makers of the future. I have used the surgeon's knife, cutting out old, loved material to make way for the new and taken the opportunity to respond to feedback I have received from readers of the previous edition. So, almost half the material in this book is entirely new or consists of new ideas woven into the old.

Screen Language: from Film Writing to Film-making is for anyone who loves film and wants to understand better the language of film and the process of telling stories on film. Learning to understand screen language is also an essential first step for anyone who wants to write for films or make films. For these readers this book can be used as a guide to the process; from the conception of the film idea, through the scripting stage, to the way the images and sounds, sequences and scenes, can be put together on the screen.

The book is divided into four parts. Part One focuses on film in microcosm. The idea of a microcosm is itself inspiring; how can it be that the whole universe is reflected in a grain of sand? Each of the seven microcosms I have chosen to explore, like those grains of sand, offer penetrating insights into the essence of the whole. They provide the opportunity to look at how film can reveal both the exterior world and the interior of an individual's mind through their dreams, memories and fantasies. They also demonstrate the use of metaphor, myth and archetype, which are fundamental to the communication of meaning in any art form.

I decided to expand the chapters on 'Dreams, Memories and Fantasies' and on 'Metaphors and Archetypes' to reflect how the film industry itself has become increasingly aware of the importance of these concepts. I have retained from the first edition much of the original material on the work of the great film maestros: Ingmar Bergman, Bernardo Bertolucci, Orson Welles, etc. Although films such as *Touch of Evil*, *Wild Strawberries* and *The Conformist* were made in the 50s, 60s and 70s, these classic films don't date; they remain as fresh, innovative and exciting in their use of film language as they were when they were first released.

Part Two looks at how the ideas embodied in a film reveal themselves in the structural dynamics of the whole. From the feedback I have received on the first edition I know that the introduction to this section is one of the most marked and used sections of the book. This is because the introduction outlines the basic principles underlying classic storytelling structure; the beginnings, development and endings and how they work – fascinating for anyone interested in storytelling and essential knowledge for anyone wanting to work in film. I have included two new film analyses in this section: Kieslowski's exploration of the nature of love, *A Short Film About Love*, and Greenaway's revenge tragedy, *The Cook, the Thief, His Wife and Her Lover*. Both films are masterpieces and examples of how the basic principles of classic storytelling are as relevant to contemporary film-makers as they have ever been. Tragically, Kieslowski died in 1996. I hope my inclusion of one of his films is a small homage to his great contribution to cinema history.

Part Three focuses on what I call 'Departures from Classic Story Structure'. Many new film-makers think that for a film to be original they must reinvent the form – classic story structure is old hat. I hope my inclusion of Greenaway's *The Cook, the Thief, His Wife and Her Lover* in Part Two will help to dispel this myth. All of 'the departures' I have chosen to explore have been made by film-makers who well understand the classic form and how their 'departure' will affect their audience. Tarantino's *Pulp Fiction* raises issues of post-modernism and of 'departing' from an established genre, in particular the gangster genre. When considering the question of multiple protagonists with conflicting aims I have chosen Mendes' *American Beauty*. As for the question of the woman protagonist, at first it appears that much changed in the decade of post-feminism since the first edition, although the profundity of these changes remains contentious. Gorris's *Antonia's Line*, a recent film made by a woman, explores how over the past 50 years women have changed their circumstances and attitudes towards them, liberating their own forms of creativity. It is also a film which raises interesting questions of how the protagonist's baton can be handed down through the generations. The chapter on Tarkovsky's *Mirror* remains the same, just as the film itself remains one of the most radical 'departures' in cinema history and one of the great films of the twentieth century.

Part Four is another of the most marked and used sections, so I am told by many readers, particularly those who want to write, produce or direct films. This is an exploration of the creative process itself. How do we get in touch with the stories we have to tell? How do ideas, images, characters, sequences, come into being? How do we develop methods of working with both our conscious and unconscious minds? How do we get the material out of our heads and on to paper, and then shape it, develop it and structure it, finally to produce a screenplay ready for the film production process to begin? I have received many reports from readers who tell me how important and useful they have found the practical exercises;

they are fun; they often reveal aspects of yourself and your talent you didn't even know were there; and sometimes they develop into major film projects. I have included in this section a one-minute film exercise inspired by Jane Campion's *Passionless Moments*, a film made when she was a student. Campion has gone on to become a film director respected on the world stage, having made films such as *The Piano* and *Portrait of a Lady*; my best wishes to those readers who aspire to have equally brilliant careers.

Finally a few thoughts on the role of storytelling in our lives. Since people first developed the power of speech, stories have had a central part to play in the life of each individual and, indeed, in the course of humanity itself. Storytelling connects us to our roots, our ancestors, the world around us and our destiny. The best stories cause us to feel the awe of such connection.

Home, which used to be the place where we sat around the fire and told stories, was also the place where, as John Berger put it, 'the vertical line crossed with a horizontal one. The vertical line was a path leading upwards to the sky and downwards to the underworld. The horizontal line represented the traffic of the world, all the possible roads leading across the earth to other places.'* So home, the place where we heard and told stories, was not only our connection with the archetypes – the Gods in the sky above and the ancestors in the ground below – it was also the heart of the family romances where we could gain insight into the intimate dramas of our daily lives, and it was the place of intersection, where we reflected on what we discovered about the world through travellers' tales told by returning voyagers.

Everything appears to have changed in the modern world. Home for many of us is merely the place where we happen to be living and our communities, and in some cases families, also change, sometimes with bewildering frequency, in our mobile global lives. Our connection with the world is instant via news-

*John Berger, *And our faces, my heart, brief as photos* (Writers and Readers, 1984)

papers, books, the telephone, film, television and the internet. The traditional spoken roots of storytelling appear to have largely died out in the western world. Or have they? Gossip, urban myths, stories about what is happening to ourselves, our friends, our family, our colleagues, celebrities, news stories which may or may not be true, serious documentary investigations into cases of injustice or attempts to discover the root causes of a tragedy, fun stories, jokes, speculations about the future and the past – our lives are saturated with stories. We rely as much on storytelling for an understanding of the world and the complexity of our exterior and interior lives as we ever did. The underlying magic of storytelling remains central to our lives. Film, as a hybrid of all the other art forms and a unique language in its own right, is the universal storytelling medium and as such one of the most profound art forms of our times.

In examining the films in this book I have chosen to describe what actually happens on screen, rather than using the original screenplays. This is because screenplays are blueprints for a film and don't include all the elements of screen language which we want to learn about here. Some of the screenplays have been published and are, of course, valuable for further study. Most of the films I have used should be available on video or DVD, although some of the older films may not be in your local library and may demand a more thorough search using your national film, video and DVD facilities – for instance, Movie Mail supply by post any video or DVD in print in the UK and specialise in foreign-language and classic films. Their website is www.moviem.co.uk and their address is PO Box 220, Hereford, HR1 2ZH, UK.

One FILM IN MICROCOSM

Introduction

A microcosm is a miniature representation which encapsulates the essence of a larger whole. My dictionary uses the example of man epitomising the universe. And it is often noted how similar the atom, with its nucleus and circling electrons, is to the solar system itself – the ultimate microcosm. There is something profound and quite magical about a microcosm because it implies the infinite.

Many feature films can be seen in their totality as microcosms. But the film microcosms I am referring to here are some of the component sequences. One of the things that distinguish great films from the run-of-the-mill is how some sequences also function as microcosms – little stories within the whole which inspire a sense of profound insight into the nature of life itself.

Most of us have seen so much film drama, often of indifferent quality, on television that we have become almost desensitized to the medium. We have become lazy and think of film simply in terms of entertaining linear stories which hold our attention because we want to know what is going to happen next. When that question is finally answered there is little more to think about and the film is quickly forgotten. Because of the prevalence of this mediocre form of the medium, which is like a drug and encourages a passive conformity in the viewer, we have learnt many bad habits almost by osmosis. To combat this we need to re-examine the very basics of film language and consider the medium as if we have never experienced it before. This will be the first step in raising our sensitivity to film.

Ingmar Bergman, one of the great film maestros of the twentieth century, said, 'The primary factor in film is the image, the secondary factor is the sound, the dialogue, and the tension between these two creates the third dimension' Ingmar Bergman.* By his use of 'the third dimension' here, Bergman is suggesting far more than creating something that is an imitation of life, he is talking about how image and sound, the two basic ingredients of screen language, can combine together, in some sort of alchemical transformation, to transcend our everyday mundane assumptions about space and time and create something closer to the *essence* of life. It is this fascination with the magical aspect of the film experience that is so exciting; this is what makes us want to see films and to make films.

Note how Bergman gave primary importance to the image and secondary importance to the sound, of which only a part is dialogue. By this he is not saying that the dialogue is not important, because of course it is. But he is saying that dialogue doesn't usually lie at the heart of the magic of the film experience, it isn't intrinsic to the basic language of film.

Most of the microcosms I have chosen to explore have a bare minimum of dialogue. This will enable us to learn about film language by focusing primarily on how the images and sounds are communicating. The relationship between the film-maker and us, via the film, is of course very complex. On the one hand, we must bear in mind that most of what we see and hear on the celluloid has been put there as a result of a conscious or subconscious decision by the film-maker. But we must also remember to experience fully the film moment itself, as we do when we are members of a cinema audience, only now we must attend far more closely than usual to each and every one of our reactions. For each 'film-phrase' we must ask ourselves, what is this making me feel? And at the same time we must ask

*John Simon, *Ingmar Bergman Directs* (Harcourt Brace Jovanovich, 1972)

4

ourselves, what is this prompting me to think? And what do I think this means? The next stage in the process is to consider what it is on film that has caused this response, or, specifically, what image and sound, separate or in combination, has caused the effect on us as audience? In this way we will find ourselves discovering the essence of the language of film.

1 What's Going on Out There in the World?

Welles' *Touch of Evil* and Goretta's *The Lacemaker*

The world is a vast and complicated place. In an attempt to understand it we break it down into a constantly shifting mass of interlocking social, political and personal structures: continents, countries, nations, states, politicians, unions, workers, unemployed, husbands, wives, parents, children, to mention just a few. Most of us spend much of our lives caught up in a turmoil of conflicts and power struggles between these groups and sub-groups and the individuals who are either upholding or subverting their interests as they attempt to communicate with each other and pursue their wants and needs and make their way in the world.

The positions people take, either consciously or unconsciously, in relation to the fray represent their moral stance or their life view. What they believe in will be manifest in their actions and the resulting consequences.

Making connections, seeing patterns in a section of this seething mass of humanity, exploring how characters relate to each other and rise and fall, is often a central theme of film drama, although it's sometimes only during the actual process of creating the artefact, deciding on the character to identify with and working through their dilemma, that the writer discovers precisely what it is that he or she has to say.

Montage in film means the juxtaposition of images that each have a separate meaning within themselves, an additional meaning when one image is added to another, and a cumulative meaning which arises from the sequence of images as a

6

whole. A story, in essence, is an exploration of a character in conflict and a sequence of events as they attempt to resolve the conflict. In film, as well as in storytelling, sequences of images also function like sequences of words in poetry – they arouse feeling and suggest meaning according to the way they are presented and ordered, and according to the rhythm, flow and accumulation of associations.

Repetition is as important as surprise. The audience needs time to absorb and reflect on what they are experiencing. Piecing together meanings which arise from separate but connected images is a gradual process. In narrative cinema the audience brings with them expectations of how the story should function based on all the stories they have ever seen and heard. The search for familiar reference points is an automatic part of their experience as they try to work out what is going on. This means that the film-maker must decide how the audience's expectations relate to what he or she is trying to communicate.

Sound is not just dialogue, it is everything you hear on the soundtrack including music and sound effects. Sound can be used in many different ways: to work in harmony with the image; to intensify or clarify a feeling or meaning; to give a sense of place; to counterpoint with the image by suggesting quite a different agenda; and to build an expectation of things to come.

The first of the two film microcosms we are going to explore in this chapter is the opening of Orson Welles' *Touch of Evil.* I've chosen this sequence because Welles is directing our attention towards the exterior social and political world. His use of image and sound to piece together a few of the ingredients of a conflict taking place between sub-groupings of the kind mentioned above illustrates not only the way his creative mind works but also the essence of a set of film-language conventions which have since become a familiar part of the American cinema.

TOUCH OF EVIL (1958)
Written and directed by Orson Welles
(Based on a novel by Whit Masterson)

Although I have broken my description down into sections, so we can consider the function and effect of each image, the entire opening sequence of *Touch of Evil* is one continuous unbroken shot and technically an extraordinary feat.

1. Black screen. As the screen gradually lightens we see an object move out of the darkness towards us. We realize that we are looking at a dark buttoned jacket around a man's midriff and the object which he holds in his hands. The object seems to be made up of a dial or timing mechanism on one side and batteries on the other. The man's fingers are carefully making an adjustment on the dial.

– Our first thought, as the object emerges out of the darkness, is 'what's that?'. We are then given the chance to examine it while the dial is being adjusted and we slowly realize that it's a homemade bomb. We immediately become alert; something dangerous is going to happen. Our first question is quickly replaced by two more: 'who is the man?' and 'what is he going to do with the bomb?'

2. We hear the sound of a couple laughing in the distance and are swung sharply round with the bomb as the man turns towards the sound. We now move away from the bomb to find the source of the laughter and see, from the man's point of view, that it's night, we're in a badly lit, down-at-heel town precinct and we're facing a long arched walkway where the couple, a man and a woman, are walking towards us in the middle distance. They turn and disappear from view under an arch on the side of the walkway. The man with the bomb darts stealthily across our path to enable him to see where the couple are heading.

8

– Notice how sound is used here to shift our attention. The distant laughter, which broke the silence of the opening image, combined with the sudden movement of the bomb, as the man swung round in reaction to the sound, gives the couple such importance that they replace the bomb as the focus of our attention. We also now have the opportunity to get an initial sense of our location, although it could be almost any town, anywhere. The couple are too far in the distance for us to get a sense of their identity and the man's movements are too fleeting for us to experience him as more than a dark, male presence.

3. The man darts back across the walkway and runs through an adjoining archway. We track along the archway wall, watching the man's shadow as it flits menacingly across an array of old peeling posters. We find him again, now in a nearly deserted parking lot beneath a skyline broken by distant, scattered buildings. He runs to a parked car, a gleaming American convertible, ducks down, opens the boot, places the bomb inside it and runs away. The music begins; at first a percussive Latin rhythm which is then overlaid with the full sound of a brass section carving out the theme as we are propelled up into a high shot of the gleaming convertible. The couple, a young blonde woman in an evening dress and an older man, walk into shot, get into the car and drive out of the parking lot. The opening titles begin.

– As soon as the couple disappear from view our attention is again drawn by movement to the man with the bomb. The image of his shadow flitting across the wall of peeling posters gives him a sense of menace and, by association, suggests that he is a part of a shadowy, sleazy underworld. The shiny convertible is the only sign of wealth in the vicinity. The straightforward action of placing the bomb in the boot of the convertible answers one of our questions, 'what is the man going to do with the bomb?' But we haven't been shown the man's face, or a single identifiable feature, before he runs away

9

and so our other question, 'who is he?', remains unanswered. The music, which begins at this point, contains two distinct characteristics: first the Latin rhythm, which is reminiscent of a bomb ticking, and second the big sound of the brass section which feels in keeping with the sleazy underworld hinted at by the images. Finally, the couple, who distracted our attention from the bomb in the opening images, become fatally linked with the bomb when they get into the convertible (note how we still only see them in long-shot and so are prevented from getting to know them as individuals) and the drama is set up – we know there is a bomb in the boot of their car but they don't, the bomb is on a time switch and, as they drive out of the parking lot, a countdown to death has begun.

4. The convertible drives out of the parking lot, through the arched walkway and into what turns out to be a busy street outside. It is halted by a policeman while pedestrians and a flower vendor wheeling his stall cross its path. It travels further down the street where it is halted for a second time to enable more pedestrians to cross. This time we move in to focus on two of the pedestrians, a new couple (Charlton Heston and Janet Leigh), as they reach the near side of the road. The man turns to glance curiously at the convertible as it passes and drives out of sight. Our attention now stays with the new couple as we watch them, talking and laughing, as they stroll happily down the street, the man with his arm placed comfortably around the woman's shoulders.

– We are surprised by the busy normality of the street outside, so close to the scene of the crime. The image of the convertible being stopped by a policeman to let pedestrians cross seems ironic; the upholder of law and order unwittingly so close to the crime. The irony is further emphasized by the sight of the flower vendor, suggesting the innocence of a community unaware of the danger that's in their midst.

It's also worth noting how the convertible is stopped twice

and it's the second time that our attention shifts to the new couple. If the car had only been stopped once we would not have had time to register the ironies mentioned above because we would still be trying to work out who the new couple are and what role they will have to play in the course of events. The reason we are giving them such significance is that they are the first characters we've met with individual identities; we can see their faces, which means we can begin to get to know them as we watch their enjoyment of each other's company as they walk along the busy street.

The moment when our focus is shifted from the convertible to the new couple is interesting, too, because the man glances curiously at the car. This glance connects him in some way to the car, although we don't yet know why – which is not unlike the way the bomb and the first couple were connected in the opening two shots. So now both couples are connected to the bomb.

5. The second couple arrive at the end of the street where there is an international border crossing. They walk past the first customs post, marked by sentry boxes and black and white car barriers, and head for the second. As they approach the customs officials, the convertible, coincidentally, draws alongside them. The couple in the car wait while the customs official questions the couple on foot.

> CUSTOMS OFFICIAL
> Are you folks American citizens?
> SUSAN
> Yes.
> CUSTOMS OFFICIAL
> Where were you born Miss?
> SUSAN
> Mrs. Philadelphia.
> Vargas hands the Customs Official two passports.
> VARGAS
> The name is Vargas.

The Customs Official reacts to this information by calling to the man in the car, which is still waiting behind.

> CUSTOMS OFFICIAL
>
> Hey Jim, did you hear that?
>
> MAN IN THE CAR
>
> Sure, Mr Vargas. Out on the trail of another dope ring?
>
> VARGAS
>
> On the trail of a chocolate soda for my wife.

Vargas takes Susan's hand and leads her away as the Customs Official reacts to the news of his marriage in surprise.

> MAN IN THE CAR
>
> (*Growing impatient about the hold up*) Hey, can I get through?

A Second Customs Official approaches as the Vargases pass by on the other side of the car.

> SECOND CUSTOMS OFFICIAL
>
> There's been a lot of talk up here about how you cracked that Grandee business. Hear you caught the big boss.
>
> VARGAS
>
> Only one of them, the Grandees are a big family.

Mr and Mrs Vargas walk away and the two Customs Officials turn their attention to the occupants of the car.

> CUSTOMS OFFICIAL
>
> Any purchases Miss? Are you an American citizen?
>
> WOMAN IN CAR
>
> Hey, I've got this ticking in my head.

The convertible drives away through the raised barrier.

> No really, I've got this ticking in my head.

– So, we're in a divided town, a border town, and the two couples arrive at the same place at the same time with the bomb, of course, ticking away in the boot of the convertible.

The dialogue is mainly exposition, which means that it refers to events that have happened before the film opens: important information for our developing understanding of the story. One of the basic skills writers need to develop for this kind of drama is how to weave expositional information into the dramatic action so that it doesn't stick out like a sore thumb but appears to be an intrinsic and natural part of the activity. In this case we conveniently have a customs official on hand whose job it is to ask the questions we happen to want to know the answer to, and who happens to have heard of Mr Vargas. This is both plausible and helpful for putting over the exposition. We learn that the Vargases are newly-weds, that Mr Vargas is a well-known law-enforcer who recently cracked a drug ring and that some important members of the ring are still at large – a foreboding of things to come. Vargas and the driver of the convertible appear to be further connected by the subject of the drug racket.

Finally, as the two couples go their separate ways, we're firmly reminded of the presence of the bomb in the boot because the woman in the convertible complains about the ticking in her head, although no one appears to be listening to her. This reminder feels opportune. The dialogue has contained a complicated agenda and, because we are trying to piece together a picture of these characters, the world they inhabit and what the dilemma at the heart of the story is going to be, we have been in danger of forgetting about the bomb and so need to be reminded for dramatic effect.

6. We track in to find Mr and Mrs Vargas walking together on the far side of the road.

SUSAN
Mike, do you realize this is the first time we will have been together in my country?
VARGAS
Do you realize that I haven't kissed you in over an hour?
Vargas and his wife embrace. Just as their lips meet we hear the explosion. They turn and we cut to the convertible, now

a mass of flames and raised momentarily in the air from the force of the explosion.

– With our reminder of the time-bomb ticking away its countdown to death we move in to watch the Vargases walking happily, arm-in-arm, on the other side of the street. The danger we feel from the bomb is transferred, via the image, from the couple in the convertible to the newly-weds. We learn that they are, for the first time, about to enter the wife's country (the border is also a divide between them) and the husband responds by wanting to kiss her. We would be forgiven for interpreting 'my country' as the wife's sexuality although we know she is literally referring to America. We could also be forgiven for thinking of her sexuality as maybe a dangerous place, as we transfer the thought of the time-bomb ticking away towards an explosion, on to her image.

The explosion takes place just as they embrace. The climax which we have been building towards since the opening image finally arrives with terrifying ferocity. The explosion breaks the kiss, literally separating the newly-weds. The sudden cut from the kiss to the explosion is also the first cut in the film and as such breaks the steady dramatic build-up of the continuous sequence and concludes the first part of the opening. We are now left with a crime to be solved in the form of the question 'who placed the bomb?', and a protagonist whose job we know it is to solve crimes and who has recently broken into a drug ring leaving some important members still at large. The danger has now been transferred to Susan and Vargas's marriage.

The incident of a car bomb going off on an international border crossing is unquestionably the stuff of drama and Welles has exploited his subject to great effect. But does drama always have to be so explicitly dramatic? The stuff of drama is happening in all of our lives for much of the time, if we only choose to value it as deserving of our attention. Earlier I mentioned that, in essence, it only takes one or more characters and a conflict or dilemma to make a story. Whether it will be a 'good' story or not will depend on the individual insight of the teller and the universality of the dilemma. The microcosm we are going to explore next, which illustrates this point, is a short sequence from *The Lacemaker*, a film by Swiss film-maker Claude Goretta. What is especially interesting in this sequence is how Goretta uses image and action, mainly focusing on simple gesture and body language, to show us all we need to know about a relationship between two young people. The resulting sequence is remarkable for its simplicity. The sequence is taken from two-thirds of the way into the film. As far as actual incident is concerned all you really need to know about the story so far is that Béatrice, a shy self-effacing girl who works in a hairdressing salon, has met and fallen in love with François, a young university student, while they were both on holiday. We have also been introduced to a rhythm, pace and atmosphere which draw our attention to those small and delicate moments between people which can have such a devastating effect on their lives. When we join the story the young couple have been living together in Paris for a number of months.

THE LACEMAKER (*La Dentellière*, 1977)
Directed by Claude Goretta
Screenplay written by Claude Goretta and Pascal Lainé
(Based on a novel by Pascal Lainé)

Sequence from two-thirds into the film

1. It is evening and we are in the living room of a student's apartment. François is sitting with a student friend, a young woman wearing a black jumper, who is reading aloud from a book while François listens.

> YOUNG WOMAN
> This is why the phenome coincides not with a

concrete phonic image but with its phonologically pertinent characteristics.

FRANÇOIS

Could you read that again please?

François' girlfriend, Béatrice (Isabelle Huppert), wearing a simple white blouse, is at the other side of the room, ironing. As François' student friend repeats what she has just read, we watch Béatrice glance briefly at the two of them while she irons. She doesn't appear to have any comprehension of what they are studying.

– François and his student friend are seated close together, and although there is no hint of a physical intimacy between them their physical proximity suggests an intellectual intimacy that excludes Béatrice. Her exclusion is further emphasized by her position in the room behind the ironing board, which acts like a barrier between her and them. There's also a striking visual contrast between the two young women; the student in her black jumper looks strong, independent, experienced. In contrast, Béatrice, in her white blouse, looks shy, self-effacing and innocent. As for the choice of study matter, it's not only incomprehensible to young hairdressers, it will also be incomprehensible to most of the audience. Goretta has chosen an example of academic jargon far removed from everyday life, particularly, in this case, from simple tasks like doing the ironing. But Béatrice, judging by her innocent glance at the two of them, doesn't have any insight into the substance, or lack of it, of what they are discussing. All she knows is that she doesn't understand.

2. Cut to a busy Paris street, shot from above. There is a traffic island in the middle of the street and some pedestrians crossing. We can just make out that one of the pedestrians is François. He sees that the second half of the road is clear and makes a dash for it. He reaches the other side and stops to look back. We follow his look and can just make out Béatrice, left behind on the far side of the road.

She manages to reach the centre island and there she gets stuck behind another sudden rush of traffic. We cut to street level and Béatrice's point of view of François as he waits impatiently for her on the far side of the road. We can tell by her expression and stance that she's embarrassed and anxious about holding him up. We then cut to Béatrice from François' point of view; she keeps trying to get across the road but the passing cars and lorries continually block her path. Eventually the road clears and Béatrice runs anxiously across to join him. But François doesn't wait to greet her, instead he turns away just before her arrival, forcing her to run to keep up with him.

– The scene opens with a high shot which prevents us from identifying with either of the characters. The shot instead invites us to think about the different ways each of them handles the hustle and bustle of daily life and the effect this difference is having on their relationship. In other words the way they cross the road together has become a metaphor for the state of their relationship. François skilfully negotiates the dangers as he hurries on his way, anxious to arrive at his destination and irritated by Béatrice who seems to be slowing him down and holding him back. Béatrice, who normally prefers a slower pace because of her timidity in the face of the hurly-burly of modern life, is trying to rush to keep up with him, ever anxious to please him, but she's trying to force herself to move at a pace that's not naturally her own. The speed of the passing traffic increases the sense of her being in danger.

Next we join the two characters at street level. By shifting the position of the camera we plunge back into experiencing directly the effect the characters are having on each other, identifying with them both in their mutual dilemma because of the point-of-view shots. We see François' impatience with Béatrice, and, because we are seeing it from Béatrice's point of view, we know that she sees it too; she sees that he really wants to rush away from her and is waiting only out of a sense of duty and guilt. Consequently we feel her hurt. We then see Béatrice from François' point of view; inept, timid, unable to keep up with him. Now we have some insight into his dilemma too. But at the end of the scene, when Béatrice, with childlike pleasure in a difficult task fulfilled, succeeds in crossing the road, François impatiently turns away from her. We now feel her hurt at his rebuff and, because the scene ends on Béatrice, we finally make a moral judgement based on our experience of her feeling; her innocence doesn't deserve his injury.

3. It is night and we are in François' and Béatrice's bedroom. The room is gently lit by a bedside lamp. Béatrice is sitting on the bed, with her back to us, unhooking her bra strap. She takes off her bra and hangs it carefully over a chair. She stands. She's completely naked. She walks shyly over to join François, who we now see is standing, fully dressed, with his back to her, looking out of the window at the night. Béatrice silently joins him by the window. They stand side by side, with their backs to us, without moving or touching. Her naked body looks young and vulnerable next to his fully-clothed figure. The soft lamp gently lights her skin and she looks more like an innocent offering than a sexual being. Eventually François moves his head very slightly, half glancing down at her and he moves his arm to rest his hand lightly on the back of her neck. Béatrice, taking this as a sign of acceptance, moves her own arm up and rests her hand tentatively on the small of his back. François takes his hand away from her neck and lets it drop again by his side. Béatrice looks up at him. Getting no response, she turns and walks back to the bed. Her naked body is turned fully towards us here; unselfconsciously beautiful, innocent and rejected. She sits on the bed and puts on her white nightdress. François still doesn't move from his position with his back to her by the window. Béatrice's head slumps down as she waits.

– In the street scene we saw and felt the danger that Béatrice was

18

in. Here we see that she still hopes that what is going wrong in their relationship will prove to be a passing phase. They are in the bedroom, a place where distance is felt all the more acutely because it is the place of greatest intimacy. She undresses, goes to the window and silently offers herself to him. Self-effacing as ever she makes no demands, she simply waits, hoping he will receive her gift of herself and hoping he will give her the intimacy and reassurance she so badly needs. We know, from the two previous scenes, that there is a fundamental incompatibility between these two young people, yet, because the scene opens on Béatrice, because we go with her action, her gesture of hope, and because throughout the scene François has his back to her and us, we wait, hope and feel with Béatrice. Her innocence and vulnerability is felt all the more keenly because of her nudity in contrast to his dark clothes and stiff demeanour. By the time he moves his arm to touch her neck we so identify with her that we too can almost feel the touch and the hope it gives, shooting through her like an electric current. But, because we have a greater insight into Béatrice's predicament than she has herself (as a result of our experiencing her from François' point of view in the previous scene), we suspect that this is a false hope. Our suspicions add to the poignancy of the moment because we want to be proved wrong.

A few seconds later our suspicions are confirmed, Béatrice's hopes are dashed. The bravery that her trip to the window took has achieved nothing. As the scene ends she is as still and silent as he is and they are both looking away from each other and from us. They appear locked into the distance between them. When Béatrice's head finally slumps down we realize she is aware of the extent of her defeat.

The danger we feel Béatrice is in, planted in our minds in the street scene, is emphasized by her almost unbearable vulnerability in this scene. The last point of hope is dashed when François takes his tentative hand away from her neck. His rejection of her feels inevitable but, given the innocence with which Béatrice has given herself so completely, leads us to ask, 'How will she cope with his rejection?'

Although in almost every way this sequence seems like the polar opposite of *Touch of Evil*, the use of film language is similar. In both sequences the dramatic build-up is through image and action, not words. Both sequences are simple and direct and go straight to the heart of the matter. Both show how much can be communicated by the physical proximity of people and their gestures. In both we know more about the protagonists' predicament than they do themselves. In *Touch of Evil* only we and the mystery man who planted the bomb know it is there. We want to warn the characters in danger, but of course we can't. In *The Lacemaker* the strength our feeling for Béatrice results from our having a greater understanding of her situation than she has herself. We want her to realize enough in time to save herself, although we know that this is beyond her capability.

Drama is as much about the predictable as it is about the unpredictable; most dramas are, after all, about familiar predicaments. Our fascination and ability to engage at a meaningful level lies not so much with the predicament itself as with the very particular nature or uniqueness of the predicament as it is portrayed. This is what causes us to see it as if for the very first time.

2 Dreams, Memories and Fantasies

Bergman's *Wild Strawberries*, Bertolucci's *The Conformist* and the Taviani Brothers' *Kaos*

How do we know when we are watching a film whether we are in the interior world of the characters or whether what we are watching is their present experience of their exterior reality? Once we are identified with a character we often take for granted the apparently seamless transition from seeing how a character is acting and responding in the world to experiencing the inner recesses of their imagination. We happily share a character's dreams, memories, fantasies and even their drug-induced hallucinations or mad delusions, without wondering how we *know* we are in their mind. But this is not a question any experienced film-maker takes for granted. Portraying on screen inner states of mind involves the most complex use of film language and unless film-makers find a way of signalling what is going on, the subsequent confusion may frustrate and alienate their audience. Film-makers also know that the solutions are not merely a matter of employing a few technical tricks – soft-focus images, cutting to sepia or black and white or employing weird sound effects. Just as our experience of dreams, memories and fantasies in our own inner imaginative world is quite different from our everyday exterior reality, the challenge for film-makers is to explore and reflect this difference.

The most exciting and productive way to begin to explore dreams, memories and fantasies is *not* to look at the work of film-makers but to use ourselves as our resource data. What are dreams, memories and fantasies? How can we tell the difference between a dream, a memory or a fantasy and our experience of exterior reality in our own lives? These questions might at first appear simple, the answers obvious – but are they?

When I ask students to discuss these questions the atmosphere in the room usually becomes increasingly heated and animated. The more we attempt to erect boundaries in order to define what each experience is, the more the boundaries appear blurred, inadequate, or a simplistic imposition on the complex nature of our experience. On the other hand, breaking free from the confines of observable, exterior reality and sharing the stuff of our dreams, memories and fantasies is exciting. The excitement is intensified by accompanying feelings of danger; the stuff of our imaginations – where our dreams, memories and fantasies reside – often feels only vaguely understood and usually beyond our control. Our imaginations lack the defences we have erected to protect us in our shared experience. We risk exposure. What might happen if we let slip intimate embarrassing details about our inner life that others might understand better than we do ourselves? And what if we become engulfed by the dark side of the experiences – nightmares, traumatic memories we have struggled to repress, fearful fantasies of horror and destruction? Once we start delving into the workings of the imagination we become increasingly aware of what feels like a mire of confusion at the levels of both content and form; we become closer to the demon chaos. The dictionary defines chaos as the disordered, formless matter supposed to have existed before the ordered universe. Our notions of order and reality are relatively recent constructions built on shifting sands. Dreams, memories and fantasies reside in our unconscious and by moving us closer to that formless matter can threaten to engulf us in a kind of madness or, as has been the case for many artists, prove to be the source of creative inspiration.

Dreams, memories and fantasies manifest themselves in a very similar language to the language of film. Film time is compressed time: an experience that may have lasted for years, weeks or hours is communicated in minutes or seconds of screen-time because only the essential ingredients of the experience are selected for communication. This process of selection and editing also takes place in our imaginations. So, by looking at dreams, memories and fantasies we will be further penetrating the nature of film itself.

If we at first attempt to explore the experiences by category we must distinguish dreams that happen when we are asleep from daydreams or aspirational dreams, which we will place in the category of fantasies. Dreams are like little films that appear in our sleep when we visit our own private cinemas and we usually play the lead in all the shows. Like stories they frequently have a sense of progression, moving towards a climactic moment which sometimes causes us to wake up and take note, often with strong feelings that we don't fully understand. The transitions between scenes, incidents and images in dreams usually transcend everyday logic. In dreams we can open a prison door and find ourselves by a raging sea or flying across a desert. Meanings are hinted at obliquely and, like works of art, ask to be understood via metaphoric, symbolic or associative connotations. It is here where we find the crucial insights into the state of our conscious lives, insights which can illuminate the nature of our present predicaments. The cast of characters who appear in our dreams, sometimes including friends or family, do not have a life separate from us as they do in reality, instead they reflect our unconscious projections on to them, they are our internalized 'others' showing us our anxieties, fears and desires. Dreams are also about our struggle for unity; we are every element in our dream and by pointing to our centre they show us the imbalances in our equilibrium. In this sense the role of dreams is similar to the role of much storytelling, which is also about exploring imbalances and conflicts in the struggle for unity.

Of course we only know about our dreams when we wake up and, if we are lucky, we can catch them by the tail and pull them back into our consciousness. Although the sensation following a nightmare is often the reverse; we wake up with it fully in our minds as if the nightmare has penetrated the very reality surrounding us as we struggle to rid ourselves of the fearful images and feelings of terror. But, whether a dream or a nightmare, the experience is known only through the sieve of our memory. As with all memories, we retain bits of what we believe the experience was, we lose bits and we even make bits up and then sometimes become unsure about what was true and what was a later invention or element of fantasy.

When first considering the difference between dreams and memories the issue of control usually arises; many people think that, unlike their dreams, they have control over their memories. Others dispute this saying they can control their dreams sometimes; they become conscious that they are dreaming and will themselves to wake up and even to re-enter the dream when they are ready. Similarly with memory, we can all of us will a memory into our minds but often, as we move through our daily life, an image, a smell, a sound or a situation will suddenly trigger a memory and we find ourselves caught up in it almost unawares. The experience of memory can feel more powerful, more resonant with strong feelings and a sense of meaning, than our experience of exterior reality. Although perhaps the notion of 'reality' is now beginning to break down, so permeated is it by our memories and fantasies; after all our memory may be dwelling on what happened just a few moments ago and our fantasy already beginning to toy with ideas of what might happen in a few moments' time.

One of the defining attributes of memory is that it is necessarily rooted in a past event. It is also very selective; we remember only what was significant to us at the time, although some details, which may themselves seem irrelevant to the 'story', can take on a special resonance; the pattern on the wallpaper, a child's toy left forgotten in the hall or the refraction of light in the bathroom mirror. It is often these details which generate the strongest sensations and feelings. Similarly with stories, the quality of storytelling lies in the resonance of the details.

As we have noted, the boundaries between memory and fantasy can become blurred in the imagination depending on the reason why we are remembering; whether our primary desire is to reach subjective truth or whether it is to reassure our egos. Most memories involve a combination of these two desires. But certain traumatic memories, which may throw our understanding of who we are into confusion or distress, become repressed by a kind of self-defence mechanism. When a repressed memory is unlocked (which is fundamental to the psychoanalytic process) it has a profound effect, although if processed properly this effect can take on the form of a kind of exorcism. This sense of exorcism, through uncovering and re-experiencing a past trauma, is crucial to much storytelling; it is Aristotle's 'catharsis', the cleansing which he saw as the effect of tragic drama (which we shall discuss later in the introduction to Part Two).

The exploration of fantasy often begins with the simple distinction that, whereas memories are about the past, fantasies are about the future. Although usually someone points out that they also fantasize about what they wish they had said or done in a past event. Maybe then fantasies are about wish fulfilment? Sexual fantasies come to mind; the perfect love-making with a stranger seen only briefly in the street, or aspirational fantasies – when you make that brilliant speech at the Cannes Film Festival, or you wear the stunning dress to the ball. The issue of control comes up again; whereas most of us don't feel in control of our dreams and we feel only partially in control of our memories, we are definitely in control of our fantasies – or are we? Wish fulfilment or desire also has its dark side, such as wanting to punish, or to express all the anger we don't dare to express in real life, or even to kill. How much are we in control of these fantasies? Or do they well up from deep within us, like our nightmares and traumatic memories? Fear fantasies also lurk beneath the surface of most of our personae: fears of the unknown future, death, Armageddon, murderers, rapists, monsters in the dark, fears of our own violent or vengeful feelings becoming unleashed – this dark side is as much a part of our fantasies as is sexual bliss or the final achievement of our goals.

It is through our fantasies that we explore, from the relative safety of our own imaginations, our most secret fears and desires – in our fantasies we can become anyone and do anything. It is but a small step from here to understanding one of the roles storytelling, in particular film, plays in our lives. Films are often categorized into genres in order to help us select the kind of fantasy we wish to indulge: horror, romance, sex, thriller, science fiction, adventure, etc. Although, of course, many classic films, like much literary fiction, transcend genre classification. But, as I said earlier, the source of much of our creative inspiration, whether or not we want to confine our form of expression to a genre formula, lies in this deeply personal interior world.

Finally, we must remember that our understanding of ourselves (and consequently our understanding of dreams, memories and fantasies) is, like film language, in a constant state of evolution and change.

A DREAM
WILD STRAWBERRIES (Smultronstället, 1957)
Written and directed by Ingmar Bergman

Opening sequence

1. Old Professor Borg sits alone in his comfortable, old-fashioned study with his dog sleeping at his feet. As he thoughtfully smokes a cigar, we hear the following voice-over:

> PROFESSOR (*voice-over*)
> Our contact with others consists mainly of discussion when we evaluate the character and conduct of our neighbour. That is why I have refrained of my own free will from almost all so-called social life. Yes, I've kept myself to myself for most of the time. The days of my life have been filled by hard work and I'm

grateful for it. First I worked to earn a living, then it developed into a love of science.

We see framed photographs of the Professor's family while he goes on to tell us about each of them.

My son is a doctor too. He lives in Lund. He's been married for years. There are no children of the marriage. My mother is still alive and sprightly in spite of her great age. My wife Karen has been dead for many years.

Professor Borg's Housekeeper appears briefly at the door.

HOUSEKEEPER

Dinner is served Professor Borg.

PROFESSOR *(voice-over cont.)*

I am privileged to have a good housekeeper.

He stands to go to dinner but first tidies his already immaculate desk.

Perhaps I should add that I am very punctilious, a quality that has made life quite trying sometimes both for myself . . .

He walks to the door, and we see the framed photo of his son in the background.

. . . and those about me.

The Professor clicks his fingers and his dog wakes and slowly gets to its feet.

My name is Eberhard Isak Borg. I am 78 years old. Tomorrow in Lund Cathedral there'll be a ceremony; the 50th anniversary of my graduation.

The dog and his master leave the study. Fade to black. We hear music, an orchestral score, over the credits which are white on black.

– We are just a few minutes into the film and already we feel that we know Professor Borg intimately. We can also detect the area of conflict which tells us what the film is to be about. Bergman, in his usual direct and economical manner, has achieved this quite simply by having his character introduce himself to us. The effect of this introduction is not at all theatrical because although Professor Borg's words are in first-person voice-over narration they are in the past tense – while he tells us about himself we see him alone in his study unaware of our watching presence.

He tells us that he is isolated through choice (he's above normal social intercourse which he believes to be idle gossip); he has a scientific (i.e. rational) mind; he's grateful for the discipline of hard work; he's obsessively tidy and although he's aware that this has caused problems (the image connects this with his son whose photo we see in the background here), he has no intention of modifying his character to suit others, which suggests that others have tried to get him to change and failed. The few members of his family are neatly framed on his desk and although there are no grandchildren to carry on the family lineage and his wife is long dead, the Professor seems quite smugly self-satisfied.

We have to ask ourselves why Bergman has chosen to give us these particular facts from Professor Borg's long life. The theme which connects each item of information is order and control. The Professor is a man of reason, not emotion, and appears to have his life neatly pigeon-holed. But something out of the ordinary is about to happen. The very next day is the 50th anniversary of his graduation, to be held in Lund, the town where his son lives. As the credits roll we ask ourselves the question, 'How could this important anniversary affect the Professor's well-ordered life?'

2. After the credits we see the Professor asleep in bed.

PROFESSOR BORG *(voice-over)*
In the early morning of Sunday June 1st I had an odd and most disagreeable dream. I dreamt that I was taking my morning walk but I had lost my way in a strange part of town. The streets were deserted, the houses were dilapidated.

The Professor is walking through the deserted streets in the brilliant early morning sunshine. He stops and looks up at a large clock hanging, like a shop sign, on the side of a building. The clock has no hands. Beneath the clock hangs a huge pair of spectacles with eyes painted on the lenses. One of the painted eyes seems to be bleeding. Professor Borg takes out his pocket watch and sees that it also has no hands. He puts the watch away, looks back up at the clock, takes off his hat and mops his brow anxiously. We can hear his heart beating. He moves out of the sun into the shade and leans unsteadily against the wall.

– Bergman tells us, in the most straightforward way possible, that we are entering a dream by showing the Professor asleep and by using his voice-over to tell us that he was dreaming. The voice-over also tells us, which otherwise we couldn't know, that the Professor is taking his daily walk when he suddenly finds himself in familiar, but at the same time foreign streets – an experience that contains opposites, that is both familiar and foreign, is something we immediately recognize from our own dreams, as we do the surreal images; the clock with no hands and the bleeding eye. So it's the Professor's own routine which has led him to this deserted place where he can neither pin down his location nor the time. His usual, rational ways of getting his bearings have gone. He's no longer in control and he's afraid. The bleeding eye contributes a sense of danger which is added to by his being deprived of all sense of time apart from the beating of his heart – he is only a heartbeat away from death.

3. The Professor walks on for a few yards, turns and walks quickly back the way he came. He stops. A man has appeared further down the street and is standing absolutely still with his back to us. The Professor walks up to him and puts his hand on the man's shoulder. The man slowly turns to the Professor who jumps in shock at the sight of his face. It is like a death mask. The man then falls to the ground. His body seems to have disintegrated

29

beneath his clothes and a watery blood trickles from where his head should have been. Funereal bells begin to toll.

– Despite his growing fear when another person appears in this apparently deserted place the Professor wants to know who it is. But the man's solid figure, as seen from behind, turns out to be an illusion; his face (identity) is a mask of death, he is a man of no substance beneath his clothes (his outer persona) and he even lacks proper thick blood (life energy). Is the Professor meeting an image that represents his unconscious view of himself?

4. The Professor continues with his walk, his face rigid with shock. He turns the corner at the end of the street and sees a nineteenth-century horse-drawn hearse lurching slowly down the street towards him and there's no sign of a driver. As he watches the hearse one of its wheels gets hooked around a lamp-post. The horses strain to pull the wheel free and continue on their journey. The wheel breaks off and rolls dangerously towards the Professor, just missing him. The hearse creaks horribly as the horses try to free it from where it remains caught against the lamp-post. The horses suddenly break free and continue on their way dragging the three-wheeled hearse behind them. The Professor watches as the coffin slides out of the hearse and falls with a crash on to the cobbled street in front of him.

– The Victorian hearse looks more like a fairytale hearse than a real one which indicates that its purpose is symbolic rather than literal. Loss of control is hurtling towards him in the form of a driverless vehicle which carries the dead. Its journey is interrupted by a lamp-post, an object which emits light, the opposite of the darkness of death. The hearse's broken wheel could have killed the Professor but it just misses him and the hearse continues on its way – death appears to have passed him by, but not quite.

5. The Professor looks curiously down at the coffin. The fall has dislodged its lid and the hand of a corpse hangs out as if offering itself to him. The hand suddenly grabs him and the face of the corpse appears. The corpse is the Professor, it's the Professor's dead self who, with a fearful energy, is trying to pull him into the coffin. Cut to the Professor in bed waking from his nightmare.

– The message of many dreams can be found in their climax. So what is this dream telling the Professor? The corpse inside the coffin is the Professor's own self but it's not death the Professor has to confront, not yet, we have just seen death pass him by. His self is attempting to do something even more fearful than death; to pull him into the coffin alive. This suggests that the confrontation and the fearful struggle the Professor has to face is with this aspect of his self. The dream then wakes him, as if asking him to attend now to its message.

6. The Professor sits up in bed, takes his pocket watch from his bedside table and checks the time. He then goes over to the window and draws the blinds. He grabs his dressing-gown and hurries through the apartment. The clock strikes three. He walks into his housekeeper's bedroom. She sits up in bed shocked by his sudden appearance.

> HOUSEKEEPER
> Are you ill?
> PROFESSOR
> Miss Agda, please make breakfast. I'm driving down.

– The Professor reacts immediately to his dream. First he checks that the real world is still in order by looking at the time and the view out of the window and, reassured that all is as it should be, he rushes to his housekeeper's room. We have a strong feeling his spontaneous and urgent behaviour is uncharacteristic, a feeling confirmed by his housekeeper's surprise at his sudden appearance in her room and her assumption that he must be ill. But we know that he has decided to change his plans for the day as a result of his dream.

In this opening sequence Bergman has chosen to make a very clear distinction between dream and reality. He tells us that we are entering the dream, in the simplest way possible, by showing us his character asleep, and likewise he tells us when the dream is over by showing his character waking up. New film-makers often feel that simple solutions like this are too obvious or clichéd. Of course it is important to be subtle, when the material demands it, but it is equally important to know when to be direct. In this case the climax of the sequence is the moment in which the Professor confronts his self in the coffin and Bergman is concerned that we fully experience this moment because of the impact it has on his character's waking life – this is the moment that causes the Professor to change his plans for the day. If we had been uncertain about whether we were in a dream or not the power of this moment would have been greatly diminished.

It's also worth noting the relationship between the pre-credit sequence and the dream. A dream is essentially about the dreamer. Our ability to understand fully Professor Borg's dream is dependent on our introduction to the character of the dreamer and the thematic link between his introduction of himself and the dream's insight into his self. At the end of the pre-credit sequence we wondered if the 50th anniversary celebration was going to upset the central elements governing the Professor's life: order and control. The dream takes up the theme and leads us, and Professor Borg, to its natural outcome, a sort of death in life, or to be more precise, life in a coffin – which stands as a metaphor for his present life. Anniversaries also tend to be confrontations with the self and the dramatic question we are left with at the end of the sequence is, 'What impact will this dream have on Professor Borg's 50th anniversary?'

A MEMORY
THE CONFORMIST (Il Conformista, 1970)
Written and directed by Bernardo Bertolucci
(Based on a novel by Alberto Moravia)

Sequence taken from the early development of the film

The film is set at the end of the 1930s. Clerici, the protagonist, is an Italian fascist now in his mid-thirties. He's been sent to France by his bosses to find and murder a left-wing university professor who was once his teacher. We join the story when Clerici and his driver are following the professor in their car with the intention of committing the murder. It is midwinter.

1. Clerici is sitting by his driver in the passenger seat of a 1930s black Citroën. They are both wearing hats and winter coats.

CLERICI
Stop. I want to get out.
The black Citroën draws to a halt. The roads are icy. The country landscape is a cold misty grey and covered with snow. Although they are passing the elegant gates of a wealthy property, there is no sign of people or even other cars in the vicinity. Clerici gets out of the car and marches ahead on foot.
CLERICI
What point is there in going? You go.
The driver opens his door and, while slowly following him in the car, calls to Clerici. His tone of voice is soft and persuasive, as if he's calling a petulant child.
DRIVER
Marcello.
Cut to a black car (a much earlier model than the Citroën) driving very slowly behind a boy of perhaps twelve years old. The boy is dressed in a sailor suit (of the kind worn by

children at the turn of the century) and has a satchel over his shoulder. It's midsummer and the scene is set in an elegant park.

Cut back to time present. The driver is still leaning out of the open car door as he follows Clerici.

DRIVER
We must be there. We have responsibilities.

Cut to the summer park. The boy runs in front of what we can now see is a black Rolls-Royce and holds his hand up like a policeman to halt the car:

BOY
Stop.

Cut to time present. Clerici walks around the front of the car to the passenger door. He bangs on the roof of the car:

CLERICI
Stop.

– The sequence opens with Clerici sitting in the passenger seat alongside the driver of the car. The two men appear to be of equal status and together on a mission but when Clerici suddenly orders the driver to stop, gets out of the car and walks in front of it, he separates himself from the driver by his odd behaviour. (In films, as in life, when a character behaves oddly the audience always wants to know why.) We know that he is having second thoughts about their mission because he says so, but the way he marches along in front of the car, especially in such miserable weather conditions, seems both petulant and childish. The driver emphasizes this in the way he responds by calling Clerici by his Christian name, Marcello, with the tone of voice of an adult trying to cajole a difficult child. It's now that we have the first cut to the summer park and the boy in the sailor suit.

Memory is usually triggered by an incident, image, sound or smell in the present. Here there seems to be a complex network of factors causing the memory. The childish behaviour of the adult Clerici, emphasized by the driver addressing him in a tone that reminds him of his boyhood, is the strongest trigger and the actual cue into the memory. Another trigger is the visual image of the elegant gates of the wealthy country estate they happen to be passing. (Clerici himself comes from a wealthy family, a fact which plays an important part later in the sequence.) The third element is the similarity of actions and words in relation to the two cars. Clerici, in the present, walks in front of a black car which slowly follows him. The boy in the past also walks in front of a black car which follows him. The boy commands the car to halt in the manner of a master addressing his servant, as does Clerici in the present.

If we look beyond the techniques of film grammar at the content of these scenes we are also learning about some very specific aspects of Clerici's character. When the driver reminds the adult Clerici of his responsibilities, Clerici reacts by remembering himself as a child aping adult behaviour by pretending to be a policeman. We then cut to the adult Clerici stopping the car in exactly the same manner. We witness the authoritarian, controlling side of Clerici's nature and at the same time learn how these characteristics were formed in his childhood and how the child within him is still operating through the man.

2. The car stops and Clerici gets into the back seat. Inside the car we see, from Clerici's point of view, the driver's back.

DRIVER
If we don't go who'll report?
Cut to the sunny afternoon in the park. The camera tracks slowly past people standing in amongst the trees. They appear to be watching something. Sounds over of children whispering.

Cut to time present. The driver's face is out of focus and we look over his shoulder to see Clerici sitting in the back of the car looking serious and thoughtful. Sounds over of the children whispering in the summer park. A slight disturbance flickers over Clerici's face in reaction to the whispering.

– The driver has reminded him of his responsibilities and
Clerici has consequently conceded to his duty and got back in
the car. His attempt, in a small way, to escape something has
failed. Although in his manner he appeared like the master, or
the man with the greater power, in both these shots Clerici's
image in the back of the car is dominated by the driver who is
now reminding him of the higher authority they both have to
report to. The image, as well as the driver's words, tells us that
Clerici is no longer his own master. It could be that this time
Clerici is deliberately using his memory in an attempt to either
escape from, or to understand, the unpalatable nature of his
present dilemma. We return to the park. This time something is
going on that is causing the adults present to watch with
interest, although we can't yet see what they're watching. This
withholding of information is a powerful dramatic device; our
curiosity is further aroused but not satisfied. The dramatic
build-up is further intensified by the whispering from the past
that Clerici hears in the car in the present. This use of sound
overlapping from one scene, time and place, into another has
the effect of taking us further into Clerici's subjective experience
(we hear the whispering with Clerici but the driver can't), and
of pulling Clerici (and us as audience) back into the memory.

3. Summer afternoon in the park. A group of boys are
playing in a huddle amongst the trees whispering to each
other. A boy, who has perhaps been on watch, runs up to
the group.

BOY
The police!

The group of boys quickly disbands. We can just make out a
boy left lying on the ground with his trousers pulled down.
The gang of boys, in their neat school clothes, tear away from
the scene of the crime on their roller skates. (The lyrical
theme music of the film is played while they skate away.)

The boy, who we now see is young Clerici, clambers to his
feet and pulls up his trousers. A black Rolls-Royce is parked

nearby. On the running board, watching young Clerici, stands an elegant chauffeur, dressed in a smart military-style uniform, black boots and chauffeur's hat. The car door is open waiting for the boy.

Young Clerici picks up his satchel from a nearby park bench, ignores the chauffeur, and walks away in the direction the boys took.

The chauffeur gets in the driver's seat and slowly follows the boy. Young Clerici walks along the road tucking his shirt into his trousers. He then runs in front of the car and, pretending to be a policeman, puts his hand up and calls the car to a halt.

> BOY CLERICI

Stop.

– We recognize this action of halting the car as a repeat of the fragment of memory we have already seen and realize that Clerici has now recalled the experience leading up to that moment. Again there is an intimate connection between the present and the past. The driver in the present reminds Clerici of the higher authorities they must report to and similarly a child in the past warns the gang of children in the park that the police (also higher authorities) are coming.

Although the boy, Clerici, is apparently a victim of the other children – he's the one left with his trousers down – the way this sequence has been constructed does not suggest that this incident is the emotional centre or the climax of the memory. This is partly because the scenes we have seen so far in the memory have been in long shot which psychologically places both the adult Clerici and us, the audience, in the position of curious observers rather than participants. (To experience the full emotional impact of the incident we would have needed to see the boys from young Clerici's point of view when they were accosting him, which would have given us some insight into how upset he was, or to have seen his facial expressions, which would also have told us about his feelings.) But instead we see his assailants skating away to the accompaniment of the lyrical theme music. The fluidity of movement combines with the music to evoke a feeling of sensuality rather than deep distress or trauma.

It's in this unexpectedly sensual mood that our focus is shifted from the boys to the elegant young chauffeur. The incident with young Clerici's school friends has immediately been upstaged by the power of the image of the chauffeur and our consequent curiosity about what is to come. Our curiosity is further aroused when the boy ignores the chauffeur and walks away along the now deserted route that his school friends took. The boy then asserts his power by making the chauffeur follow him in the car and then stopping the car when he is ready. But how much power does he really have? He is, after all, merely a young boy in the back seat with a startling-looking man in uniform driving the car.

4. We cut to young Clerici inside the car as it drives past his school friend assailants. He watches them out of the back window as they skate after the car. The car soon leaves them behind and the boy turns and looks at the chauffeur curiously:

> CHAUFFEUR
> What's your name?
> BOY CLERICI
> Marcello Clerici. And yours?
> Cut to the exterior of the car. It's now high above the city, cruising along an elegant driveway past palm trees and well-tended lawns.
> CHAUFFEUR
> Pasqualino Semirama, but call me Lino.
> The car draws to a halt.

– As the car speeds past young Clerici's assailants the image tells us about his potential power, and his desire for power, because we now see his relation to them in quite a different light. He is no longer their victim, he is now the rich boy in the powerful car while they are reduced to ordinary mortals whom he looks down on out of the window.

Next he turns his attention to his chauffeur who, we gather from the way they ask each other's names, is a new employee. It's worth noting here how film can create its own sense of time. Young Clerici asks the chauffeur his name very soon after they leave the gang of boys behind. We hear the chauffeur's reply over an exterior shot of the car arriving in a new location high above the city – in the split second between the question being asked and hearing the reply we have entered another world; the world of a very wealthy Italian family. The chauffeur gives his name in full but also tells the boy his nickname, which suggests a desire for an intimate rather than formal master-servant relationship, and this is our introduction to whatever is to follow in this new time and place.

The dramatic question is now, 'What is going to happen (or, given that we are in a memory, what once happened) between young Clerici and the chauffeur that is relevant to the journey the adult Clerici, a fascist assassin, is now making?'

Earlier we saw how, in *Wild Strawberries*, Bergman made quite sure that we knew when we were entering the dream and when the dream had finished. We also noted how he adhered to the conventions of dream language while in the dream. But in life, as well as in films, the boundaries between sleep-dreams and conventional notions of reality are quite distinct. The boundaries between our experience of reality and our experience of memory are considerably less distinct. But in this sequence Bertolucci has likewise chosen to make sure his audience knows when we are in the present time, as experienced by his protagonist, and when we are entering his memory, taking great care to illuminate the very specific nature of Clerici's character by exploring each associative detail of his memory process. He has done this because, again like Bergman, the meaning he wants to communicate lies in our being able to make the connection between what happened to Clerici in the past and our understanding of the motivation for his actions in the present. The child within the man is still

39

acting on the man. This is crucial both to what this sequence, and to what the whole film, is about.

Also, look at how, at the end of the sequence, the dramatic thrust within the memory is still energetically moving us forward. We are certainly not yet ready to leave this memory. We want to know what happens next and we feel sure it will be more illuminating of the present-time dilemma than what we have already seen. We passed over the child being molested by his friends in the park, which for many people would in itself have been a traumatic event, relatively easily so we know that there must be another, more significant event pulling the memory forward and we want to go on to find out what it is. In this sequence Bertolucci has not only achieved a complex exploration of how memory itself works, he has also used its complexity to dramatic effect by carefully observing the urgency of the relationship between memory and present action.

A FANTASY?

KAOS (1984)
Written and directed by Paolo Taviani and Vittorio Taviani
(Based on short stories by Luigi Pirandello)

Sequence taken from the opening of the fifth story

Kaos is a film made up of five stories each set set in the area of Sicily known as Kaos which was also Luigi Pirandello's childhood home. The stories are loosely linked thematically in that together they create a portrait of a place, its inhabitants, its history, its sorrows and its magic. In this final story the protagonist, who is Pirandello himself, returns to Sicily after the death of his mother.

'CONVERSING WITH MOTHER'
(titles white on dark blue)

Dreams, Memories and Fantasies

1. When the film opens we hear the familiar chugging of a train for a few moments before we cut to the interior of a train compartment. It's empty but for one smartly dressed, middle-aged man. This is Luigi Pirandello. His head rests uncomfortably on his arm on the hard wooden table in front of him. We move into a close-up of his balding head as it's rocked by the motion of the train and then down to his free arm, which is dangling lifelessly. In spite of his obvious discomfort Luigi appears to be in a deep sleep. His hat, which rests on the wooden shelf above him, is also being rocked by the motion of the train. It suddenly rocks to the edge of the shelf and falls.

We then cut to the exterior of the train as it hisses to a halt. It's entering a tiny country station which appears to be the only building in this flat empty landscape. There is a rhythmic clanging of metal as the train waits for a small group of people to climb aboard. The train begins to pull out of the now apparently deserted station when a door is flung open. Luigi jumps awkwardly out of the train and on to the platform, clutching his hat and coat in his arms. As he gains his balance his bag comes flying out of the window and lands unceremoniously at his feet.

– Long train journeys; time out from the normal routine of life, submission to the superior power of the duration of the journey; dreaming and dozing lulled by the familiar, rhythmic chugging of the wheels on the tracks. It's no accident that, after the title has faded and we are left with a dark blue screen, we hear the sound of the train for a few seconds before the image of the train compartment appears. Those few seconds, like a passing whiff, are just enough to remind us what it feels like to be a dreamy submissive traveller and to set the mood for the appearance of our sleeping protagonist.

Although he is fast asleep and we can't see his face, our interest in him is aroused, partly because there is nobody else in the compartment to distract our attention, but mainly because, with the close-ups of his balding head, his dangling

41

hand and his hat, the film is inviting us to contemplate nothing other than this man's total submission to dead sleep.

The hat, which falls off the luggage rack, apparently of its own accord, just as the train happens to be entering the station, then reminds us of forces beyond the control of man, whether they be purely coincidental, or have that wayward quality of dreams, or even suggest a more mystical significance. The sudden movement of the hat's fall also has the effect of energizing the sequence and moving it on, preparing us for something to happen, which in this case is the arrival of the train at the man's destination.

And what a beautiful way to construct a scene of a man getting off a train! The dreamlike atmosphere we've been introduced to in the opening scene is sustained. The station is a little like a station in a dream in that it's unlocated, or in the middle of nowhere. And the strange rhythmic clanking which accompanies the train as it pulls into the station adds to the feeling of otherworldliness. The distant figures have climbed on to the train and it's already departing when our man abruptly appears, as if he is being rudely disgorged by the train, with his baggage flung out of the window after him. Apart from being funny, this too has a dreamlike quality about it. We know the man was fast asleep when the train entered the station (although maybe the falling hat woke him up), and we also know that he was alone in the compartment, so who is flinging his forgotten baggage out of the window after him?

2. Luigi is alone on the platform, trying to get his bearings. He picks up his bag, looks curiously after the departed train, smiles to himself and shakes his head wonderingly. He then seems to become aware of his new location and the sudden silence. He looks over the rails at the station building; broken mouldings and stucco are peeling off the walls and a wayward vine is creeping over the unreadable, aged station sign. We hear a gentle, haunting music. Luigi turns his attention to the dull, flat landscape around him, as if he's still trying to understand where he is. He then looks

over to the platform on other side of the rails where something attracts his attention.

We suddenly see a boy's face filling the screen. He must be eleven or twelve. He has thick dark hair and dark eyes which seem to look optimistically into the future. He is a beautiful boy, full of life, health and vitality. The haunting music swells and he raises both his arms into the air as if they are wings.

We cut back to a close-up of Luigi transfixed by this image of the boy. We then cut to the boy in long-shot. Now we can see that he's wearing a striped top and knee-length trousers and is standing on top of a small pyramid of white sand, which has been left on the station platform. He's holding his arms up in the air as if he is about to fly. But instead he allows his body to go limp, sinks on to the pyramid of sand and rolls down on to the station platform. A second boy appears, runs to the top of the sand and takes his turn rolling to the bottom.

We track slowly from the boys' game, back over the rails, to find Luigi still standing where the train left him, with his bag and coat in his arms, looking totally bewildered.

– When Luigi looks curiously after the departing train and smiles to himself he seems to be asking the same question as we in the audience are: 'Who could it be who threw his bag out of the window?' And by the way he shakes his head wonderingly, we know that the question will remain one of life's mysteries. It's clearly not of consequence to our story, beyond adding to the growing sense of our reality not being quite as well ordered, structured and logical as perhaps it ought to be. In this mood Luigi looks at the world he has tumbled into. The relative comfort of the train has gone and the silence adds to our feeling his aloneness.

Then, as he looks at the ageing station building, the name illegible, the foliage suggesting that it is somehow being reclaimed by nature (maybe by the same forces as those that toppled the hat off the shelf and threw the baggage out of the window?), the gentle, haunting theme music appears on the soundtrack preparing for us to be transported into another world. This is the moment when Luigi's attention is attracted by something on the other side of the tracks, and the boy magically appears.

The reason we experience the boy as magical and hypnotic is the result of a number of different factors in combination. The first is the culmination, throughout the sequence so far, of small strange moments, just unsettling enough to disturb our sense of time, place, cause and effect. The second is the image of the boy himself; he is unusually beautiful and has an optimistic innocence in his eyes that is wholly captivating. The third element is the shot itself; we cut to the boy after Luigi's attention has been attracted by him – we want to see what our character is seeing. But we don't see what he sees. Or do we?

A moment of pure film magic happens here. The logical shot which should follow, arising from our desire to see what Luigi is looking at, would be a shot of the boy from Luigi's point of view, which would be a long-shot. The boy is, after all, on the other side of the tracks. But instead of that we are given an image of the boy that Luigi could not possibly, realistically, be seeing; a big close-up of the boy's face filling the screen. Because the shots building up to this moment have been communicating Luigi's subjective experience, and the shot following the appearance of the boy is a close-up of Luigi, transfixed by the boy's image, we believe that this must also be his experience. The only way we can rationally comprehend the moment is by deciding that Luigi has imagined, or fantasized the image or that maybe it's in his memory. But the next shot shifts our point of view again. This time we view the boy from a neutral point of view (not from Luigi's) which enables us to see that the boy is actually there, playing in what we had previously thought was an empty station. Therefore, we deduce, he can be neither a memory nor a fantasy, he must be real.

The film goes on to stress this reality, first by bringing another child into the game, and second, by panning from the boys' game, over the tracks, to where Luigi is standing watching them. In other words, if the boys and Luigi are together in the same unbroken shot, it logically follows that they must be in the same place at the same moment in history! But, in spite of this assertion, the moment we experienced earlier, when the boy magically appeared, remains so powerful we are forced, by the conflicting elements in the grammar of the film, to contemplate the multi-layered nature of Luigi's experience, and therefore of the nature of subjective experience itself. It is as if Luigi, and we the audience, are, like the station building, somehow being reclaimed by the foliage, or by time itself.

3. Luigi steps down on to the rails, crosses to the platform and, while we follow him as he walks past the station buildings towards the exit, we hear the following:

> LUIGI *(voice-over)*
> I had slept through the two-day journey to Sicily, my first visit since my mother's death. Somebody had called me back. I never really understood who, but I had willingly left my house in Rome where the effort of living had lately become intolerable; my work, my children, my age. I don't want to explain the in-explicable. Still tired from sleep I wondered if I was still asleep.

Luigi stops walking, puts his foot on a station bench and fixes the buttons which have come undone on his shoe.

– The sequence up until this scene has been absorbing but also disorientating. Luigi's words now ground us in a number of simple ways and in doing so kick off the story. First we are given reasons for his disorientation; Luigi's journey has been long, he's slept for two days and he describes a mysterious feeling; he has somehow been 'called back', as if forces beyond his conscious and rational mind are operating on him. There's no suggestion that these forces are supernatural: he describes a feeling I'm sure most of us have experienced, when our actions cannot be explained in terms of our conscious will. The title of the film is 'Conversing with Mother' and we now learn that he is visiting a place of huge emotional significance, his childhood home, and that this is his first visit since his mother's death. We are also told that living for him has recently become intolerable in all the important areas of his life; his work, his children, his age – so he is not only a man who has been mysteriously 'called' back to his roots and the home of his mother but he is also a man who, because he is going through a crisis of meaning, is in great need. This information enables us to formulate the question, 'Given Luigi's need will he find solace, or even a way forward, in the place where he is going?' The story has now begun.

In *Wild Strawberries* and *The Conformist* Bergman and Bertolucci both used film language to ensure that we, the audience, were quite clear about what was dream or memory and what was their protagonists' present reality. In both cases this clarity served the thematic and dramatic intentions of the sequence.

In *Wild Strawberries* Bergman's central concern was that we ask how the Professor's dream will affect his waking life, given that the Professor appears to be complacent and self-satisfied, yet the dream suggests the need for a dramatic confrontation with the self. It was necessary that we were able to distinguish clearly between dream and present reality because the issue was how the dream would affect his reality. In *The Conformist* Bertolucci was likewise concerned that we were able to distinguish clearly between Clerici's present preoccupation – his mission as a fascist assassin – and a specific memory from Clerici's past, because he wanted us to consider how what happened between Clerici as a boy and the chauffeur Lino is relevant to the adult Clerici's journey.

In *Kaos*, the Taviani brothers are concerned that the boundaries between present-time reality, normality, memory and fantasy are blurred. Just as the character Luigi says, 'I wondered if I was still asleep', in other words reality for him feels like a dream. Although we are seeing Luigi in the present on a journey, just like we saw Clerici in the present on a journey, the focus and dramatic thrust of the *Kaos* sequence points towards the past. Whatever he has been 'called' for, and therefore must soon confront, lies in the past, whereas in *The Conformist* what Clerici soon has to confront lies in the present.

What is emerging here is that the way we handle dream, memory and fantasy is always rooted in the character's experience, the dramatic question which motivates the character and, finally, in what the film-maker is trying to say. The film language, in each of these examples, serves to illuminate these three aspects with no irrelevant or extraneous information to confuse the audience. All the camera set-ups and scenes contribute to the central focus of the sequence. Even in *Kaos*, where the Taviani brothers want us to experience a complex concertinaing of time, the present being reclaimed by the past, or the past leaking into the present, they take great pains to use film language to make clear the specific moments when something strange is happening, or when something from the past leaks through to the present. Each time they break a rule of film grammar they are doing so consciously in order to contribute to what the sequence is about.

All storytelling, in our case fiction films, is rooted in the life experience of a character. Even if that character is portrayed as an animal or a creature from outer space, it is usually endowed with the human ability to experience life. And our everyday life experience is not purely linear. We encounter our present through our past, our memory and our dreams. We have the capacity to imagine our distant ancestry and to fantasize a desired future. There are very few film-makers who have contributed significantly to international film culture who have not entered this terrain. As new film-makers establish themselves new boundaries are broken and our perception of ourselves is once more altered.

3 Metaphors and Archetypes
Leone's *For a Few Dollars More* and the Taviani Brothers' *Kaos*

As with dreams, memories and fantasies, metaphors and archetypes are also a part of the continuous, complex and diffuse nature of our everyday experience. They are concepts which are fundamental to all art forms. Many film-makers find that the very first idea or inspiration for a new project often comes into their mind in the form of an image that is also a metaphor. The metaphor grounds the idea in visual form and frequently acts as a guiding light throughout the writing and film-making process. In the sequence from *Kaos*, the lonely, aged station building stands as a metaphor for Luigi's state of mind, and the boy, who so magically appears with his arms held up as if he is about to fly, is an archetype representing the optimistic child about to embark with innocent enthusiasm on the journey of life – an image many older people look back on with a sense of nostalgia and loss. But these are just two of the numerous examples of metaphors and archetypes which have occurred in the sequences we have explored so far. The purpose of this chapter is to isolate these two concepts and to look at them in greater depth.

A metaphor is a compressed similarity. In film it is an image or sound which has both a literal meaning and at the same time suggests another meaning through resemblance, implication or association with something else. The power of the metaphor derives from the relevance and compression of the comparison. In *The Lacemaker* we are not invited to consider the image of crossing the road and the relative dangers to the

48

pedestrians literally. Goretta is suggesting a similarity between the way his two protagonists cross the road and the internal conflicts within their relationship. In *Wild Strawberries* the film focuses on Professor Borg's trip to the town where he graduated as a young man; the journey, which takes less than a day, stands as a metaphor for Professor Borg's entire life. We are not invited to consider how interesting it is that life is like a journey, in some abstract way – the film *is* the journey. The power used by the film-maker to compress the comparisons into a microcosm explodes into meaning. It is through metaphor that we experience depth, complexity, insight and, most importantly, unity – the way all things interpenetrate.

This process of recognition and identification clarifies and affirms what we feel our experience to be and connects us to the larger whole. This connection with something much larger than ourselves and the specifics of our unique experience, through the microcosm reflecting the macrocosm, can feel like the point where art and transcendental or spiritual experience meet; they are both addressing similar needs, concerning wholeness and unity.

An archetype is an image which is both a metaphor and a microcosm of a myth (a myth, by definition, is an archetypal story) which has recurred, although in many different guises, throughout history and has a universal meaning. Jung, whose understanding of the human psyche was largely based on the concept of archetypes, described them as 'the instinct's perception of itself or as the self-portrait of the instinct'.* Freud, who referred to archetypes as 'archaic remnants', also recognized their significance when he placed the Oedipus myth, which embodies some of our most familiar archetypes, at the heart of his psychoanalytic theory.

The myth of Oedipus is about a young man who, unaware of the truth of his parentage, murders his father and marries his mother. When he discovers the truth he gouges out his own

---

*Quoted by Jolande Jacobi, *Complex Archetype Symbols in the Psychology of C. G. Jung*, trans. Ralph Manheim (Princeton UP, 1959) p. 36.

eyes. Freud saw how the story represented a rite of passage in the universal conflict between son and father. In order to achieve a separate identity the son unconsciously desires to replace the father and possess the mother. The catharsis in the story is the horrific self-blinding which is intended to have the effect of cleansing or purging the guilt.

The hero is one of our most common archetypes and is the focus of numerous myths, ancient and modern, irrespective of culture. The hero myths tend to have a universal pattern: 'a miraculous but humble birth, his early proof of superhuman strength, his rapid rise to prominence or power, his triumphant struggle with the forces of evil, his fallibility to the sin of pride, and his fall through betrayal or heroic sacrifice that ends in his death.'* I'm sure most people will recognize how, with a few adjustments of emphasis, this structure even applies to the familiar story of Christ, although we tend to think of Christ as a spiritual leader rather than a hero. The great heroes of mythology were men such as Theseus, who entered the dreaded labyrinth to destroy the minotaur in order to rescue Ariadne, his damsel in distress; or the Knights of the Round Table overcoming seemingly insurmountable obstacles in their quest for the Holy Grail; or Jason's great journey to find the Golden Fleece which he needed in order to regain his lost kingdom. It was Medea who eventually enabled Jason to find the Golden Fleece and when Jason later betrayed her for a younger woman she took her revenge by murdering the two children she had with Jason. The Holy Grail, which some believed to be a cup containing the blood of Christ, and the Golden Fleece are both archetypes representing the ultimate elixir or meaning of life.

Archetypes of women are often split into two categories representing the good and the bad mother: the earth mother, the Virgin Mary, the princess, the fairy godmother, the nurse, the saint on one side, and the Medusa, the witch, the whore, the siren, the wicked stepmother on the other side.

*Man and His Symbols, Carl Jung ed. (p. 110).

The Lacemaker
Because the scene opens on Béatrice, because we follow her
actions, her gesture of hope, and because François has his back to
us, we wait, hope and feel with Béatrice.

Wild Strawberries
Surreal images, such as the clock with no hands and the bleeding
eye, and experiences that contain opposites, that are both familiar
and foreign at the same time, are things we immediately recognise
from our own dreams.

The Conformist
We witness the authoritarian, controlling side of Clerici's nature
and at the same time learn how these characteristics were formed
in his childhood and how the child within him is still operating
through the man.

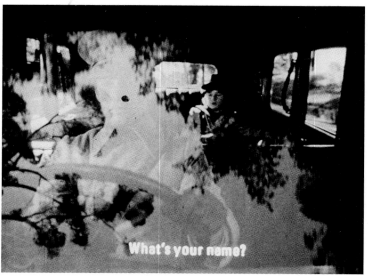

The Conformist
What is going to happen (or, given that we again enter Clerici's memory, what once happened) between young Clerici and the chauffeur that is relevant to the journey the adult Clerici, a fascist assassin, is now making?

Kaos

The only way we can rationally comprehend this moment is by
deciding that Luigi has imagined or fantasized the image of the
boy, or that maybe it is in his memory… Luigi, and we the
audience, are, like the station building, somehow being reclaimed
by time itself.

For A Few Dollars More

By placing the feminine aspect and the inexorable nature of time in the heart of the scene Leone penetrates beneath the surface agenda of the duel and invites us to understand its meaning in a new light.

Kaos

The raven, a carrion bird normally associated with ill-omen and doom, in this case is a cock raven nurturing new life and both the father-bird and its eggs are in danger from the predator: man. But what can this combination of associations mean?

Kaos
When Salvatore rescues the raven, ties the bell around its neck and
gives it freedom, he enables us to escape from ignorance and
callousness and to soar up into the sky with that wonderful feeling
of elation and transcendence. He has also created a new metaphor
giving insight into how destruction and creation are inextricably
linked in the creative act.

Both Freud and Jung agreed that the source of our archetypal images resides in the unconscious although they differed on the role archetypes have to play in our conscious lives and on the precise nature of the unconscious. The Australian Aborigines, on the other hand, would tell us that archetypes are spirits who reside in the Dreamtime and have an existence in the desert, the rocks, the trees and the sky, entirely independent from man – a perception of the spirit world common to many primitive cultures. The ancient Greeks would have claimed something similar for their archetypes, which they also believed had a parallel existence in the world of their gods and goddesses. In the later monotheistic religions most of the archetypes have become woven into the fabric of storytelling, which forms a bridge between man and spirit.

Pier Paolo Pasolini chose to set two of his finest films, *Oedipus Rex* and *Medea*, largely in ancient Greece. When George Lucas made *Star Wars* he took the mythic story of the Odyssey and adapted it for his futuristic journey into outer space. Lucas was well aware of the power of archetypes and mythological stories when he employed Joseph Campbell, the American authority on mythology, to aid the development of his screenplay. In *The Fisher King* Terry Gilliam brings the Arthurian legend to modern-day New York. In the myth the Fisher King, Keeper of the Holy Grail, is sorely wounded which causes his loss of faith and the land to become a Waste Land. Joseph Campbell explains this archetype of the Maimed King as 'the knowledge of the anguish of existence as a function . . . of being.'* Nietzsche later described this in *The Birth of Tragedy* as 'the Hamlet Condition'. Whether in ancient Greece, Shakespearean England, late-nineteenth-century Germany or contemporary New York the fundamental questions concerning the human condition remain the same, as do the underlying archetypes although many of their motifs or

*Joseph Campbell, *Creative Mythology – The Mask of God* (p.424).

visual manifestations are constantly evolving in our ever-changing world.

The first of the two microcosms we are going to explore is a sequence taken from the climax of Sergio Leone's spaghetti western, *For a Few Dollars More*. At the heart of most westerns lies the archetypal confrontation on the frontier between lawlessness and civilization. Sergio Leone was the pre-eminent spaghetti western director. His films demonstrate an insight into the western myth which, as well as being an expression of his personal concerns, also takes a specifically European existential perspective. (The term spaghetti western was first coined in the 1960s to refer to a genre of western made by the Italians and mainly shot on location in an area of southern Spain which bears a striking resemblance to the desert landscape of south-west America.)

FOR A FEW DOLLARS MORE (Per Qualche Dollari in più, 1965)
Written and directed by Sergio Leone

Sequence taken from the climax of the film

Manco (Clint Eastwood) and Colonel Mortimer (Lee Van Cleef), who is the older of the two and a war veteran, are both bounty hunters in America's Wild West. They find themselves in competition because they are after the same man, Indio (Serg Volonte), a crazed murderer. The Colonel has a personal vendetta to settle with Indio. We don't yet know the precise nature of this vendetta but we do know that both men carry identical pocket watches with a photograph of the same beautiful young woman in the lid. Indio is obsessed with this photograph and (as we have recently learnt through memory flashback) many years ago while he was raping the young woman she reached for his gun and shot herself.

We join the film towards the end of the final shoot-out when Indio's murderous gang have been shot by Manco and Colonel

Mortimer. Indio is left to finish the battle alone. The setting is amongst a small group of deserted whitewashed adobe houses, way out in the desert.

1. Indio suddenly emerges from one of the adobe houses and shoots the Colonel's gun clean out of his hand. He walks deliberately towards the Colonel until he reaches a suitable duelling distance. He puts his gun in his holster and takes his watch out of his breast pocket.

> INDIO
> When the chimes end pick up your gun. Try and shoot me Colonel, just try.

He flicks the watch open and the gentle tinkling chimes within begin to play a simple melody.

The Colonel glances at his gun which is lying on the ground a few feet away and looks again at Indio.

Indio takes a few steps towards the Colonel but his attention is increasingly drawn to the watch. As he listens to the simple tune the crazed killer seems to fall into a trance. The chimes are joined by the strings of an orchestra. We cut to Indio's point of view; his hand holds the open watch and the portrait of the young woman faces us. In the background is the duelling distance between Indio and the Colonel whose dark figure stands legs astride with his hands by his hips. Behind the Colonel a horse grazes beneath a tree and in the distance, beyond the desert, a mountain range stretches across the horizon.

– This image feels timeless and quite beautiful in spite of the horrifying agenda; the sequence is, after all, about killing and death. But unlike the chaotic carnage of random killing in the previous scenes, all the ceremonial elements of a ritual duel are now carefully being moved into place. Indio could easily have shot the Colonel, his mortal adversary, but instead even the crazed murderer recognizes the solemnity of the moment. He appears to submit to a higher order. He walks deliberately over to the correct distance from the Colonel and sets in motion the basic ingredients for the honourable duel, apart from the fact that his gun is in his holster and the Colonel's lies on the ground. The scene is very familiar; the force of good, the gunman who is on the side of the law, confronts the force of evil, the bad gunman or the outlaw, and the setting for the final confrontation is the wasteland on the very boundary or frontier of civilization.

Indeed Leone has pared this archetypal confrontation down to only its essential elements and most important, and totally surprisingly, he has placed at the centre, in the very heart of the scene, a pocket watch which plays a gentle melodious tune and contains a photograph of a beautiful young woman. As Indio stares at the photograph, and is transported by the chimes, a feeling which is deliberately emphasized by the addition of the orchestral strings, we see from his point of view all the essential elements in relation to each other: in the immediate foreground the image of a woman placed inside a watch, the feminine and time contained together, and, behind her, the Colonel, his mortal adversary, the horse, man's only true companion in the wasteland, the desert wastes and the distant mountain range. These images are the very opposite of domestic entrapment – here man may be alone but at least he's free. Or is he? And free from what? By placing the feminine aspect and the inexorable nature of time in the heart of the scene, Leone penetrates beneath the familiar surface agenda of the duel and invites us to understand its meaning in a new light.

2. Cut to a long-shot of Indio from the Colonel's point of view; Indio's dark figure stands in front of the small group of white adobe houses.
    Close-up of the Colonel watching Indio.
    Close-up of Indio watching the Colonel.
    Big close-up of the Colonel watching Indio.
    Big close-up of Indio watching the Colonel. The chimes seem to be slowing down.
    The Colonel looks down at his gun lying on the ground.

His hand begins to move, as if getting ready to go for his gun.

The chimes of the watch are very slow now, the mechanism has nearly wound down. But suddenly they begin again with a renewed vigour. Both the Colonel and Indio turn their heads in surprise looking in the direction of this new sound.

We see another hand holding an open pocket watch and again the desert and mountains in the distance behind.

The Colonel puts his hand to his waistcoat pocket and pulls out a gold chain – his watch is missing. He looks at Manco, who now appears holding his watch.

A dramatic Mexican guitar is added to the soundtrack. The faces of the three men watching each other suspiciously are intercut. Indio is about to go for his gun but stops when he realizes that Manco, who is holding the pocket watch in one hand and a rifle in the other, has taken control of the situation.

> MANCO (*to the Colonel*)
> Very careless of you old man.

Manco walks to the Colonel's side. He takes off his bullet belt and gives it to the Colonel.

> Try this. Now we start.

To the accompaniment of a solo trumpet Manco walks back to his position which is an equal distance between the two men, careful to keep his gun pointed at Indio, and sits on a small wall which we now see circles the duelling area. He looks from one man to the other. We cut to the dark figures of both Indio and the Colonel as they face each other, silhouetted against the desert landscape. They watch each other and wait. Manco looks down. We cut to a big close-up of his hand holding both his rifle and the pocket watch with the lid open. The image of the young woman again faces us as the chimes begin their countdown to death.

– The dramatic build-up to the final shooting and the inevitable death of one of the adversaries has begun. But, just as the chimes slow down, a new element enters the arena in the form of Manco, who appears like a God or a Fate, holding an identical pocket watch which plays an identical tune. The ritual cycle has been interrupted. The Colonel looks at his broken watch chain and realizes that Manco has stolen his watch. Manco then refers to the Colonel as 'old man', emphasizing his own relative youth, and the aspect of father-son or teacher-pupil in their relationship, as he gives the Colonel back his gun and lends him bullets. The familiar solo trumpet, so reminiscent of the US cavalry, is also significant here. It plants the idea that order and justice, values associated with the frontier spirit, have at last arrived.

We now see that even the space where the duel is taking place, a circle created by a low wall, reminiscent of both a magic circle and a theatre arena, has a primitive ritual element. And Manco, like Indio before him, submits to the higher order of the ritual, but this time by adhering absolutely to the unwritten rules, first by making the two men equal in arms, and then by sitting an equal distance between them on the edge of the circle. Manco, the young man, the pupil, the son, is now also the adjudicator controlling the action both with his gun and, now he too is in possession of the pocket watch and so the image of the woman, with the chimes. The chimes begin the final countdown and Manco's attention, like Indio's before, is almost hypnotically attracted by their melodious sound. This time from Manco's point of view, the woman, time, the gun and the countdown to death are fatally linked.

3. The chimes slow down and finally stop. The two men draw. Indio falls to the ground but he's not quite dead, he lifts his gun in one final attempt to shoot the Colonel. He fails and his head slumps forward.

MANCO
Bravo.

The Colonel flicks his gun back into his holster and goes to check that Indio is really dead. He puts his foot on Indio's wrist, releases the watch from Indio's fist and takes it. He opens the watch and runs his thumb over the picture inside the lid. Manco walks to his side.

> MANCO
>
> There seems to be a family resemblance.
>
> Here.

Manco hands him the other watch.

> COLONEL
>
> Naturally, between brother and sister.

– The electric moment of life just before death, which everything has been building up to, is over. The Colonel's retribution, which was apparently his motivation, has been completed. He goes on to tell Manco that the woman in the photograph, who was murdered by Indio, was his sister, but somehow this information seems flat. Knowledge of the specific nature of the Colonel's relationship with the woman seems of little importance, compared to how we now see her placed in the heart of the duel. Each of the men, in turn, connect with her image in separate but almost identical ways, which unites them in relation to the feminine archetype, just as they are united in their relation to the masculine tragedy. And although the Colonel's revenge is achieved he seems relatively unmoved. Revenge has so dominated his life that he has very little identity beyond the quest. He is destined to be a traveller alone in the wasteland, searching for more ways of repeating the cycle, as is Manco, his son-figure and pupil.

The ritual has been so carefully constructed, with each image specifically placed in its relation to the others, that we are invited to probe for deeper meanings. Freud's interpretation would probably be: man fleeing his sexual fear of woman by running into the arms of Thanetos, or the death instinct. Jung might suggest that the raped and murdered woman in the photograph is the feminine archetype representing the men's anima, or the feminine part of their own psyche, and it is this that they are fleeing, just as the duel represents the eternal combat with the Shadow, the dark side of his psyche. Sartre would point to the existential quest of man, the road to freedom leading to the inevitable confrontation with death. Manco says 'Bravo' with the flat cynicism of a man who has seen it all before and has just watched yet another re-run of an old show which has many more performances to go.

If, as Jung suggests, archetypes are self-portraits of the instincts, then the duel is a self-portrait of the death instinct. The final microcosm we are going to explore could conversely be described as a self-portrait of the life instinct, although, as you will see, this is something of an over-simplification. The microcosm is the pre-credit sequence of the Taviani brothers' *Kaos*.

KAOS (1984)
Written and directed by Paolo Taviani and Vittorio Taviani
(Based on short stories by Luigi Pirandello)

Pre-credit sequence

1. Blue sky. Foliage growing on the rocks. A young peasant's dark curly head slowly rises into the frame. He has a hunter's gleam in his eye and is totally absorbed in watching something on the ground in front of him.

Cut to a nearby rock. The head of a second young peasant rises into frame to peer over the rock at what is moving on the ground in front of his companion. His face, which is ensconced in a sort of balaclava made of sheepskin, lights up when he spots his companion's prey.

Cut to a third peasant. This man is also watching but he is much older and frowns as if he doesn't know what to make of what is going on.

Cut back to the curly-haired peasant who suddenly grabs his prey and, although we can't yet see what it is, we hear the cackle of a captured bird.

CURLY-HAIRED PEASANT *(calling excitedly)*
Saro!

Saro, the peasant with the sheepskin balaclava, jumps down to the ground just in front of the captured bird. His face lights up with delight.

The captured bird, a black raven, squawks furiously as the curly-headed peasant pins it to the ground with his hand firmly planted around its neck.

The curly-haired peasant looks up at Saro and smiles gleefully.

CURLY-HAIRED PEASANT
It's a cock raven sitting on eggs.

He lifts the raven from the nest and reveals six large white eggs.

The older peasant picks up one of the eggs, looks at it suspiciously and then puts it to his cheek.

OLDER PEASANT
It's warm.

CURLY-HAIRED PEASANT
Cock, are you hatching eggs?

— The sequence opens with the sky and the earth, the most basic dichotomy, and the peasants rise into the frame as if they're so much a part of the earth they're almost growing out of it. The animal skin Saro wears around his head still further emphasizes the primitive simplicity of these men's lives and their closeness to the land.

The peasants are so totally absorbed in what they're watching that we immediately become equally absorbed in watching them. They are alert, like animals, which gives us the feeling that they're hunting something. Their apparently innocent excitement and pleasure is catching, we feel that excitement too. What is it that's so captivating them? The older peasant frowns uneasily. What is it that causes such excitement and such an uneasy frown on the face of the older, wiser man? The more we are prevented from knowing what is going on the more our involvement and curiosity grows. (This withholding of information is an age-old dramatic device and will remain effective for as long as human beings remain curious.) The build-up of drama peaks when we see the curly-haired peasant pounce on his prey, we see his pleasure, we hear a captured bird squawking, and finally the cause of such intense excitement is revealed to us; it's not just a bird but a cock raven.

The raven is, of course, simply another of God's creatures. It's also a black, scrawny creature which feeds off carrion left to rot by others, although, according to the mythology of many cultures, the raven symbolizes a foreboding of terrible calamity and doom. But our encounter with this particular raven is more complicated than that. When we first see our raven it's a captured creature squawking in terror; it is the victim and the prey of man. In spite of the apparent innocent enthusiasm of the men, and the sinister mythic associations of the raven, we find ourselves feeling sorry for the bird. Adding still further to this complexity is the information we are given that the raven is a cock, a male, and it's in the process of hatching eggs. In other words the male is behaving unnaturally by acting like a nurturing female. The six eggs lie in a small vulnerable cluster in the nest. We look at them and feel awe at the mysterious beginnings of life and acutely aware of the danger to new life now their parent has been snatched from them.

So, the raven, a carrion bird normally associated with ill-omen and doom, in this case is a cock raven nurturing new life and both the father-bird and its eggs are in danger from the predator, man. But what can this combination of associations mean? What is the metaphor? We need to look at some more of the film to find out.

2. Cut to a long-shot of the scene. A huge rock is revealed on the top of a hill. Our three peasants are crouched around the raven at the foot of the rock. Nearby, three other peasants are settled around a fire.

CURLY-HAIRED PEASANT (*calling to his companions*)

Look at this! A cock-bird hatching eggs! Shame on
you! What sort of cock are you?

Two of the peasants by the fire run over to see the bird. The
sixth man doesn't seem interested. He stays alone by the fire.

The curly-haired peasant runs to a position near the fire
and holds the raven up in the air by its feet.

CURLY-HAIRED PEASANT

He who hits it, gets it.

The nest containing the eggs is carried to the scene of the
sport. Saro takes an egg out of the nest and hurls it at the
bird.

Another young peasant has a throw. His egg smashes
against the curly-haired peasant's arm.

CURLY-HAIRED PEASANT

Missed!

– We are now able, because of the long-shot, to place the scene
in the wider context of the peasants' remote hill-top environment. This shot also enables us to see that there are not
three but six peasants in the group, five who join in the fun
while the sixth man chooses to separate himself from his
companions by remaining alone by the fire, which singles him
out for our interest. The long-shot also marks a radical change
in rhythm and so begins the next stage of the drama – the
setting up of the game.

Drama within scenes and sequences often moves in little arc-
like shapes: the drama set up by the question 'what is it they are
watching?' peaks with the capture of the bird and is resolved
when we see that the bird is a raven. But within the answer to
the old question lies the germ of the new question and so as one
arc peaks and is resolved the next arc begins to build. It is also
worth noting that just as the dramatic build-up of the opening
sequence of scenes focused our attention directly on to the
metaphor, so the metaphor remains at the centre of the drama
in this next build-up. We now want to know what the discovery of a cock raven hatching eggs means. The rough, simple
peasants have no doubts; the bird's behaviour is unmanly and

as such it deserves to be an object of fun, derision and punishment. When the egg misses the hapless bird and smashes against the peasant's arm the innocent glee on the men's faces is in sharp contrast to their destructive actions. The peasants' glee is reminiscent of how callous children in groups can be and is also a reminder of ourselves as children. The sight of an innocent creature being mocked, pilloried and stoned by the ignorant group is a familiar motif throughout human history.

3. Cut to a long-shot where we see again that only five of the peasants are joining in the sport, the sixth is still alone by the fire.

Cut back to a close-up of the curly-haired peasant holding the hapless bird up as a target. The sixth man, Salvatore, then suddenly jumps in front of him and snatches the bird from his grasp.

PEASANTS

Salvatore, what are you doing?

Salvatore calms them with his hand. He then takes a goat's bell from inside his sheepskin jacket, holds it high in the air and shakes it.

SALVATORE

Music!

We hear the clear high-pitched ringing of the bell and see it silhouetted against the sky.

Salvatore then crouches down on the ground, ties the bell around the now calm raven's neck, stands, looks up to the heavens and releases the bird by launching it up into the clear blue sky.

The raven flutters against the blue sky. The lyrical theme music of the film begins.

Saro and his young peasant companion watch in awe as the raven circles in the sky above them.

Salvatore watches with a kind of quiet paternal concern.

SALVATORE (*quietly*)

Go on.

We soar with the raven, higher and higher, leaving the peasants way behind as we see the world below from the raven's point of view. We soar over the steep escarpments of the barren hills, past little villages clinging to the cliff edges and circle around the ruin of an ancient Greek temple.

Opening credits.

– Now we see why the sixth peasant, Salvatore, chose to remain separate from the others. He sees something that they don't see. He feels something that they don't feel. And he acts on his feelings by saving the bird. As he calms his companions' protests with a gentle hand gesture we see the power of the man; he is like an actor, a teacher, or a prophet who has the power to hold his audience enthralled and to communicate to them something that they hadn't previously seen. When he holds the simple goat's bell up in the air, rings it and tells us this is 'music', the simple sound, against the blue sky, becomes the most pure music. And when he ties the bell around the raven's neck and launches the bird on its journey our spirits are lifted up to the heavens with the bird's flight.

Salvatore, by tying the bell around the raven's neck and giving it freedom, has put together a combination of images which gives us our much-needed insight into the significance of the metaphor. The male raven hatching eggs suggested both a foreboding of death and a nurturing of life. The opposites, destruction and creation, are united in this image, just as these equally potent forces are inextricably linked in the creative act. But, as has frequently been the case throughout history, when a work of art is not understood, it has been mocked and pilloried by the uncomprehending or ignorant. Salvatore is the only one of the peasants who understands what the discovery of a male raven hatching eggs means. When he ties the bell around the raven's neck he returns this meaning to the bird and, by creating a new metaphor for creativity, gives us the insight which enables us too to escape from ignorance and callousness and to soar up into the sky with that wonderful feeling of freedom, elation and transcendence.

As we soar with the bird the ironies of the image begin to emerge; the bell is a heavy weight around the raven's neck, could this be a last soaring before death? Is the bird, which was liberated and set free by the bell, also going to be destroyed by the bell? Life and death are as always locked together – but is this so terrible while, for the moment, we feel the intoxication and exhilaration of glorious flight? The land below is illuminated with a sense of timelessness and we see antiquity, in the form of an ancient Greek temple, presiding over the present from its position on the hill-top. The artist Salvatore's creative act has transformed our experience and given us meaning and hope.

As Bergman said, the primary factor in film is the image (the cock raven hatching eggs, masculine and feminine united), the secondary factor is the sound (the bell) . . . and the tension between these two creates the third dimension (film art). Finally, this archetypal metaphor has been about film itself.

Two

THE MACROCOSM OR THE WHOLE STORY

Introduction
The Basic Principles of Classic Story Structure

Every art form appears to have an inner structure which is innate to the medium itself. For instance, the ancient Greeks defined certain principles underlying the relationships between shapes within the rectangle. These basic structures can be seen in the underlying geometry of much of European fine art and architecture, and in modern movements which have stripped away the surface layers of content to present pure form. The ancient Greeks, in particular Aristotle, also defined certain basic principles which they felt underlay dramatic narrative form, which for them, of course, was restricted to the Greek amphitheatre. Some of these basic structures can be traced through the history of western storytelling forms and the evolution of dramatic art right through to contemporary feature films.

The dynamic energy or force generated by the structures themselves would suggest that they represent something essentially human and unchanged by time. From the ancient Greeks to the present time represents a single epoch in the history of civilization and so we are naturally adhering to a continuity of thought about ourselves, society and art. But each new artist's dynamic relationship with structure is also crucially affected by convention; the customs and practices of their period in history which overlay these basic inner structures often become so accepted by popular culture that many believe them to be innate to the form itself.

The medium in our case is the feature film, which makes the

67

question of what these basic principles or structures are that much more complicated, because feature film is not only one of the newest art forms, it is also a hybrid: the theatre and the novel are its obvious first cousins, and photography, painting, music, sculpture (Tarkovsky chose to call his own book about film-making *Sculpting in Time**) and poetry are all important relations. In the following chapters we are going to focus on the classic narrative structure film has inherited from storytelling and dramatic art, which, as I mentioned earlier, can be traced back to Aristotle. We can then move on to explore the philosophical basis of classic narrative and consider some of the implications of departing from the form from the points of view of both the audience and film-makers.

A Brief Outline of the Basic Principles

Classic narrative is basically linear. It is like a river which has a source in an inland spring. The water bubbles up from the ground and sets off on a journey, pushed forward by the energy generated at its source. It twists and turns and gains momentum according to the obstacles in its path, as if it always has one aim in view; to finally reach and unite with its destination, the sea.

Premise: The premise is the source of the river. It is the initial set of circumstances that generates the conflict and so the energy which causes the water to bubble forth and begin its journey to the sea. Some of these circumstances may have been born way back in the past life of the protagonist, or way back in the history of events which turn out to be intimately connected to the protagonist's life. When these gestating elements combine with one, or some, crucial new ingredients, like a chemical reaction, the premise is formed and the journey begins.

Andrey Tarkovsky, *Sculpting in Time: Reflections on the Cinema*, trans. K. Hunter-Blair (Bodley Head, 1986)

Protagonist: The protagonist is the character who embodies the central conflict generated by the premise. The key attribute of a protagonist is that he or she has an overriding and conscious want or aim that is difficult to achieve.

Aim: In our river analogy the aim is to get to the sea. So, to extend the analogy a little further, the aim is like a lighthouse at the river mouth. The flashing beacon represents the vision or ideal that the protagonist is striving to reach. The story begins when the struggle to achieve the aim begins and the story ends when the aim is either finally achieved or when it is finally lost, or ceases to have its hold over the protagonist. The aim, therefore, provides the backbone for the story.

Obstacles: The obstacles are everything that stands in the way of the protagonist achieving his or her aim. These are usually a mixture of other people and external circumstances or events which come into conflict with the aim. Obstacles can also be facets of the protagonist's own personality, unconscious needs which may prove to have a stronger hold over the protagonist than what they think they want, and character traits which thwart the protagonist's progress.

The Dramatic Question: The dramatic question arises from the conflict between the protagonist's aim and the obstacles. Providing the necessary ingredients to enable the audience to formulate the dramatic question is an essential part of the opening. From then on each sequence takes up the previous sequence's dramatic question, like a relay baton, but which, according to the course of events, is each time reformulated into a new but closely related version of the original question posed by the opening.

Characterization and Motivation: Motivation is the character's incentive, or what causes their aim or desire. As we have just noted, the protagonists are motivated by a complex mixture of conscious wants and unconscious needs or desires. They also have highly individual personality traits, of which some hinder their progress while others provide the key to their possible fulfilment. Characterization is the totality of what a character wants and needs and their character traits, in combination with some idea of their motivation. Characterization is obviously especially important in relation to the protagonist because it's he or she who embodies the backbone of the story structure. But all of the major characters in a drama have their own aims and their own motivation, which is either in conflict or in harmony with the protagonist's aim and so provides the rich textural body of the story. Therefore equal attention needs to be paid to the characterization of all the major players.

Identification: Identification is when we experience and feel what is happening in the story from the point of view of the protagonist. Their hopes and fears become our hopes and fears.

Exposition: Exposition is the information about events which have taken place before the story begins that is necessary to our full understanding of the story. In the traditional theatre exposition is usually communicated through dialogue. In film we have the additional visual possibilities and voice-over narration, flashbacks and memory-flashbacks to give us insight into such past events.

The Beginning or Opening: This is the first section of the story when most, if not all, of the above ingredients have been made manifest.

Development Sequences: These are the sequences in the central body of the story which, although intricately interwoven into the flow of the story, can also, under close examination, often be seen to have a beginning, middle, ending and dramatic question of their own. Each development sequence either moves the protagonist nearer to, or further away from, his or her aim. If the development sequence takes us quite a long way from the aim, to a point where we are in danger of losing sight of it, the aim is usually reaffirmed, which puts the story back on course. The early development sequences are usually devoted to exploring the initial obstacles. In the late development sequences a momentum is usually gathering, together with a sense of urgency, as we move towards the ending.

The Plant: This is when our attention is drawn to an object, a piece of information, or an incident that has little or no direct bearing on the present action but arouses our curiosity because we feel it might have an important part to play later in the story.

Dramatic Irony: This is when the audience knows something that the protagonist or major characters don't know. It has the effect of making us more aware of their vulnerability – we want to warn them, or tell them what they need to know, but, of course, we can't. In this way it increases our emotional involvement with their plight.

The Ending: This is the final part of the story when the following ingredients become manifest:

Crisis: This is an incident, near the ending of the story, which can loosely be described as the straw that breaks the camel's back, or the point of no return. It sparks off the climax, which usually follows immediately or soon after.

Climax: The climax is the inevitable outcome of the crisis. It is the incident which the entire story has, directly or indirectly, been building up to. And it always contains the final answer to the central dramatic question posed at the beginning of the story. It is in the climax that the protagonist's aim is either finally achieved or finally thwarted. In Aristotle's view, in tragedy this is the moment of catharsis, when the audience is purged or cleansed by pity or terror and so healed by the experience. (Opening and development sequences also very often have their own mini-form of crises and climaxes, but these are never so momentous that they end the story.)

Resolution: The resolution is the inevitable outcome of the final major climax. We see how the protagonist has changed (if they have survived the climax!) now that their aim has finally been disposed of. The other threads to the story are also finally wrapped up.

Theme: The theme refers to the meanings of the film or what it is about. Most of us have had the experience of leaving the cinema with friends and finding ourselves, whether we like it or not, plunged almost immediately into an intense discussion about what the film was saying. The focus of this discussion is usually the climax, the outcome of the film, and from there we work backwards. This is because, although many sub-themes may have been touched on during the course of the film, the central theme, which is of overriding importance because it is what the film's author is saying and is therefore the moral standpoint of the film, invariably comes to the surface in the climax. The climax, which is usually a highly dramatic incident, is the watershed that brings about a radical change in the protagonist, it's everything the film has been leading up to, it's the final outcome. And in films, just as in life, when a watershed incident takes place our thoughts about meaning are provoked because we want and need to understand.

Unity: 'The various incidents must be so arranged that if any one of them is differently placed or taken away the effect of wholeness will be seriously disrupted. For if the presence or absence of something makes no apparent difference, it is no real part of the whole' Aristotle.* Aristotle's original defini-tion, when closely examined, is difficult to better. A sense of

Classical Literary Criticism, Aristotle/Horace/Longinus, trans. T. S. Dorsch (Penguin, 1965) p.43.

unity is what many screenwriters and film-makers still strive for. It means that every image, scene and sequence, whether it directly relates to the unfolding narrative or is concerned with mood, atmosphere, metaphor, or simply with telling us, in the way film does so well, about the kind of place we are in, is a carefully considered part of an organic whole. And it reminds us to think of the economy of our work, and to consider our reasons for what we want to include and what should perhaps be left out because it doesn't have an intrinsic place in the overall scheme of things.

Many of the above points are mentioned in Aristotle's writings on the nature of drama. Since then numerous works about the structure of drama have been written, both about the theatre and more recently about film. Some of these works have looked at radical innovations and others have turned the form into a dogmatic formula, even going so far as to assert that the ingredients of the opening should have been dealt with by a specific page number, and by the next specified page number you should have revealed your next plot point!

Aristotle's writings are part of the beginning of a new epoch when there was a radical shift in man's view of himself, which can perhaps best be summed up as humanist. In *The Poetics* Aristotle writes that 'the unravelling of the plot should arise from the circumstances of the plot itself, and not be brought about *ex machina* . . . there should be nothing inexplicable about what happens, or if there must be it should be kept outside the tragedy'.* *Deus ex machina* literally means a god from the machine. In Aristotle's time, and throughout the preceding epoch, most people believed not only that there were hundreds of gods and goddesses acting out the most incredible and extraordinary dramas in another dimension but that these gods and goddesses and dramas had a direct effect on events in earthly, everyday lives. The significance of Aristotle, demonstrated in the above quote, is that he shifted the

*Ibid. p.52

responsibility for events away from the gods and firmly placed it on man himself.

Aristotle also said in *The Poetics* that 'in deciding whether something that has been said or done is morally good or bad, not only should we pay regard to the goodness or badness of the saying or deed itself, but we should also take into account the person by whom and to whom it was said and done, the occasion, the means, and the reason – whether for example, to bring about the greater good, or to avert a greater evil'. In other words, if there should be nothing inexplicable about what happens, man must also bear the moral responsibility for events and this moral responsibility can only be judged in the light of all the information we need to enable us to understand 'the occasion, the means and the reason'.*

The importance of Aristotle for understanding modern narrative conventions is that the philosophy on which he based his approach to drama has dominated western thought for the past twenty-four centuries. The philosophy is linear and rational – for everything there is a reason, if only we have all the information we need to understand it. Man is no longer a victim of forces outside of himself and beyond his control, if he is a victim of anything at all he is a victim of himself. Within the broad confines of this philosophy there are, of course, a multitude of arguments to be resolved, as the history of western philosophy demonstrates. We will be exploring some of these conflicts when we look at departures from the classic form. But first we need to see how the classic form, outlined above, manifests itself in feature-film storytelling.

If we tried to explore entire feature films in the same kind of detail we employed for the microcosms, this book would become far too heavy, so I've decided to concentrate on just three films: Schlesinger's *Midnight Cowboy*, Kieslowski's *A Short Film About Love* and Greenaway's *The Cook, the Thief, His Wife and Her Lover*. The three films are from three different

*Ibid. p.71.

74

cultures – American (although Schlesinger himself is British), Polish and British. But I have chosen them primarily because of their excellent and very individual use of screen language and because they each conform to the classical narrative tradition outlined above. I have broken our exploration of the three films down into their three main parts: the beginning, the development sequences, and the ending. For each part I have described only the key aspects of the developing story (rather than go into the complex network of screen language which we looked at in our exploration of microcosms), and I have followed each description with my observations about how the basic story structure can be seen to emerge from the texture of the developing films.

As I mentioned earlier, the danger of this kind of structural analysis may be in thinking of form as a formula; a set of rules which function like an empty vessel. All the screenwriter has to do is learn the formula, pour in fresh content and, hey presto, you have a screenplay. Although this attitude to form is prevalent in the film business it's not very conducive to producing original work. We have already taken the first step in breaking free from this formula-based approach, which is to think of the form as a philosophy of man rather than an abstract vehicle. My intention with the following film analyses is not to fit the films to the form but to see how the form emerges organically from the rich texture of the films. This will enable us to connect the form with its philosophical roots. Also, in this way, we will be able to get a feeling for three very different and highly personal interpretations of the form, while at the same time developing a real understanding of the concepts of story structure by exploring how they manifest themselves in screen language.

4 Schlesinger's *Midnight Cowboy*

MIDNIGHT COWBOY (1969)
Directed by John Schlesinger
Screenplay by Waldo Salt
(Based on the novel by James Leo Herlihy)

The Beginning

Part One

1. Familiar sounds of a gunfight (taken from an old western). We then see a huge cinema screen standing against the vast and empty Texan desert landscape. But the screen is blank and the drive-in movie theatre is deserted.

2. In a cheap motel room a handsome young man, Joe (John Voight), soaps himself in the shower and sings 'Whoopie ti yi yo, git along little dogies, you know New York will be your new home . . .' He then enthusiastically sprays his arms and crotch with deodorant and dresses in his brand-new clothes: bright red shirt, thigh-clinging pants, Stetson, and, finally, a magnificent pair of cowboy boots. This process is intercut with scenes from the scullery of a fast-food restaurant. First Ralph, an ageing black worker, calls for Joe Buck, then a sweating waitress peers over a growing pile of dirty dishes and demands to know where he is, and finally the irate manager takes up the cry.

76

Joe, as if in answer to the commotion he is causing, turns admiringly to his now fully adorned image in the mirror and says, 'You know what you can do with those dishes. And if you ain't man enough, I'll be happy to oblige.' With this proud statement, and now ready to take on the world, he kicks open the door of his seedy motel room and walks out into the sunshine.

3. We track with Joe as he walks energetically through the sprawling Texas backwater, with his brand-new horse-hide suitcase swinging in his hand. The credits roll and we hear the title song '. . . I'm going where the sun keeps shining through the pouring rain, I'm going where the weather suits my clothes . . .'

4. Joe walks proudly into the busy fast-food restaurant and tries to ask his boss for the back pay owed him but the manager ignores his request, demands to know what he's doing in such a ridiculous get-up and tells him to get on with his work. Nobody seems bothered with Joe's departure except for the ageing black man, Ralph, his fellow dish-washer, who asks him what he's going East for:

> JOE
> There's a lot of rich women back there Ralph, begging for it, paying for it too, and the men, they're mostly tootie-fruities . . . So I'm going to cash in on some of that, right. What do I get to stay around here for? I've got places to go.

With that Joe walks back out into the street.

5. Joe passes the window of Sally's, a derelict beauty salon. He peers through the window and (in superimposition) we see a twelve-year-old boy massaging the shoulders of an attractive middle-aged woman who sighs and moans with pleasure. The image suddenly disappears (as if Joe has

pushed it out of his mind) and is replaced by a FOR RENT sign. Joe hurries on his way.

6. Joe jumps on the Greyhound bus bound for New York.

Notes

1. The opening image tells us we are in contemporary southwest America which answers our first question – 'where are we?' But this image is also pure cinema; on the soundtrack we hear a western gunfight but the cinema screen we see is as empty and barren as the Texan desert behind – although, as the soundtrack reminds us, this was once the battleground of the new frontier, heartland of the American Dream.

2. Our next question is 'who?' and this question is also immediately satisfied. We meet Joe Buck in the shower and the sequence is spent getting to know him. Each new piece of filmic information gives us an additional clue as we try to work out what the basic situation is that will generate the coming film and give us an idea of what it's going to be about.

First we have Joe's song – which again contains a strange mixture of the old West and a vision of the East, New York, as now being the desirable place to go.

The energy of Joe's preparations, and his brand-new clothes, tell us that this is a very special day – the final burst of deodorant on his crotch even suggests that sex may be high on his agenda.

The commotion in the restaurant scullery not only shows us the nature of Joe's work but also, as we learn from his imaginary confrontation with his boss, what he's intent on escaping from.

3. We get still more insight into what Joe's escaping from when we walk with him through the sleepy suburb where his infectious optimism is further heightened by the words of the title song, which is also about making a journey to a new life.

4. When Joe arrives at the restaurant we finally learn the

precise nature of his aim, and hence the situation at the root of the film. He's going East, to New York, to make his fortune as a male prostitute. We are given this crucial information in a simple and believable way – in response to a question Ralph would naturally ask at such a time. The restaurant scene also gives us a further clue about the complexity of the situation. First, in spite of Joe's bravado, he doesn't have the nerve to get his back pay from his boss. And second, the naivety of his image of New York, as a city paved with rich, frustrated women and men who can't give them what they want, gives an insight into the unrealistic nature of Joe's expectations and hence into the possible obstacles and dangers ahead of him.

We now know the protagonist's aim and the first obstacle to his achieving that aim, and so the dramatic question can now be formulated: 'How will Joe Buck, given his naivety, survive as a male prostitute on the streets of New York?'

5. But we are given one final piece of information before we climb on the Greyhound bus and this is portrayed by the image of the boy massaging the woman's shoulders in Sally's beauty salon. The salon is derelict, which means we have entered Joe's unique interior world of either memory or fantasy and the image seems to relate directly to Joe's aim in that the young boy is somehow servicing the older woman's sexual needs. But the way the image suddenly disappears and is replaced by the immediate reality of the FOR RENT sign is almost brutal and seems to leave Joe, and us, with a sudden sense of loss. We don't yet know for sure who the boy or the woman are but this scene suggests that the motivation for Joe's journey is not purely material; his deeper motivation relates to certain unresolved issues from his own past. In other words there are two aspects to what is motivating the aim: what the character consciously wants and what he unconsciously needs.

Part Two

1. As the bus speeds out of the suburbs into the desert Joe tries to strike up a conversation with the driver, who totally

ignores him. Snubbed and hurt Joe retreats to the back of
the bus where he manages to impress two giggling teenage
girls. Reassured, he gives his new boots a quick polish with
his handkerchief and then turns to stare out of the window
at the familiar Texan landscape. The momentousness of his
departure from his home environment now seems to close
in on him.

2. Dissolve from Joe's thoughtful face through to the
hesitant smile of the boy we saw earlier (in Sally's beauty
salon). He's now standing outside a cowboy hat shop and
we hear his grandma in voice-over: 'You look real nice
lover boy, real nice. Make your old grandma proud. You're
the best-looking cowboy in the whole parade. You're going
to be the best-looking one there.' We think these words are
meant for young Joe but we now cut to the boy's point of
view and see that he is watching his grandma take another
cowboy, a full-grown man, into her arms, leaving Joe
somehow excluded and alone. We next see grandma telling
young Joe that his TV dinner's in the oven because 'old
grandma's got herself a new beau'.

3. Joe's memory is interrupted by a young mother who is
now on the next seat asking for some gum for her little girl.
Joe takes the opportunity to proudly tell the mother that
he's going to New York. She smiles politely but soon falls
asleep and Joe plays peek a boo with the little girl; Joe
hiding behind his cowboy hat and the little girl behind her
Wonder Woman comic.

4. Joe once again drifts into his imaginary world. On the
soundtrack we hear a girl whispering words of love and we
see:
– Anastasia, a beautiful teenage girl, running through a
field of corn towards a house.
– Joe as one of a pack of local youths, following Anastasia
down a dusty street.

80

– The pack of youths chase Anastasia across a desert landscape.

– Back at the house Anastasia runs into Joe's arms. They make love with Anastasia whispering to Joe that he's 'the only one' and 'the best one'.

5. Joe seems disturbed by his memories and looks to the next seat hoping to be reassured by the mother and child, but their seat is now empty and he is suddenly very alone.

6. An old man now sits in the next seat. Joe tries to make conversation by asking the old man if he knew his grandma, Sally Buck, but the old man simply shakes his head and looks away.

7. It's night and the bus speeds past lurid neon signs as we intercut with more of Joe's childhood memories: in bed with his grandma and one of her lovers; at the rodeo; as small boy in military uniform being left with his grandma by two young women; rocking on the front porch.

8. It's day and the bus is now filled with drunken servicemen. Joe hears the New York announcer on his radio and whoops with joy as he realizes they are at last entering New York City. His optimism has now fully returned.

Notes

The bus journey, taken as a whole, feels like a transition from the known to the unknown. In the first part of the opening we focused on Joe's optimism and although we realized there were dangers in the naivety of his expectations we were swept along by his confidence and energy. Now his hopes and fears, and our hopes and fears for him, are being pitted against each other in dramatic conflict, the tension growing as we near his destination.

1. The snub by the bus driver is a first reminder of how

indifferent strangers can be and Joe is heading for a world where everyone will at first be strangers! This rejection is quickly counteracted by his momentary success with the giggling girls, and when he polishes his boots we are reminded of the optimism of his sexual agenda.

2. Joe is leaving his home environment, probably for the first time ever, and his thoughts and feelings turn naturally towards his home and past. We have already been given a hint that there are complexities in Joe's childhood that are motivating his present action. We now enter a more disturbing memory. We think grandma's loving words are meant for young Joe and feel a real shock when we realize that the boy is simply an onlooker, displaced and excluded by grandma's new beau.

3. The young mother and child sitting next to Joe revive our hopes by reminding us of the potential friendliness of strangers. And the game Joe plays with the little girl also serves to remind us of the childlike traits in Joe's character; cowboys, like Wonder Woman, populate the world of children's fantasy. Joe's childlike traits are endearing but they also remind us of the danger his naivety may put him in.

4. Joe's next venture into his world of memory is even more unsettling. The images of himself alone with Anastasia are beautiful but also seem idealized, memory tinted with fantasy, and when we see him as a member of the local gang of youths chasing Anastasia we feel a strong hint of danger and potential violence. Anastasia's words of love, 'you're the only one', when put together with Joe's earlier memory of being displaced by grandma's new beau, remind us of Joe's unfulfilled need, only now we learn the very specific nature of this need; to be loved and to be the only one. But the memory/fantasy sequence as a whole raises more questions than it gives answers, implying a larger agenda behind Joe's deep motivation and leaving us wanting to know more.

5. Finally, as the bus draws nearer to New York, we are increasingly filled with fears for Joe's future, fears emphasized by the disappearance of the mother and child, the indifferent old man, the lurid neon signs in the night and the appearance of the drunken servicemen, each suggesting the very opposite dynamic to the optimism encountered in the motel room and the sleepy Texan streets. But, nevertheless, Joe whoops with joy as the bus enters New York City. This new, unknown world may be fearful and alien but Joe Buck will find a way, or will he?

In the beginning as a whole Joe Buck has been firmly established as the protagonist. His aim has been clearly stated, he's going to New York to become a male prostitute and this is the basic situation which is driving the action forward. We've been told enough about Joe for us to believe that he is capable of achieving his aim: he's handsome, he's got a beautiful body, he takes pride in his appearance, he's charming, he's energetic and enthusiastic, and his childhood experience seems to have prepared him for the work. The obstacles, or dangers, which threaten the fulfilment of his aim have also been clearly set up: he's naive, he has difficulty confronting authority (i.e. asking his boss for money), he has unrealistic expectations, his motivation seems to relate to some dangerously unresolved issues from his past, he's easily hurt when snubbed by strangers, he has childlike needs for reassurance, and, finally, the alienation and indifference he encounters on his way to New York will probably be ten times worse in the big city itself.

Joe's motivation has been touched on, both at the level of want and need. The motivation behind his want is his desire to start a new, and hopefully lucrative, life, and at a deeper level it looks like he may want to re-enact a sexual pattern he learnt in childhood with his grandma. His deeper needs for the security of love, to be 'the only one' and possibly to resolve a violent incident in his youth, have taken us still further into the complexity of the situation.

Finally, when the film opened, our hopes for Joe were

paramount, we believed he was capable of achieving his aim, but by the end of the beginning our fears for him have definitely moved into the ascendant. The stakes against him are high but the potential in his character, manifested by his sheer enthusiasm, gives us hope that he may be able to find a way.

Development Sequences

Earlier I mentioned that the central body of most feature films can usually be broken down into somewhere between six and eight development sequences and when we explored micro-cosms we discovered that, amongst other things, each sequence, whether it was from the opening, development or ending of the film, had its own shape – with a beginning, a middle, an ending and a dramatic question of its own. Our aim now is to get a sense of the unity of the central body of the film, or how the parts add up to a whole, while at the same time looking for the basic dramatic principles underlying the development of the story.

ONE: Joe's first pick-up

Joe settles into his hotel, and then goes out into the teeming streets. There are plenty of middle-aged women on their own but how does he go about picking them up? After a few abortive attempts he finally manages to proposition a middle-aged woman, but omits to tell her the precise nature of their liaison before they go to bed. When he is dressed and ready to leave he finally asks her for payment. She's so insulted that she bursts into tears and Joe ends up lending her money for a taxi.

– Joe's stated aim in the beginning was that he was going to New York to find work as a male prostitute and this sequence is structured entirely around his attempt to achieve his aim in the most straightforward way possible. But it turns out not to be so easy as he had imagined. The streets are certainly full of women on their own, but how does he know which ones are in need of his services? How does he approach them? And how does he do the deal? Remember how, in the beginning, Joe didn't have the courage to ask his boss for back pay that was rightfully his. We see now how this character trait is becoming a real obstacle.

At the end of the sequence Joe's central aim has remained the same but the dramatic question has become more specific: 'How is Joe going to find the women, and even if he manages to get that far, given his shyness about money, how is he going to manage the financial side of his business?'

TWO: First meeting with Ratso

Joe is sitting in a bar contemplating his difficulties when Ratso (Dustin Hoffman), a sharp young man with a crippled leg, admires Joe's 'colossal shirt'. Joe warms to him immediately and when Ratso warns him that the woman making eyes at him is in fact a man in drag Joe is impressed. He decides to tell Ratso his problems and ask for advice. Just as Ratso convinces Joe that what he needs is 'management' the transvestite approaches again, this time warning Joe that Ratso is a pickpocket. For a moment Joe doesn't know what to believe, but he soon decides to trust his new friend Ratso and leaps to his defence.

Limping and diminutive beside Joe, Ratso leads him through the New York streets to the prospective 'manager's' apartment. On the way he kicks a taxi that he accuses of trying to run him over, tries all the telephone booths for loose change, greets bewildered strangers as if they are old friends and generally shows Joe the streetwise ropes. He asks for twenty bucks for his services and leaves Joe at the 'manager's' apartment door.

– We have immediately begun to address the dramatic question posed by the previous sequence. At first, meeting Ratso seems to Joe, and to us, like a possible solution to his problems. We agree that he does need 'management'. But another element is also at work here. We learnt from the beginning that Joe also needs to be loved, or at least cared for. At this stage in the film we don't imagine that Ratso could fulfil this deep need but at a simple level we realize that he could be a friend and confidant. As soon as we see the two of them walking together in the street we realize that Joe's good looks and brawn complement Ratso's streetwise wits and we become alerted to their potential as a team. But at the same time, Joe has chosen to ignore the warning about Ratso given by the transvestite, and we are getting increasingly worried that Ratso is going to rip Joe off. So our hopes for the potential in the relationship are pitted equally against our fears, exacerbated by our knowledge of Joe's naivety.

Whilst Joe's central aim remains the same the dramatic question becomes still more specific: 'Who is Ratso's "manager" and what effect will the encounter have on Joe's prospects?'

THREE: Management?

For a while Joe doesn't realize that the so-called 'manager' is in fact a Christian soul saver, not until the man throws open his bathroom door which, with its flashing neon effigy of Christ, doubles as an altar. The man tries to drag Joe down on to his knees to pray. The scene is intercut with images of young Joe being baptised and obviously hating every moment of it. Panic-stricken, Joe runs from the apartment building and in a blind fury searches the streets for Ratso.

The extent of his anger seems to generate still more memories from his troubled youth and we see violent images of both Joe and Anastasia being raped by the gang of youths we saw in the beginning. When Joe finally arrives back at the bar, where he met Ratso, the transvestite, realizing that Joe has been conned, laughs at him. Joe picks up a bottle in anger but suddenly remembers himself as a boy smashing his grandma's beauty salon. He puts the bottle down and leaves.

– Since the beginning we've felt that Joe's naivety will be one of his biggest obstacles and now it lets him down badly. The dramatic effect of our realizing, long before Joe does, that this man is not the 'manager' he hopes for, is very powerful. We watch in agony as they talk at cross purposes, and when the altar is eventually revealed, in its full neon horror with the lavatory behind, it is both funny and tragic. During Joe's rage, when he searches desperately for Ratso, we learn more about the incidents in his youth first introduced in the beginning. But now we are given a horrifying new revelation; both Joe and his girlfriend were gang-raped. Although the drama is still left unresolved: there is an unsettling sense of ambiguity about the incident because we know that Joe was also a member of the pack. When we finally see Joe as a boy smashing his grandma's beauty salon we realize, for the first time, that anger and violence are deeply embedded in his character. The potential for this inner violence to surface yet again functions in the drama as another obstacle which may threaten Joe's ability to succeed.

Joe's aim remains the same but the dramatic question now seems more general: 'Given the extent of the obstacles against him, his recent failures, and our growing awareness of his deep needs, how will he survive alone in this indifferent city?'

FOUR: Lonely New York

Days and nights pass and Joe roams the streets without success. One evening he arrives back at his hotel to find he's been locked out of his room for not paying the bill and all his belongings have been taken as collateral.

Joe watches the young men washing dishes through a restaurant window. Dejected, he buys coffee and sits opposite a young mother and her child, hoping for some comfort. But this young mother seems high on dope and her child is equally weird. Joe spills ketchup all over his pants and to make matters worse tries to wipe the mess off with a coffee-stained napkin! Finally, with nowhere to sleep, he wanders the deserted late-night subway looking for forgotten coins in the slot machines. He catches sight of his reflection in a slot machine mirror and says, with obvious fear, 'You know what you've got to do now, cowboy.'

– The theme of this sequence is indeed survival. Things go from bad to worse. He loses the roof over his head and his treasured horse-hide suitcase (which in the beginning represented his optimism for the future). He watches the men washing dishes – remembering his former self. He seeks a little comfort from the mother and child, but they're a far cry from the mother and child we remember from the bus and only serve to further alienate him. He spills ketchup on his pants and we remember how proudly he first dressed in his new clothes, so sure that the key to his success lay in his appearance. When finally, homeless and destitute in the subway, he catches sight of himself in the slot machine mirror, again we remember the beginning and contrast the depths he has now reached with his former confident exuberance.

In fact, throughout this entire sequence, the images we got to know in the beginning, which related to Joe's hopes and aspirations, are re-encountered in the new light of Joe's present circumstances. The effect is devastatingly sad. The contrasts serve to emphasize the change in Joe's fortunes and enable us to empathize with his present plight. If we were at all in danger of distancing ourselves from the protagonist at the end of the last sequence, because of his possible complicity in the horrific violence of his past, we are now, once again, fully identified with him and so care about his survival.

At the end of the sequence things are so bad that we think he might have lost sight of his aim. But the dramatic question is as specific as ever: 'What is it that Joe knows he has to do and that he is clearly so resistant to doing?'

FIVE: The gay pick-up

Joe joins the studs outside a gay pick-up cinema. He's soon

approached by a gawky young student. They go into the cinema and Joe stares doggedly at a film about the space probe while the student makes love to him. The frightened and ambivalent expressions on Joe's face are intercut with scenes of him making love with Anastasia, but his recollections are confused between an ideal lovemaking and Joe lining up with a queue of youths for the gang-rape.

Joe and the student go to the men's lavatory for the pay-off but the student throws up in a basin and fearfully confesses to Joe that he doesn't have any money.

– Again the dramatic question is answered immediately; it may be difficult to hustle women in New York but it's easy to hustle men. Joe now learns what life as a prostitute can really be like, exacerbated for him by his fear of gay sex. Becoming a gay hustler is clearly not going to be the answer to his problems. At the same time we learn some more about his youth; Joe is bearing the burden of guilt for being a participant, as well as a recipient, in the gang-rape. Finally, his inability to ask for payment in advance lets him down again and he seems further from achieving his aim than he's ever been. The dramatic question is simply, 'What is Joe going to do now?'

SIX: Second meeting with Ratso

As Joe crosses the street he's almost run over by a taxi. He kicks the taxi in defiance and we're reminded of his first meeting with Ratso. He then walks past a café and sees Ratso sitting inside. He lights up with all the joy of seeing a friend before he remembers Ratso's con and his anger is rekindled. But Ratso is now much sicker, his cough sounds terrible and he hasn't got any money either. He offers Joe his last cigarette butt and a roof over his head instead.

Ratso takes Joe to the derelict building where he lives. There's no heating or lighting and the only colour in the squalor is in the pictures of Florida oranges Ratso has stuck up on the walls. Joe immediately falls into a deep sleep and Ratso watches over him with an almost maternal concern.

We now see a series of violent images from Joe's dream. Images from the gang-rape, again with Joe both as victim and rapist, are intercut with young Joe's grandma sadistically spanking his bare bottom and with Anastasia accusing Joe of rape and of being 'the only one' who did it. We see Joe being imprisoned and finally the world tumbling around him. In his dream even his new friend Ratso is out to get him. Joe wakes in a terrified sweat and accuses Ratso of stealing his boots. Ratso manages to calm him down and to reaffirm their friendship. Joe falls asleep content.

– When Joe kicks the taxi we are both reminded of Ratso and shown how Joe is being changed by the city; he's become more like Ratso. Ratso has changed too, he's sicker and even more broke. We remember the potential we saw in their relationship when they first met; now they seem to really need each other. So, when Ratso takes Joe home with him, in spite of the appalling squalor, we are filled with a new hope.

Joe's dream takes us further into the traumas of his past. It's now clear that Joe was both a victim of rape and a rapist, but we are also given some new information. Joe's beloved grandma spanked him with such sadistic cruelty that this too was a kind of rape. And Anastasia not only accused Joe of rape, she told the police that he was 'the only one' and he was subsequently imprisoned. The images culminate with an overwhelming feeling of terrible violence and betrayal between Joe and the two most important women in his life, with Joe as both victim and instigator, which has resulted in an intense confusion, fear and an all-embracing paranoia.

But something very interesting happens next: Ratso deals quite calmly with Joe's paranoia and not only manages to calm him but also shows a familial concern for his well-being. So, although we've been taken still further into the depths of Joe's traumatic past, at the end of the sequence we feel that, emotionally at least, with Ratso, the streetwise cripple, he's in good hands.

Joe's aim, for the time being, has been forgotten. The

dramatic question now is, 'How will Joe and Ratso survive together?'

SEVEN: *Joe's new life with Ratso*

With Joe's good looks and brawn and Ratso's wits and cunning, together they make a good team. Ratso tells Joe his dream which is to go to Florida where he will get well and Joe will find more lonely rich widows than anywhere in the country. They decide that to get the money for the trip they need to clean Joe up and this time Ratso will act as manager. They wash his clothes, steal his hat back, clean his boots and finally he is once again standing admiringly in front of the mirror ready for action.

But their attempts to find Joe work fail. Winter sets in and they're freezing and hungry. They pawn Joe's radio, sell blood, walk the streets and watch the building next door being demolished, but throughout this adversity their friendship and interdependence grows. One day Ratso takes Joe to the cemetery where his dad is buried and afterwards, while they're sitting in a café discussing the possibility of an afterlife, an eccentric young couple appear and give Joe a party invitation.

– We see here how the central dramatic thrust of the story is reasserted and Ratso becomes a part of Joe's aim rather than an obstacle. Florida is both a place where Ratso will get well and where the beaches are paved with rich widows just waiting for a hustler like Joe to come along. Also, if we remember from the beginning, Joe's need for love underlay his desire to work as a hustler. This need is now finding fulfilment in his friendship with Ratso and so Joe's aim now naturally extends to include Ratso's need to get well.

To get to Florida they need money and so, once again, Joe goes through the now familiar preparations for work. When he confronts his revived image in the mirror we are reminded of the optimism he felt in the beginning and once again we become hopeful for him. His attempt to get work fails again but, as we watch their friendship growing in the face of terrible adversity, we find that a big shift has taken place in our hearts; our hopes are now more focused on the success of Joe's friendship than on the success of his work endeavours. The fulfilment of his need is ultimately more important than the fulfilment of his want. Although this too is under threat: Ratso is slowly getting sicker.

Finally, when they are reduced to exploring the possibility of their dreams being fulfilled in the afterlife, given that their hopes of fulfilment in this life are looking so slim, a wonderful act of God, or coincidence, takes place. Out of the blue they are invited to a party.

We end on an unrealistically hopeful note – 'Will the party somehow get them to Florida?'

EIGHT: The party and Joe's first successful pick-up

The party turns out to be a 1960s extravaganza of eccentricity and drugs but Joe, much to his surprise, is picked up by a wealthy woman. Ratso negotiates the deal and for the first time since the film began Joe has actually got work as a stud. The only problem is that Ratso is so sick he can hardly stand. On the way out Ratso falls down an entire flight of stairs. The taxi pulls away, with Joe and the wealthy woman in the back. Joe is filled with anxiety as he looks at his friend, diminutive, sick and alone in the bitter winter snow.

Joe goes to the woman's apartment but finds, much to his humiliation, that he can't make love. The woman teases him by accusing him of being gay. This so riles Joe that he forces himself to prove her wrong. The next morning the woman is so pleased with the experience that she phones her friends to get Joe more work and Joe goes home to find Ratso and tell him that success is theirs at last.

– The party turns out to be a blessing in disguise as far as Joe's work prospects are concerned, but his anxiety for his sick friend outweighs all his excitement about finally achieving his aim. He now realizes that his need for the kind of familial love provided by his friendship is far more important to him. The dramatic question we are left with now is, 'Will Joe's financial success come in time to save his friend?'

In the development as a whole Joe's central aim, although receding somewhat in the middle sequences, has essentially remained the same throughout. (On the one occasion when we seemed to lose sight of it altogether the following sequence was devoted entirely to re-establishing its importance.) Each sequence has a beginning, development and end of its own, structured around the exploration of a specific dramatic question, which in each case relates directly to the preceding sequence. The ending of each sequence arrives at a different but closely related dramatic question. The sequences each focus on, and explore in depth, either the obstacles to Joe's achieving his aim, or the rebuilding of his hopes. All these obstacles, and his hopes, were raised in the beginning, either directly or obliquely – even the violence in Joe's past was hinted at in his early memories.

Almost all the motifs which appeared in the beginning are also repeated in these development sequences. But when we encounter them for a second, and even a third, time we see them in a very different light. Because the motifs represent Joe's hopes and fears this serves to accentuate and add poignancy to the changes in Joe's feelings and fortunes. Our hopes for Joe are always pitted against our fears resulting from the obstacles. But although things go from bad to worse, we never entirely lose sight of hope; when Joe reaches his lowest ebb Ratso reappears. Hope energizes the drama. The obstacles provide conflict.

Each development sequence changes Joe although his aim and his deep needs remain the same. But in the late development sequences a significant shift takes place; we are now far more aware of Joe's deep need. Consequently we now find that our hope is more centred on his finding fulfilment for this need than on achieving his aim. At the same time the chief obstacle also shifts: Ratso is getting sicker and their poverty is a real danger to his health. The success of Joe's aim has now become essential for the fulfilment of his need and, by the end of the development, a sense of real urgency is building: time for Ratso is running out.

The Ending

Crisis and climax are concepts we associate with danger in our everyday lives and, as we saw in the introduction to classic structure, they are also concepts which, along with the theme and the resolution, have a crucial role to play in determining the classic ending. The question facing us now is how these concepts manifest themselves in the texture of the film and how a full understanding of the meaning of these four concepts sheds light on the classic structure as a whole.

The Crisis (part one)

At last it looks as if Joe's fortunes have turned. His night with the woman he met at the party was a success and he's got another job lined up for the end of the week. He returns to the derelict building, clutching food and medicine, eager to tell Ratso the good news that they won't have to steal any more. But Ratso is now sicker than he's ever been. He's sweating and shivering so much he can hardly hold the mug of soup Joe makes him, let alone eat. He confesses to his friend that he can no longer walk and he's scared. Joe is momentarily annoyed with Ratso; how can he have got so ill just as Joe's on the verge of success as a hustler? He suggests getting a doctor, but Ratso thinks doctors, like the police, are dangerous. Florida, he insists, is the only answer. But to get there they need more than the twenty bucks Joe earned the night before and they can't wait for the job at the end of the week; Ratso might not last that long.

– Joe's annoyance with Ratso for getting so ill just as he's on the verge of getting a proper income from hustling expresses the conflict between what he has been wanting throughout the film

94

and his devotion to Ratso. But the dramatic question we were left with at the end of the development was, 'Will Joe's success as a hustler come in time to save Ratso?' This question is now restated with an even greater urgency. Ratso is so ill that they cannot even risk waiting until the end of the week for Joe's next job, they have to get to Florida as quickly as possible. There is, of course, an easier option in their present predicament and that is to fetch a doctor, which is why it becomes necessary to deal with Ratso's fear of doctors at this point (for the sake of the believability of the rest of the film). Florida, if we remember from the development, became a part of the aim – in Florida Joe will find it easier to get work as a hustler and Ratso will recover (or so they believe). At the end of the scene the stakes are higher than they have been at any point previously in the film – Joe's ability to find money is now a matter of life and death.

The Crisis (part two)

Joe goes back out on to the streets, desperately worried about his friend and determined to find the money somehow. He phones the woman he scored with the night before, but she's left town. He's in an amusement arcade, shooting at tin cowboys while trying to think of a plan, when Towny, a lonely middle-aged businessman, approaches him. Joe's need to help his friend is greater than his fear of the gay hustle and he goes with Towny to his hotel room.

– Again the obvious solution to the problem has to be dealt with first, which is to ask the woman Joe spent the previous night with for money. So he phones her only to find that she's left town. But more importantly, it now becomes clear that Joe's deep need for a loving friendship, a need we detected in Joe way back in the beginning of the film, outweighs his desire to achieve his aim. This shift is made visually clear with the image of Joe shooting tin cowboys; the motif which has stood for Joe's pride in himself as a hustler throughout the film now becomes a cheap amusement and an object for destruction. There's also a hint of danger here – shooting is, after all, a desperate act. The irony here is further emphasized when we discover that Towny has approached Joe because he's attracted by his cowboy image. We've seen Joe resort to a gay hustle before (in the development), so we know that for him it's a solution only to be resorted to in the most desperate of situations.

The Final Crisis and Climax

While Towny phones his mother Joe practises asking him for money in the bathroom mirror: 'Listen,' he mutters urgently, 'I've got a sick boy on my hands and I've got to get him south as quick as I can.' But when Towny finishes his call he's changed his mind about the deal. In an agony of masochistic guilt, he asks Joe to leave. The scene now becomes intercut with images (from Joe's imagination) of him carrying Ratso's sick body out of the building and through the freezing streets of New York to the bus station. 'Listen,' he tells Towny through clenched teeth, 'I've got family,' and in a desperate fury he strikes him and takes the cash he needs from his wallet. But Towny has fallen by the telephone and manages to grasp hold of the receiver to call for help. Joe grabs the phone and rams the receiver brutally into Towny's already bleeding mouth.

– The opening image, of Joe practising asking for money in the bathroom mirror, serves to communicate the complexity of the conflicting emotions going on within Joe by reminding us of so many different moments in the film: the pride and optimism in the beginning, when he put on his new cowboy clothes in front of the mirror and practised giving notice to his boss; the moment when he first met Ratso, who admired his 'colossal shirt' in the bar mirror; the moment when he was desperate, alone and trying to pluck up courage for his first gay hustle in the subway mirror; the revival of hope, when his cowboy outfit was again clean and he was ready to go back on the streets with Ratso as his manager. In this scene the motif is again Joe's attempt to find courage and hope, but it's now combined with Joe's paternal words about having a sick boy on his hands which reminds us, once more, of the seriousness of Joe's present plight. So, when Towny changes his mind about the deal we know immediately that this is the crisis, the straw that breaks the camel's back.

Joe can't walk away this time, he's 'got family', as he says, and he's 'the only one' who can help Ratso. (Remember how in the beginning he wanted to be 'the only one' for Anastasia and his grandmother.) The intercut images of Joe carrying Ratso to the bus station further demonstrate how Joe's mind is fixed on his objective, he must save his 'family' whatever the cost. And the cost is great. Most of the major obstacles have been dealt with in the development sequences but two crucial ones are left: his difficulty in asserting himself over money matters and the deep inner violence born in his personal history. Although Joe is basically a loveable person he's been involved in some horrifying incidents in his past and when under extreme pressure he's capable of equally extreme violence. These two character traits are both crucial causal elements to the crisis and climax. The violent side of Joe's character takes him over. The climax, which is the tragic consequence of the crisis, is Joe's attack and probable murder of Towny.

The Resolution (part one)

Ratso, coughing and bathed in sweat, sits next to Joe as the bus speeds through the New York suburbs. Joe gently tucks the blanket around his friend. 'You didn't kill him, did you?' asks Ratso. 'You've got blood on your jacket.' Joe says he doesn't want to talk about it. Night falls and then a new day dawns as the bus speeds south. Joe wakes to find Ratso crying. 'I'm falling apart here,' Ratso says and confesses that he's wet his pants. Joe makes a joke of it to cheer Ratso up and asks him what size pants he wears. Through the window we can now see the blue sky and palm trees of Florida. Joe emerges from a store near the bus stop wearing a pale yellow short-sleeved shirt and inconspicuous pants. He dumps his cowboy jacket, Stetson and boots in a nearby garbage bin and heads back to the bus. As the bus continues on its way south he dresses

Ratso in a brightly coloured shirt decorated with palm trees and tells his friend his new plan: 'When we get to Miami I'm going to get some kind of a job,' he says, 'because hell, I ain't no kind of a hustler. There must be an easier way of making money than that. Some kind of outdoor work? What d'you think?' He glances at his friend who, although his eyes are strangely staring, appears to be asleep. Realizing that something is wrong, Joe tries to shake his friend awake, but Ratso is dead.

– This penultimate sequence of the film is the first part of the resolution. Ratso asks Joe the question we want to know the answer to: Was it murder? Joe doesn't want to talk about it, instead he tucks the blanket around poor, shivering Ratso. He's done what he had to do, he's got Ratso on the bus to Florida, and at this moment his concern for Ratso, who is still physically deteriorating, blots out all other concerns. Also, we can imagine that Joe probably got out of that hotel room so fast he doesn't know the answer.

The long bus journey south brings to mind Joe's bus journey in the beginning of the film. Joe is once again travelling towards a new life, only this time the predominant feeling is of an era ending. The motif of his cowboy outfit, which through most of the film represented his determination to achieve his aim, is finally disposed of in a garbage bin, and Joe, wearing the inconspicuous clothes which now represent his future hopes, tells Ratso that he no longer wants to be a hustler, he's decided to get a real job. But Ratso, like the hustler era in Joe's life, is dead.

The Resolution (part two)

The bus pulls to a halt as Joe tells the driver what's happened. The driver asks Joe to close his friend's eyes and tells the curious passengers that there's nothing to worry about, just a little illness and they're only a few minutes away from Miami. The bus continues on its final leg of the journey. In response to the curious passengers who are staring at Ratso's body, Joe protectively puts his arm around his friend's shoulders and holds him tight. The bus cruises into Miami and we watch, through the reflections of the passing buildings on the bus window, Joe's face as he holds Ratso's body in his arms. Ratso looks somehow peaceful, protected from life. Joe looks bewildered, devastated, sad, but somehow, in his fresh new clothes, stronger and more able to cope with life than we've seen him before. Fade to black.

– Joe, as on his first bus journey, has to confront the in-difference of strangers and, as we watch his face through the reflections of the city buildings, we realize that he is also once again arriving in an alien city environment. But he has changed since that first journey. He now has a new strength, born of his recent experience. He wants to make something of his life rather than become consumed by the criminal underworld. This is stressed by his change of clothes and by the way, in spite of his obvious fear of death, he holds his friend's body so protectively. This image also seems to tell us that he is not alone, his relationship with Ratso will remain a part of him – he's changed as a result of it, he's learnt that 'family' is the most important thing for him. Although Ratso is dead his newly found self-knowledge is crucial to our hopes for Joe's future.

Finally, the way the reflections of the buildings pass over Ratso's body is enormously sad, speaking somehow of his death, and even of the nature of death itself, as Ratso's spirit seems to pass both into Joe's history and back into the city landscape.

So, all the major strands which were set up in the beginning and pursued through the development have now reached their natural, and perhaps inevitable, conclusion in the climax and resolution. Joe's unconscious need for love, which we detected in the beginning, is now fully conscious and has proved to have a more powerful influence on his life than his conscious aim. And in the resolution we learn that his aim, like the motif of cowboy clothes, has been finally disposed of.

But what of the theme which is, of course, the moral standpoint of the film? If we remember, from the outline of the basic principles of classic drama, the theme inevitably rises to the surface in the climax. Anybody who has seen the film will recall the full horror of Joe's attack on Towny. This horror is not wholly a result of the explicit nature of the violence itself. The reason why this particular image of violence so offends people is that, in spite of his involvement with a gang-rape earlier in his life, most of us have grown to love Joe Buck. And now this climax scene is asking us to love a character who has not only been a participant in a gang-rape but has also committed an act which probably resulted in murder. This presents us with a considerable moral dilemma.

The resolution of the film does not relieve us of this moral dilemma, instead it focuses on Ratso's death and Joe's hopes for a new life. Consequently at the end of the film we are forced to return to the scene of the crime and to ask ourselves what it means. Each of us will, of course, finally have to come to our own conclusion about such a difficult matter. But the film as a whole, by inviting us to love Joe Buck, seems to be saying that we cannot judge this kind of violence purely by the act alone, we have to take into account all the extenuating circumstances, or, to use Aristotle's words 'the occasion, the means and the reason'. We don't have to morally condone the violence but we do have to abandon simplistic notions of good and bad. And, by being asked to consider and understand the complexity of the good and bad within Joe Buck's character and the world he lives in, we also have to consider the complexity of these things within ourselves.

5 Kieslowski's *A Short Film About Love*

A SHORT FILM ABOVE LOVE (1990)
Screenplay by Krzysztof Kieslowski & Krzysztof Piesiewicz
Directed by Krzysztof Kieslowski

A Short Film About Love was originally made for Polish television as an episode of a drama series called *The Decalogue* – a contemporary cycle of ten films based on the Ten Commandments. Stanley Kubrick said in his foreword to the published screenplays: 'By making their points through the dramatic action of the story they gain the added power of allowing the audience to *discover* what is really going on rather than being told. They do this with such dazzling skill, you never see the ideas coming and don't realise until much later how profoundly they have reached your heart.'*

Two of *The Decalogue* films, *A Short Film About Killing* and *A Short Film About Love*, were also made as feature films for worldwide cinematic release.

The Beginning

Part One

1. Silence followed by the gradual introduction of the lyrical notes of a slow and haunting piano theme (which plays

*The Decalogue (Faber & Faber, 1991)

throughout the sequence). A wrist wrapped in a surgical dressing is lit up in the darkness. A woman's hand comes to rest gently on the dressing. An older person's hand takes the woman's hand away. The camera pans from the surgical dressing up the arm to rest on the face of Tomek, a sleeping nineteen-year-old youth. Although his face looks relaxed with just the hint of a smile he also looks very ill. We move closer in to his face which twitches slightly as if he is dreaming.

2. Through an open window, half concealed by curtains, Magda, a beautiful woman in her late twenties, sits at a table playing patience. She seems to hear something, stands and walks to the fridge. She now has her back to us. Our attention is drawn to her white knickers and bare thighs as she reaches up for something out of our sight.

3. Tomek still sleeping.

4. Again we see Magda through a window. She is now wearing a man's shirt which fits loosely and dancing quietly with an artist's paintbrush in her hand. We are struck by how there are two images of Magda – this is an optical effect caused by a section of circular glass within the window which, like a fish-eye lens, encapsulates her second image in miniature within the frame.

5. Tomek's sleeping face is cast into shadow.

6. A glass window crashes into tiny pieces on the wooden floorboards in the corner of a gymnasium at night. Tomek jumps down on to the floor and cautiously leaves the gymnasium. As the credits roll Tomek hurries through the corridors of a deserted school. He arrives in a storeroom and searches the shelves with his torch, lighting up computers, video recorders, televisions, until he finds a small telescope. He smiles with satisfaction, tucks the telescope inside his coat and leaves.

7. Cut to a big close-up of Tomek's hand pulling focus on the telescope which is now set up in his room. Through the telescope we see the grey concrete façade of a post-war apartment block and come to focus on a particular apartment window. Tomek stands back with a smile and begins to dismantle a pair of binoculars which have previously been fixed into a position facing the apartment.

Notes

1. The opening shot instantly plants dramatic questions in our minds: Whose wrist is it? What has happened? How did this person get hurt? These questions are quickly followed by more. Who is the woman whose hand gently moves to touch the surgical dressing? Whose is the older hand which takes the woman's hand away? Why does she or he remove the woman's hand? What is the connection between these three people? And how are the two hands connected to the wound? Not only is our curiosity already excited, our emotions have also been aroused – it is as if we have been invited to share an intimate concern for the wound. With this in mind we pan up to Tomek's sleeping face – the answer to our first question. As we move slowly closer, although he is wounded and looks ill, we see that his face is relaxed with a hint of a smile. The effect of moving in closer makes us feel as if we are beginning to get to know him. The process of inviting an audience to identify with a character has begun. Already we find ourselves wondering what is going on in his mind?

2. As if in answer to our question, we see Magda playing patience. The way we are looking at her, through an open window half concealed by a curtain, places us in the position of a voyeur – we are observing her from outside without her knowledge as she believes herself to be alone. This sense of being a voyeur is emphasized as she gets up and goes to the fridge to reach up for something – the image of her bare thighs and white knickers is beautiful and also makes us think of her sexuality.

3. This time when we return to Tomek's sleeping face we wonder if this is what he is thinking – is he dreaming of Magda, or remembering seeing her like this? Are we sharing a moment when he too is enjoying her sexuality?

4. Our next image of Magda is more complicated. We both see her through the window and at the same time see a second miniature image of her encapsulated within the fish-eye section of the glass. It is as if we are seeing her through a lens which adds a new dimension to the meaning of the image – it is also about the complexity of seeing. The effect makes us even more aware of our position as unseen observer. As Magda dances with the paintbrush in her hand she appears to be alone and completely unaware that she is being watched. But any sinister connotations with the role of the voyeur are somehow smoothed away by the gentle harmonious piano notes on the soundtrack. The music lulls us into viewing the woman with pleasure. Is it this pleasure that is causing Tomek's relaxed smile?

5. This feeling we have, that we have been sharing what is going on in Tomek's mind, is confirmed when we see the final shot of his sleeping face. The shadow casts him into darkness and casts us out of his mind ending the pre-credit sequence. The connection between Tomek and Magda has been firmly established. We know he's thinking about her and we felt his pleasure in the experience by sharing it with him. But the questions planted in our minds by the opening shot still remain: What has happened to wound Tomek? How is the wound connected to Magda? And who is the third person?

6. The glass crashing on the floor of the gymnasium breaks the hypnotic trance-like mood of the pre-credit sequence. We have been looking at Magda through a window and now a window is smashed – they are not the same window but there is an unconscious association. When Tomek jumps down into the gymnasium we recognize him immediately and also notice

104

that his wrist is *not* bandaged. Could the glass crashing on to the floor, which so definitively breaks the mood of the pre-credit sequence, also mark the beginning of the story of what has happened to Tomek which eventually led to his wounded wrist? The assumption we make is that we have gone back in time. As Tomek hurries through the deserted corridors of the school we realize that he has broken in. We now want to know why. What is he looking for? Is this going to be a film about a burglar? (Remember, we are still trying to get our bearings in the film, still looking for clues which will tell us what the film is to be about.) This question is quickly dispensed with. A common burglar would take any stuff that is valuable. But Tomek is not interested in the computers or video recorders. He is only interested in one thing, a telescope. Note the economy of Kieslowski's storytelling. He has not included what may well have been superficially dramatic exterior shots of Tomek breaking into the school at night. Kieslowski is only concerned to show details that focus our minds on the one thing that matters – that Tomek wants a telescope – which is central to the film's theme.

7. For similar reasons of economy Kieslowski dispenses with Tomek's journey home. He cuts instead to a shot telling us why Tomek wants the telescope by showing him focus on one particular apartment window. The exterior of the apartment block tells us about the anonymous alienating exterior of Tomek's home environment. As he dismantles the binoculars, his former apparatus, we learn that Tomek has been watching this apartment before, only now he has upgraded his viewing equipment.

A major question facing all writers is where to begin a story. The frequently quoted reply is to begin at the beginning. But in fact the more experienced writer knows that it is often far more dramatic to begin in the middle of things. (A narrative device suggested by the Roman writer Horace 2000 years ago – but just as applicable today.) Although it might be interesting to see the first time Tomek began spying on the apartment opposite and to know what was going on in his life at the time, it is more dramatically compelling to enter the story when the binoculars are no longer sufficient – Tomek is already in the grips of something that is now causing him to take risks, to commit a burglary, and who knows what it will lead to next? We are dramatically engaged by the urgency of this question.

Part Two

1. Magda goes into the post office where Tomek works. She hands Tomek a money order notice and while she waits she takes off her high-heeled shoe, shakes it and knocks it on the counter as if there is a stone in it. She is indifferent to Tomek – to her he is a stranger who serves behind the counter. Tomek tells her the notice sent to her was a mistake and she should come back another time. She leaves angrily slamming the door behind her.

2. Tomek is learning a foreign language in his room at home. There is a knock at the door and a middle-aged woman, his landlady, enters to tell him that Miss Poland is on the television. Tomek obligingly follows her into the sitting room of the cramped apartment. His landlady sits in front of the television clearly hoping that Tomek will join her, but he's not interested. An alarm clock goes off in his room and he takes the opportunity to escape. Back in his room he removes a red cloth which cloaks his telescope, folds it methodically and looks through the telescope. We see what he is seeing. Magda comes into her flat, looking through her post, and takes off her high-heeled shoes which she places on the table. The lyrical haunting piano theme begins on the soundtrack and we notice her double image through the same fish-eye lens in her window that we saw in the pre-credit sequence. We also see that her attention has been drawn to a large painting on the wall which she looks at while she slips off her trousers and blouse. Tomek walks through the sitting room to fetch a cup of water from the bathroom. His landlady turns from the Miss

Poland competition to look at him – she still wants him to keep her company. But he returns to his room where he makes himself coffee and prepares something to eat, all the time glancing through the telescope. Magda, now wearing only her underwear and a loose shirt, goes to the fridge and takes out a bottle of milk and something to eat while she works on her painting.

3. Tomek reaches for the phone and dials. Magda answers her phone. 'Hello,' she says, 'hello.' But there is silence. 'Enough of this idiocy. Who is it? I can hear you breathing, you bastard.' She hangs up. Tomek looks guilty. He dials again. When she replies angrily he says, 'I'm sorry,' and hangs up. We hear the lyrical theme music as Magda looks thoughtfully at the phone. The picture we have of her through the window again contains the fish-eye lens with her miniature image encapsulated within it. She then appears to react to a sound, hurriedly clears the bedclothes from the bed and goes to answer the door. A man comes in. They begin making love almost immediately. Tomek looks disturbed and pushes the telescope away.

Notes

1. Just as in real life, when we are getting to know someone we often want to know what they do for a living. We now learn that Tomek works in a post office. We also learn a little about Magda's character. She appears strong and assertive – the kind of woman who bangs her shoe on a post office counter, slams doors and gets angry with her time being wasted by others' mistakes. It is worth remembering the notice sent to her by mistake – could this be a 'plant' for a future part in the drama?

2. In the next scene we get to know more about Tomek. He's learning a foreign language. The apartment he shares with his landlady is cramped and she seems lonely; there is only one armchair in front of the television when she tries to get Tomek to watch Miss Poland with her. The decision to have a beauty contest on television is no accident. It tells us that Tomek is not

a normal voyeur, if he were he would no doubt want to watch the nation's beauty queens lining up for the camera. But Tomek shows no interest, instead he takes the first opportunity to slip away. Once back in his room we learn of the extent of his obsession. He sets his alarm clock so that he can be ready to watch Magda arrive home. There is something neat, organized and even ritualized about the way he carefully folds the cloth which covers his telescope and settles down to eat while watching Magda. We learn more about Magda too. Whatever her day job she is also an artist. Like Tomek she appears to have her familiar habits and routines when she arrives home: checking her post, putting her shoes on the table (the same high-heeled shoes we saw in the post office), slipping off her day clothes, taking milk from the fridge and something to eat while she works on her painting. It is as if, unbeknown to Magda, Tomek is sharing her life with her, he is even joining her for his evening meal and this has been his evening routine for some time now.

3. What happens next threatens to disrupt the calm atmosphere of the routine – Tomek breaks an unseen boundary by telephoning Magda. She is understandably annoyed with her nuisance caller. When she says 'Enough of this idiocy' we get the impression that this too has happened before. But we are struck by his guilt when he calls back to say he is sorry, and so is she. The shot of her through the window with her image again repeated in the fish-eye lens, accompanied by the lyrical theme tune, reminds us once more of the pre-credit sequence when we saw that Tomek was hurt. By phoning Magda and speaking to her Tomek has lowered the guard of his anonymity and this feels dangerous. The arrival of Magda's lover and Tomek's response, pushing the telescope away and refusing to watch, adds a final crucial ingredient to enable us to understand the nature of the story. Tomek is *not* watching Magda purely for sexual titillation. He does *not* want to see her making love. This single action forces us to look elsewhere for Tomek's motive for watching her.

All the ingredients of the opening are now in place. We know that Tomek is the protagonist because the answer to the question, what does he want or what is his aim?, is clear – he wants Magda. His desire for her image is central to everything we have seen so far, his desire for her is so great that it has become the major obsession which governs his life. Although what wanting Magda actually means to Tomek remains unclear. Could it be love – as suggested by the title of the film?

What are the obstacles to Tomek achieving his aim? Magda is a beautiful older woman, strong, assertive and experienced. In contrast Tomek appears barely a man, inexperienced, shy, not the kind of person Magda would think of as a lover. She hardly noticed him in the post office. What's more, we have learnt that she has a lover already – this man could certainly be an obstacle to Tomek fulfilling his love. We don't yet know the role that Tomek's landlady will play, although she seems lonely. We are still wondering whose was the older person's hand in the opening shot? What if Tomek did declare his love to Magda? How could a relationship between them possibly overcome this inauspicious beginning? Tomek has, after all, been spying on her without her knowledge and making nuisance phone calls. This would appear to be an almost insurmountable obstacle. If Magda was to learn of his spying surely she would despise him? And how might this affect Tomek?

It's worth noting here how Kieslowski has used all his skills as a film-maker to prevent us from despising Tomek for his voyeurism. Although we know that Tomek's spying is morally indefensible we have identified with him. In order to understand how we must return once more to the first image of Tomek in the pre-credit sequence. He is hurt and vulnerable. Some in the audience may suspect, even from this single shot, that the surgical dressing could be a result of slashed wrists. There is a lesson here; identification has a lot to do with vulnerability, because vulnerability suggests an openness, a way in to a character's soul. Even if the character appears bad, if we can see our way through their defences we begin to care about them. So by opening the film in this way Kieslowski is not only presenting us with the dramatic question, how did this happen to Tomek? He is also inviting us to care about Tomek by showing him as vulnerable and inviting us to share his most intimate thoughts. Kieslowski also uses music when Tomek is watching Magda, to suggest that his activity is gentle and harmless, rather than having sinister connotations. In this way the feeling of caring stays with us and we find ourselves wanting to understand Tomek, not to judge him.

At the end of the beginning, uppermost in our minds, is the danger to Tomek not Magda. When a person allows their life to be ruled by an obsession the greatest danger often appears to be the prospect of their obsession being taken away. What will happen to Tomek if he gets found out? Might his landlady expose him? What might happen if Magda finds out? Here there may be a faint ray of hope. Magda's characterization is already quite complex. She is an artist and is uninhibited sexually. Although she is angry with her nuisance caller she is also thoughtful when he calls back to say he is sorry. Might she be unconventional enough to show some understanding? But this ray of hope is slim and the obstacles to Tomek's achieving his aim appear to be almost insurmountable. At the same time our identification with Tomek is strong. The central dramatic question is how, in spite of our doubts about the morality of his obsession, can Tomek find a positive way of surviving this situation, or how can something good come out of what appears on the surface to be bad?

Development Sequences

Again we will see how the central body of the film can be most easily understood by breaking it down into development sequences, each with its own beginning, middle, ending and a reformulation or addition to the central dramatic question which leads us on to the next sequence.

ONE: Tomek interferes with Magda's love life

Tomek is in a supermarket when he notices Magda complain to the supervisor about her milk not being delivered. The supervisor tells her that they have a staff shortage.

That evening at home Tomek is as usual watching Magda. Again Tomek appears disturbed when he sees her making love, this time with a different boyfriend. He reaches for the phone, calls the gas board and reports a leak in Magda's apartment. While he waits for his plan to take effect his landlady tells him about a letter she has received from her son who is away seeing the world. She is very affectionate towards Tomek and tells him that although her son may return it won't be for long and she would like it if Tomek stays with her. She says that her son has an Arab girlfriend and asks Tomek if he is 'seeing someone'. Tomek hesitates before answering 'No'. His landlady looks concerned. She talks about how girls only pretend to be casual, really they like a little tenderness and says if Tomek would like to bring a girl home she wouldn't mind. He mustn't be shy. Tomek listens politely and assures her that he hasn't anybody. Back in his room he watches the gas board arrive at Magda's apartment. Magda's evening of lovemaking is ruined. Tomek laughs at the success of his plan and punches the wall, breaking a wooden panel, in his exuberant expression of triumph.

– As the issue of the milk in the supermarket does not appear to have any immediate dramatic purpose we deduce that it is a 'plant' to be paid off later in the story. The scenes with Tomek's landlady serve to give us more information about his life. His landlady's affection for him, and his polite and fond response, are touching, although we worry whether she is at the same time using Tomek to fill the loneliness in her life. There is an obvious irony when she asks if Tomek is 'seeing anyone', an irony which Tomek appreciates by his smile and hesitation before he says no. When she asks if he has a girlfriend she also expresses our concern – why hasn't a young man like Tomek got a girlfriend? Is it shyness? Or is there something deeper going on?

The drama is picked up when Tomek again reacts with distaste when he sees Magda making love with another man and this time decides to interfere directly with her life by phoning the gas board. He succeeds in stopping her love-making but his success leaves us feeling disturbed – this is underlined by his punch of triumph which damages the wooden panel. The dramatic irony here is that as Tomek takes increasingly greater risks, becoming more pleased and sure of himself, the audience can see the potential danger this may lead to but Tomek can not. The dramatic question now is how long can this go on before Magda suspects?

TWO: Milk, blood and tears

Tomek asks the supermarket supervisor for a job delivering milk, shrugging off the prospect of rising at five a.m. as not a problem for him. Early next morning he arrives outside Magda's apartment. First he hides her empty bottle and then he rings her doorbell to tell her she has forgotten to put her empty bottle out. Half asleep, Magda fetches him a bottle and closes the door in his face.

In the middle of the night Tomek is woken by screeching car brakes. He looks out of the window and sees Magda in the car park having a row with one of her boyfriends. The boyfriend drives off and Magda goes into her apartment block alone. Tomek watches as she comes into her apartment and takes a bottle of milk from the fridge. She places the bottle on the table and accidentally knocks it over. We move into a close-up of the milk spilling across the table as Magda sits with her head in her hands, her whole body is shaking with tears.

Tomek's landlady calls to him from her bedroom. She asks him why he isn't asleep? 'Why do people cry?' he asks her. 'Don't you know? Haven't you ever cried?' his landlady replies. Tomek tells her that he did cry once a long time ago when he was left. The landlady tells him that people cry for various reasons; when someone dies, when they are left alone, when they can't stand living any more, when they are hurt. Tomek asks if they can't do anything about it. She tells him of a time when her son had toothache, in order to alleviate the pain he held a hot iron to his shoulder – he soon forgot about the toothache.

Back in Tomek's room he places his hand on the table and with a pair of sharp pointed scissors begins to rhythmically stab the spaces between his splayed fingers. He shuts his eyes and continues stabbing until the point stabs into his finger. He thoughtfully sucks the blood. Cut to Magda's apartment where, exhausted from crying, she is now slumped on to the table running her fingers aimlessly through the spilt milk.

– The 'plant', of Tomek watching Magda complain in the supermarket about her milk delivery, is now paid off and as a result the drama intensifies – Tomek has discovered a way of getting even closer to Magda. Also we know that milk is important to Magda, it is always the first thing she takes out of the fridge when she gets home, and in the next scene this is precisely what she does. But we now see her in a completely different light – when she sits down and cries, literally over the spilt milk, for the first time we see her vulnerability. A row with a boyfriend may have sparked off her tears but as we watch her body shaking with sobs the extent of her anguish feels great – almost as if she is crying for her life.

'Why do people cry?' Tomek asks his landlady and like her we are struck by the strangeness of his question. His landlady's affectionate patience with him is touching as she tries to explain. Her reasons – because people die, or are left alone, or lose their reason to live, or are hurt – all give us an insight into what may have been her life. We also learn an important fact about Tomek's life, that he was once 'left', in an orphanage we assume. This helps to explain why his sensibilities are different from normal young people and gives an important clue to his motivation. The story the landlady tells about how her son alleviated his pain leads directly to the next scene. We know what Tomek is doing when he stabs the scissors between his fingers until he draws blood – he is both alleviating his pain and sharing Magda's. When we cut, from Tomek sucking the blood from his finger to Magda aimlessly rubbing her fingers in the spilt milk, the scene takes on spiritual dimension. Kieslowski is inviting us to think about the basic simplicity of milk, normally associated with nurturing, now spilt, and of blood – two elements which are essential for life. He is inviting us to contemplate suffering, the need for nurturing and the need to share pain.

Our feelings for Magda have been transformed by this sequence. Until now we have seen her as strong, assertive, on top of her life. Now we learn that she is also vulnerable and has within her a huge reservoir of sadness. Now we can identify with her as well as Tomek. Although Magda and Tomek are in fact quite alone, in the film they appear to have moved much closer to each other. Our fears remain; that Tomek might never be able to achieve his aim, which is to fulfil his love for a woman like Magda. But for the first time our hope has been raised – there may be a good outcome for Tomek's story after all.

THREE: Tomek's confession

On his morning milk-round Tomek pushes a note into Magda's post-box. Later Magda comes into the post office and hands Tomek another money order. Tomek again tells her it is a mistake. But Magda does not accept this, she demands to see the manager. A row between Magda and the manager ensues resulting in the manager accusing Magda of forging the money orders. Magda is humiliated and leaves the post office in distress.

Tomek runs after Magda. He catches her up in a deserted precinct and confesses to her that he sent the money orders. 'Why?' Magda asks. 'Because I wanted to see you,' Tomek replies simply. Upset and uncomprehending, Magda walks away. Tomek stares after her and shouts impulsively, 'I saw you crying.' Magda stops, walks back to where Tomek is standing and asks him how. Tomek confesses that he has been watching her through the window. Magda is horrified and pushes him away from her in disgust. Rejected, Tomek wanders sadly back the way he came. Magda shakes her head as she watches him go, puzzling over what she has just learnt, she raises her hand as if she is about to call him back, but then changes her mind.

– The beginning of this sequence connects with the opening of the film when we first saw Magda take a money order into the post office. Now we know for sure that Tomek has been sending her the money orders as a way of getting her to come to the post office where he can enjoy seeing her at close quarters. Dramatically this sequence is a major turning point in the story. It contains all the ingredients of an ending. The increasing risks that Tomek has been taking to get close to Magda have led to the crisis in the post office which, because Tomek cannot stand to see Magda humiliated in public on his account, inevitably leads to the climax, which is Tomek's confession. One of our greatest fears for Tomek, that if Magda knew about him spying on her she would despise him, has now happened. Or has it? A stage in the story has ended but there is also the suggestion of a new beginning. We watch Magda's face as she watches Tomek walk away. We see what she sees: a strange and sad young man. Her expression is more one of compassion than disgust. When she nearly calls him back we have the impression that she wants to understand something. Our new dramatic question is: What will Magda do now?

FOUR: Punishment

Tomek is again watching Magda from alone in his room but this time she knows. She peers out of the window looking for him. She then takes off her coat revealing a sexy black dress and drags the bed to where it can be clearly seen through the window. She picks up the phone and gestures that Tomek should call her. He looks scared, but does as she wants. She points out that she has moved the bed for him to have a better view and tells him to 'have fun'. Her boyfriend arrives and she pulls him to the bed while taking off his clothes. They begin to make love and then we see, from Tomek's point of view, that she has told the boyfriend. She laughs, while her boyfriend scrambles to hide from the window, and throws his clothes at him.

The boyfriend appears in the gardens below Tomek's window. He shouts up to Tomek, 'Hey, come here you bastard.' Tomek obediently goes down to the garden. The boyfriend knocks him down with one punch. Back in the apartment Tomek's landlady lovingly attends to his bleeding nose.

– Our question is quickly answered. Magda has assumed that Tomek is an ordinary voyeur wanting sexual gratification and has decided to teach him a lesson by playing a game with him. By the way she throws her boyfriend's clothes at him and laughs, we get the impression that she is playing a game with him too. Tomek's obedience, when he goes down to the garden to face her boyfriend, suggests that he knows that he is guilty and must be punished. The dramatic irony here is strong – we know that Magda has got it wrong, she doesn't understand Tomek or his motivation. The dramatic question is now: How can Tomek redeem himself in her eyes?

FIVE: Redemption?

Tomek, nursing a black eye, delivers Magda's milk. She opens her door so suddenly he is knocked off his feet. She asks him if he wants to come in. He shakes his head. She asks him why he has been peeping at her. At first he is too embarrassed to reply. He looks out of a small window at the end of the corridor and says, 'Because I love you.' 'And what do you want?' she asks. He says he doesn't know. She makes suggestions: to kiss her? to make love to her? to go away with her? To each he says 'no'. 'So what do you want?' she asks. 'Nothing,' he says and turns and runs.

He runs on to the roof of the apartment block and stands looking out over a landscape made up of identical grey concrete apartment blocks. It's cold up there. He finds two thin blocks of ice and holds them against his ears as if to cool the heat of his embarrassing confession of love. He then sucks the ice and an idea occurs. He rushes back down to Magda's apartment. 'Could I invite you out to a café for some ice-cream?' he asks Magda politely. Cut to Tomek running excitedly in the gardens below, dragging his milk trolley with one arm and waving the other, circling in wide arcs like an excited bird. He passes a stranger, a man dressed all in white carrying a heavy suitcase, who watches Tomek with pleasure and wonderment.

– Tomek delivers Magda's milk. The routine of life goes on. And the extent of Tomek's obsession is such that he is not going to give up hope so easily. By the way that Magda opens her door we know that she has been waiting for him. This tells us that she is not indifferent to him. For her his punishment is not the end of the story. She already suspects that something more mysterious than simple voyeurism is going on. When Tomek tells her he loves her she assumes it is the superficial love of a callow youth. Her questions are those we asked ourselves at the beginning of the film, but now we know Tomek better they seem inappropriate. But when she finally expresses her exasperation and asks again 'so what do you want?', we too want to know the answer. We are with Magda now; with her struggle to understand him.

The scene on the roof is one we can all understand; the embarrassment we felt when we first told someone we loved them, an embarrassment that heats from within and burns the cheeks, despite the outer cold. The world Tomek inhabits is made up of concrete tower blocks – this love he feels is the human being within us all fighting back against this alien environment. Finally he sucks the ice and we have a visual association – we know exactly where his idea has come from when he rushes back down to Magda's apartment to invite her out, just like any normal young man. Again note the economy of storytelling here – we cut away before hearing Magda's reply. We know she has said yes by the sheer abandoned joy Tomek expresses when he runs through the garden. His excitement is infectious. For the first time since the film began, our hope that Tomek might find a way to fulfil his love for Magda is in the ascendant. Just as in our own lives, when we feel the total excitement of being in love all our doubts are suspended. We don't know who the stranger is, his presence at this moment in the film appears to be entirely symbolic. The choice of white clothes might suggest innocence or purity and his suitcase indicates a journey – life's journey, perhaps, as he witnesses Tomek's transcendent moment of joy. The dramatic question now is: Will the date fulfil Tomek's expectations?

SIX: The date

Magda and Tomek are sitting opposite each other in the café talking. Magda asks him to repeat what he told her that morning. 'I love you,' he smiles shyly. 'There's no such thing,' she replies. Tomek looks shocked. 'There is,' he insists. 'Apart from loving me and working in the post office what else do you do?' Magda asks. Tomek tells her he is learning Bulgarian because he knew some Bulgarians in the orphanage. He says he has a good memory, he even remembers his birth. But when Magda asks about his parents he says he remembers everything except them. Their talk turns to an ex-lover of Magda's who went to Australia and never wrote. Tomek confesses that he has been intercepting her post. He takes a bundle of letters from his jacket pocket and gives them to her. Magda opens a couple of letters, glancing briefly at the contents. 'You besiege me,' she tells Tomek angrily and lists all the bad things he has done to her. She then loses interest in her anger and tosses the letters aside. 'It doesn't really matter,' she says. Their talk moves on to Tomek's one friend, the landlady's son and how it was he who first showed Tomek how he could watch Magda with a pair of opera glasses. The conversation is interrupted by the waitress. After they have given their orders Magda takes Tomek's hand in hers. A close-up of their hands shows us Tomek's extreme nervousness at her touch. Magda glances at a young couple kissing in the corner of the café and tells Tomek that he has a lot to learn.

Magda and Tomek leave the café and walk towards the bus stop. They see their bus arriving. Magda grabs Tomek's hand, 'If we catch it you're coming to my place. If not no. Agreed?' They run, but too late, the bus pulls off. A moment later it stops for them.

– We suspected, at the end of the beginning of the film, that Tomek's aim was to fulfil his love for Magda. Now most of the obstacles to Tomek achieving his aim have been overcome; Magda's boyfriends have proved not to be a problem, Tomek no longer needs to devise ways of interfering with Magda's life, Magda knows all about his spying on her and doesn't despise him for being a voyeur or for 'besieging her life'. Instead she has put what has happened into the past. This is confirmed when she even tosses aside the letters Tomek has stolen from her ex-lover – the past no longer matters to Magda, she is interested only in the present. As we suspected early in the film, any real hope for Tomek must lie in Magda's character, her individualistic approach to life. It is her disregard for convention that remains his only hope.

With the other obstacles out of the way the theme of love now emerges in a more distilled form. 'I love you,' Tomek tells her again and without hesitation or bitterness Magda replies, 'There is no such thing.' Tomek is shocked and, because we are identified with Tomek, so are we. But we have also begun to identify with Magda – we shared her vulnerability and loneliness the night when she cried over the spilt milk, and we now feel the emptiness underlying her life view. Magda learns a little about Tomek's past; the orphanage, the loss of his parents, enough to see that he is no ordinary young man, enough to arouse her curiosity and pity. But an obstacle remains – she does not understand what he means by love. When she holds Tomek's nervous hand and indicates the young couple kissing in the corner, the suggestion is that for Magda love is about sex and this is what Tomek has to learn.

The conflict now pits Tomek's innocent belief in love directly against Magda's experience and disillusion. It is this which forms the final dramatic conflict as we move into the ending.

In his introduction to *The Decalogue* Kieslowski writes, '. . . to understand where you are in the present, it is necessary to retrace the steps of your life and isolate the parts played by necessity, free will and pure chance.'* Kieslowski now evokes this element of chance: 'If we catch it [the bus],' Magda says, 'you are coming to my place. If not no.' Magda's sudden impulse, to hand Tomek's future over to the capricious hand of fate, is bewildering. Whatever our fears for Tomek if Magda takes him home, we want that bus to stop and are relieved when it does. As with all great dramas, we don't want Aristotle's *deus ex machina* to intervene. We know that whatever is happening between Tomek and Magda has to be resolved through the playing out of their actions and reactions in order to reach the inevitable catharsis necessary for us, and them, to gain insight and understanding.

The ending

Crisis and Climax

Tomek walks around Madga's apartment, as if wondering at the strangeness of actually being there rather than watching through the window. He takes a glass ball from his pocket. Magda comes out of the bathroom, her hair wet from the shower and wearing only a short gown. Tomek tells her the glass ball is a souvenir and gives it to her as a present. Inside the ball is a little house in the snow. 'I'm not good,' Magda says, 'don't give it to me.' 'I don't care, I love you,' Tomek replies simply.

In Tomek's room we see that the landlady is watching them both through Tomek's telescope.

Back in Magda's apartment Magda asks Tomek to describe

The Decalogue (Faber & Faber, 1991)

what he sees when he watches her with men. Tomek says it's called making love. 'It's got nothing to do with love,' Magda reproaches him. Tomek attempts to describe what he sees, showing her how she lifts her hands above her head. She laughs and asks him if he has ever had a girl. 'No,' he replies, nervously. 'Did you do it with yourself when you watched me?' Tomek puts his head in his hands to cover his embarrassment and says, 'I used to, not now . . . Now I think only about you.' Magda crouches in front of him. She tells him she has nothing on under her gown. 'When a woman wants a man she becomes wet inside,' she says, 'I'm wet now.' She takes Tomek's hands and places them on her bare thighs, telling him not to be afraid. Tomek is overcome by the feel of her thighs. By the expression on his face and the sounds he utters we know that he has ejaculated before even beginning to make love. He cries. 'Already?' Magda says and adds dismissively, 'That's all there is to love.' Tomek is unable to look at her. He accidentally knocks her over as he rushes out of the apartment.

Magda looks worried and goes to the window. Outside in the darkness she sees Tomek run into the garden below. He slows down as he passes the man in white we saw earlier, still carrying a heavy suitcase. Tomek goes into the block opposite. Magda looks up at the windows trying to work out which is Tomek's. She searches in an old box of things and finds a pair of opera glasses. She looks again for Tomek's window. She lifts the phone signalling for Tomek to call her.

Tomek is in his bathroom filling an enamel bowl with water.

Magda writes on a large piece of paper: 'I'm sorry. Please come back.'

Tomek rolls up his sleeves and takes the blades out of a razor.

Magda holds her message up to the window.

Tomek cuts his wrists and holds his hands in the bowl of water. He concentrates hard as he watches the water turn red with his blood. He rests his head against the toilet and closes his eyes.

– This is the first time Tomek has actually been inside Magda's apartment and we know that for Tomek he is walking on hallowed ground. The glass ball he takes from his pocket connects with the visual motif of the lens and reminds us of the many different times we have seen this motif in the film; the lens of the telescope and the fish-eye lens in Magda's window containing her miniature image. The glass ball, which Tomek gives to Magda, takes this motif a stage further. The charming little house in the snow protected by the globe of glass is like a Christmas card image. The house is the kind of place where an idealized loving couple might live; it evokes feelings of domesticity, harmony and security. This is the clearest image yet of the childlike purity of Tomek's dream. As if recognizing this Magda rejects the ball. By saying 'I'm not good' she is also telling Tomek that she is not who he imagines her to be. Her project is to show Tomek the reality, not to nurture his illusions of reality.

The cut to Tomek's landlady, now watching through the telescope, adds quite a new dimension to the drama. We already know that she feels protective towards Tomek, but what is she up to now? This unanswered question serves to sustain the dramatic tension through to the end of the film.

Back in Magda's apartment it becomes clear that Magda's plan is to initiate Tomek sexually. He becomes increasingly nervous and embarrassed in the face of her direct questions about what he has seen when watching her having sex and whether he masturbates when watching her. His dream of the perfect love is finally dashed when he ejaculates prematurely and Magda coolly says, 'That's all there is to love.' In dramatic terms this moment is the crisis, the straw that breaks the back of all Tomek's hopes. What happens next is the inevitable outcome of the crisis and leads directly to the climax of the film, which is Tomek cutting his wrists because he feels that he has nothing left to live for.

Note here how the narrative structure of the film splits. While Tomek's story reaches its climactic moment, Magda takes up the baton of the protagonist. This is because in a classic love story there are usually two protagonists united by their common aim which is their quest for love. In more traditional love stories this unity of aim is set up at the beginning. Because this is a more unusual love story, it is only now, when Magda has all but destroyed Tomek's love, that her own feelings are awakened. Kieslowski demonstrates this by shifting the narrative to her point of view: Magda looks for Tomek out of the window, she tries to work out which apartment is Tomek's in the block opposite, she finds opera glasses and looks again, she tries to reach him with the telephone and the message she scrawls on the sheet of paper – all images which we associate with Tomek and show how Magda has now taken on Tomek's obsession. The intercutting provides the dramatic irony – we see what Magda does not: unbeknown to her, while she is trying to communicate with Tomek he is in the bathroom slitting his wrists.

Finally, let's consider the moment when Magda watched Tomek run across the gardens below; she saw him pass the man in white with the heavy suitcase. This is the second time in the film this man has appeared and again his appearance seems purely symbolic. The first time he witnessed Tomek's transcendent moment of joy; this time he witnesses the opposite extreme, Tomek's moment of extreme suffering which, as we soon discover, leads to his attempt to die.

The Resolution

Magda picks up Tomek's coat, which he has left behind. The doorbell rings and she hurries to answer it, hoping it might be Tomek, but is disappointed when through the spy-hole she sees the distorted image of one of her boyfriends. She refuses to answer the door. Back in her room she looks down to the gardens below and sees an ambulance drive away. Tomek's landlady makes her way slowly back into the apartment block.

Magda takes Tomek's coat and goes over to his apartment block, searching for his apartment. Finally she presses a doorbell. She has guessed correctly; Tomek's landlady answers and reluctantly invites Magda into Tomek's room. The landlady tells Magda that Tomek is in hospital, although it is not serious, he will be out in a few days. Magda asks what happened. The landlady says with obvious distaste, 'You will probably find it funny. He fell in love with you . . . He made a bad choice.' 'Yes,' Magda agrees. Tomek's landlady goes on to say, 'I don't need much but I am afraid without someone in the house.' Magda doesn't know how to reply to this and goes to the door. She asks if she may phone to ask after Tomek. The landlady says she doesn't have a phone and closes the door. As Magda walks away she remembers something. She knocks on the landlady's door again and asks for Tomek's name. 'Tomek,' the landlady smiles sarcastically and closes the door in Magda's face.

In the morning Magda wakes, still wearing her coat. She sleepily goes to her table where a game of patience is in progress. She plays a card and thinks. Outside she hears the tinkling of the milk trolley. She goes eagerly to the window and looks down to the garden – but instead of seeing Tomek she sees the landlady delivering Tomek's milk for him. Magda goes to the post office to look for Tomek. His usual position is closed. We notice that Magda now wears her hair up and very little make-up as she waits in the entrance hall of her apartment block. When the postman arrives she asks him about Tomek. 'It seems that he cut his wrists out of love,' the postman tells her. Magda asks for Tomek's name but the postman doesn't know.

It's night, the phone rings in Magda's apartment. At first there appears to be nobody on the line. Magda thinks it must be Tomek. 'I've looked for you in several hospitals,' she says, 'to tell you . . . you were right.' There is still no voice on the other end of the line. She hangs up. The phone rings again, this time one of her boyfriends speaks and tells her it was him just now, there was a problem with the line. Magda hangs up angrily. She goes to her bed and lies curled up like a foetus.

Outside in the early morning drizzle the landlady helps Tomek out of a taxi. Magda stirs but does not wake. Slowly Tomek and his landlady walk together into their apartment block. Later in the morning, as Magda is getting dressed, she hears her milk being delivered in the hall. She opens the door and asks the landlady if Tomek is back yet. The landlady says no.

Magda continues to watch Tomek's apartment through the opera glasses until one day she sees two figures at the window behind the lace curtain. Joyfully she grabs her coat. The landlady shows her into Tomek's room where he is asleep in bed. Magda begins to walk to his side but the landlady places herself between Magda and Tomek, as if defending him from danger. Magda walks around the landlady and sits at the end of the bed. She looks at the dressing on Tomek's wrist and moves her hand to touch it. The landlady firmly removes Magda's hand.

Magda goes to Tomek's telescope and looks through it at her own apartment. Through the telescope she sees herself as she was when she arrived home late at night; taking the milk out of the fridge, placing it on the table, knocking it over, sitting at the table crying. Still looking through the telescope she smiles slightly and closes her eyes. Back in her apartment Tomek's figure appears. He places his hand gently on Magda's shoulder and looks at her with concern as she sobs uncontrollably. Magda's sobbing subsides, she moves her head to rest on Tomek's hand and reaches her hand up to his face. Fade to black. End credits.

– Now Magda has taken up the protagonist's baton: her need to find Tomek is as great an obsession as was his need to fulfil his love for her. Her refusal to answer the door to her boyfriend tells us clearly that she has no interest in anyone except Tomek. Luckily Tomek has left his coat behind which gives her an excuse, if she needs one, to go looking for him. The scene with the ambulance suggests that Tomek's landlady might have found him in time to save his life.

The landlady now becomes the remaining obstacle to be overcome. Her attitude towards Magda is accusing – Magda is already feeling guilty and the landlady adds to her guilt. Her judgemental attitude to Magda, although perfectly understandable given the circumstances from the landlady's point of view, also reinforces Magda's idea of herself that she is bad. We have seen the landlady being affectionate and loving towards Tomek, as a mother towards a son, but we have also suspected that her affection might be as much in her own interests as Tomek's. When she tells Magda that she is afraid without someone in the house, we see more clearly than ever before how it is in the landlady's interests to keep Tomek tied to her. This sense of her being a danger to what both Tomek and Magda need is emphasized further when the landlady first lies to Magda by telling her that she does not have a phone, and then refuses to tell Magda Tomek's surname.

Magda wakes and goes to play patience at her table and we are instantly reminded of the first image we saw of Magda in the opening sequence of the film. This sense of unity with the whole film is reinforced as we watch Magda's search for Tomek and continually see images that remind us of Tomek's earlier attempts to reach her; the post office, the milk deliveries, watching Tomek's apartment through opera glasses, the phone call when there appears to be nobody on the line. We are struck, during this period, by how Magda has changed – this change is emphasized by her wearing her hair up and little make-up, which makes her look younger, more open, less in control of her life, and is crystallized when she lies curled up foetus-like on her bed. She is in this position when Tomek arrives home in the taxi. The dramatic irony here is that although Magda stirs in her sleep she doesn't wake – we know that Tomek is home but she doesn't. This irony is underlined when she asks the landlady if Tomek is home yet and again the landlady lies to her.

Magda finally discovers that Tomek is home by watching through the opera glasses. Her joy is palpable and we share it. The landlady has realized that she can't keep the truth from Magda any longer, although she still tries to defend Tomek from the danger she believes Magda represents. Here Magda again seems to have changed – she is not angry or confronting, as the person we met in the post office at the beginning of the film might have been. Instead she is patient with the landlady, although without relinquishing what she wants. When she sits on Tomek's bed and moves her hand to touch Tomek's dressing we recall the first image of the film. The story has now arrived full circle. We know now that the hand is Magda's, the hand which removes hers is the landlady's, and we now understand the full story behind this moment.

In the final scene in the film Magda sees herself through the telescope. The image Kieslowski has chosen to show us here is of Magda when she was at her most vulnerable. She looks at herself sobbing by the spilt milk and she smiles lovingly, as if seeing herself through Tomek's eyes has enabled her to feel for herself the love that Tomek felt for her. As she closes her eyes we are invited to share what she is imagining (just as in the opening pre-credit sequence we shared what Tomek was imagining). In Magda's fantasy she accepts Tomek's love, her sobbing subsides and she is able to reach out to him and accept his comfort.

All the strands which were set up in the beginning of the film have now reached their natural conclusion in the crisis, climax and resolution. *A Short Film About Love* is clearly and unequivocally a love story, although an unusual one. Both the protagonists have changed as a result of this story. Tomek's change happened in the final scenes before the climax. He learnt that he could come out of the lonely world where he could only view the woman he loved from a distance. He discovered the joy of talking to the woman he loved and of actually being able to say 'I love you'. Although his journey was painful and very nearly fatal, when he finally recovers Magda will be there to help him understand what has happened to him. Because we now know that Magda has also changed, we trust that she will be able to help him understand with the new-found love of her own. We will never know whether their feelings for each other will develop into a relationship. It may well be that their different characters and the age difference are such that there is no future for them as a couple. But that is not necessarily important. Not all love stories are for ever, some are short, their significance lying not in their longevity but in their intensity and meaning for the short period that they last and their effect on the future.

The theme of *A Short Film About Love* can be clearly understood from the climax of the film. Magda's cynicism and disillusion have led her to believe that love is purely sexual. Her attempt to teach Tomek this very nearly destroys him. Tomek's understanding of love is deeply felt, spiritual and the only thing that gives him hope for the future. We know that Magda learns this when she finally sees herself, as if through Tomek's eyes – through Tomek she has learnt to love herself, which will enable her to love another. Through this strange, sad and deeply moving love story Kieslowski is reminding us of fundamental truths about the nature of love itself.

6 Greenaway's *The Cook, the Thief, His Wife and Her Lover*

THE COOK, THE THIEF, HIS WIFE AND HER LOVER
(1989)
Written and directed by Peter Greenaway

Students are often surprised when I include *The Cook, the Thief, His Wife and Her Lover* in an exploration of classic narrative structure because Peter Greenaway is not usually associated with traditional storytelling and the film appears to them to be radically different from anything they have seen before. The mistake they are making is to assume that if the construction of the scenes is not naturalistic, if the use of image and sound appears daring, exciting and new, then the narrative structure must also be experimental. My reason for including the film is to show how, if you want to be daring, experimental and part of the film-making avant-garde, you don't, at the same time, have to invent the storytelling equivalent of 'the wheel'. In fact it is the conviction many aspiring film-makers have, that they must reinvent story structure in order to be original, which most frequently stalls them at the outset. They have a vision, but can't find a structure for it and they shun using the traditional form, fearing that it will somehow subvert or even destroy what they have to say and turn them into an 'ordinary' storyteller. One of the lessons we can learn from *The Cook, the Thief, His Wife and Her Lover*, which I consider to be a masterpiece, is that far from turning Greenaway into a conventional film

129

storyteller, his use of classic narrative has liberated his totally original vision of the world.

The classic form that Greenaway has chosen for his story is known in the theatre as revenge tragedy. One of the earliest examples is the *Oresteia* by the ancient Greek playwright Aeschylus. In the *Oresteia* Clytemnestra murders her husband Agamemnon in revenge for his sacrifice of their daughter to the gods in order to ensure a fair wind to sail his ships against Troy. Some of Shakespeare's plays also conform to this genre, of which *Hamlet* is the supreme example. One of the more gory is his early play *Titus Andronicus*, which contains the somewhat challenging stage direction: 'Enter Lavinia, raped with her hands cut off and her tongue cut out.' The Queen's sons, who had raped Lavinia, have cut off her hands so she could not point to who did it and cut out her tongue so she could not tell who did it. As his act of revenge Titus, Lavinia's father, has the Queen's sons killed, baked in a pie and served to their mother for dinner. As we shall see, this play may have influenced Peter Greenaway.

We discovered with *Midnight Cowboy* and *A Short Film About Love*, how a classic narrative can usually be broken down into the beginning, a series of development sequences and the ending. This also applies to *The Cook, the Thief, His Wife and Her Lover*. In fact Greenaway has made this structure even more explicit – after the opening sequence which takes place at La Hollandais restaurant, he introduces each of his development sequences by showing a menu card headed with the following day of the week, until the final menu card heralds the resolution of the film.

The Beginning

Part One

The film opens at a low level as a pack of dogs feed on animal carcasses. Slowly, as Michael Nyman's music plays on the soundtrack, the camera tracks up through backstage scaffolding to a higher level, where two men, wearing distinctive red costumes, pull back heavy stage curtains revealing, not a stage, but an empty parking lot at night. Cars and delivery vans drive up, a group of men get out of the cars, two men drag a third man into the lot. This man is stripped and beaten by the gang of thugs. Albert Spica, their boss (Michael Gambon), shoves animal faeces into the man's face – apparently the man owes him money. Albert's wife, Georgina (Helen Mirren), calls from the car, where she is waiting for Albert, to leave the poor man alone. But Albert continues to humiliate the man until he is ready to stop. He then, with Georgina and his henchmen, goes through large double doors into a vast restaurant kitchen.

A kitchen boy sings with a perfect choirboy's voice while he washes up. Georgina stops to listen intently. Albert tosses a coin into the boy's washing-up water and shouts for the French Cook, who is busy plucking a duck. Albert wants the new neon sign of his name, Spica, switched on to mark the three-month anniversary of La Hollandais restaurant's opening. An egg falls and breaks on the floor amongst the pile of duck feathers. The neon sign is switched on, which promptly causes a power cut. A waiter rushes in to say that the restaurant has gone dark. 'Thanks to Mr Spica's generosity it is dark everywhere,' the Cook says ironically. 'No power, no light,' he adds as we cut back to the parking lot where the hapless naked man is struggling to stand while the pack of barking dogs circle around him.

In the kitchen Albert attempts to read the French menu while the Cook hands out candles to his kitchen staff. Georgina corrects Albert's appalling French. Instantly the lights come back on. Albert is humiliated by his wife's perfect accent and smacks her in the face with the menu. He tells the Cook that he has bought two van loads of food. The Cook is not impressed, insisting that good cooks always buy their own food to ensure quality. Albert says he is the only person who offers quality around here, 'quality and protection'. 'Protection against what?' the Cook asks. 'Protection against the rash tempers of my men,' Albert replies and follows his wife and men into the

131

restaurant. As soon as Albert has gone the Cook helps the poor beaten man; he offers him a chair, asks his kitchen staff to wash him and hands him a brandy. The humiliated man weeps with gratitude while the kitchen boy sings as if in a cathedral choir.

Notes

The opening images immediately invite us to consider the film as a theatrical metaphor. Greenaway is not concerned with realism, instead he makes us aware of the set and how it might represent different levels of consciousness; the scavenging dogs at the lower level, the underpinning scaffolding suggesting the idea of structure, the men in red costumes who pull back the curtains revealing the parking lot on the higher level where much of the action of the film will take place. As we witness the violent assault in the parking lot, the image of the scavenging dogs at the lower level resonates – the dogs are doing what animals do while the men, although supposedly at a higher level, behave like animals. With the opening of the grand stage curtains we have been brilliantly introduced to Albert's crude and brutal world, where he is boss, his men do what he says and his wife, Georgina, although she pities the beaten man, is powerless to intervene.

Although we are made aware by the vans in the parking lot that the scene taking place is in the present, there is also a timelessness about Albert's world. This is suggested by the lace collars, cuffs, silk sashes and high boots worn by Albert and his men, the opulence and excess of the vast kitchen, which is reminiscent of the kitchens of aristocrats or royalty, and by Michael Nyman's music – modern but with echoes of the baroque. The opulence also tells us about Albert's wealth and pretensions – as the new owner of this restaurant he is moving up in the world. The beauty and purity of the kitchen boy's voice stands in stark contrast to the brutality and excess and also introduces us to another important difference between Albert and his wife: Georgina appreciates the boy's voice, Albert tosses him a coin, as if to a dog.

There is a wonderful irony when the blackout is caused by

Albert's insistence on seeing his name in lights, an irony underlined when the Cook points out that far from bringing light to the world Albert has caused 'darkness everywhere'. The cut, at this moment, to the naked man, covered in faeces, struggling to stand, surrounded by barking dogs, is poignant; the image is reminiscent of a renaissance painting of hell. There is further irony when Georgina corrects Albert in perfect French and instantly the lights return – as if her respect for culture brings light to Albert's dark world. The Cook also has a different sensibility; when we first meet him he is plucking the downy white feathers of a duck which suggests that, like a craftsman he has an intimate, tactile connection to his work. There is something harmonious and beautiful about the way he hands lighted candles to each of his staff; he respects quality, there are levels of meaning containing wisdom in his words and finally, by helping the beaten man he restores to him a modicum of dignity.

So, we have met the Cook – a refined, wise, caring man; the Thief, a gangster running a protection racket; and the Wife, who is dominated by her husband's brutality but is also caring and sensitive. We are now wondering who her Lover might be.

Part Two

The camera tracks with the two men who opened the stage curtains (we now realize their red costumes are waiter's uniforms) through to the stunning opulence of the restaurant where the rich and successful are dining in style. On the wall behind them is a vast reproduction of a Franz Hals painting of a group of Dutch burghers. The predominant colour in the restaurant is red. The tracking shot comes to rest on Albert's table where he sits with Georgina by his side, his main acolyte, Mitchell (Tim Roth), on his other side and his henchmen all around. Albert's talk is crude and he harangues everyone around him.

Georgina notices a single man sitting at a nearby table reading a book. She watches the man, Michael (Alan Howard), with increasing interest. Michael notices her and they exchange smiles. Albert's incessant talk turns to the idea of an artist – he insists that the way he combines business and pleasure means he is also an artist. 'Money is my business, eating is my pleasure, and Georgie is my pleasure,' he says, banging angrily on the table when he sees that Georgina is not listening. The Cook arrives with Albert's dinner. Georgina notices Michael leave for the toilets. She takes the opportunity to follow him.

In the spacious white ladies room Georgina fixes her make-up. Michael wanders in, as if by mistake. He leaves but waits outside in the red corridor, where Georgina passes him. Again they exchange smiles. In the restaurant, as Georgina walks past Michael's table, she looks at his book. The Cook notices this with interest. Georgina returns to her table where Albert is still holding forth. She notices Michael return to his table. Again she leaves for the toilets. Michael catches her up in the red corridor. The sexual chemistry between them is powerful and they return to the ladies toilets where they begin to make love in the privacy of a cubicle. Albert comes into the ladies room looking for Georgina. Michael manages to hide by standing on the toilet seat where he can not be seen from beneath the cubicle door. Georgina nervously convinces Albert that she is just having a quiet smoke – he hates her smoking. Albert pretends to leave but lies in wait for Georgina. A few moments later he pounces on her when she comes out of the cubicle but he still does not notice Michael. Almost as if he smells sex Albert crudely propositions Georgina but she manages to escape his advances and they return to the restaurant.

Notes

The restaurant depicts a world of sumptuous excess, further emphasized by the designer's use of the predominant colour red. The vast reproduction of the Franz Hals painting of Dutch burghers, the wealthy and powerful merchants of Hals' day, invites comparisons with the rich and successful in the present time – this again adds to our awareness of the timeless nature of the themes being explored. We notice how Georgina is first attracted to Michael because he is reading a book – he is a cultivated literary man, quite different from her crude husband. We have already seen how Georgina was moved by the kitchen boy's singing – she needs something beautiful and pure to give her hope in the relentless brutality of her life with Albert. As we observe her courting ritual – the discrete eye contact, small smiles, the way she and Michael contrive to bump into each other and finally their beautiful erotic foreplay in the ladies room – we realize that Michael is the Lover. For Georgina Michael represents escape and perhaps hope for the future.

The stylized use of colour and the design of the sets serves the themes of the film. When Georgina walks into the ladies room her dress, which appears red in the restaurant, becomes white and, despite the love scene taking place in a toilet, the spacious whiteness brings a virginal purity to this first love scene, even though the lovers are both nearing middle age.

It is now clear that Georgina is the protagonist. She wants her lover and everything that he represents to rescue her from Albert and his world. The obstacles are equally clear. When Albert ignorantly claims to be an artist Greenaway is telling us how powerful men like Albert attempt to dominate, possess and brutalize not only their wives but everybody and everything, including literature, the arts and high cuisine. From the outset Georgina's love is in great danger. This is clear from the way Albert lies in wait for her in the ladies room. But she does have an ally; the Cook has observed her interest in her lover and we have already been shown how the Cook respects human dignity and how he likes Georgina, who shares his sensibility. The Cook is also the one man whom Albert cannot dominate – Albert needs the Cook to reflect the image he wants of himself as a successful man. The dramatic question at the end of this sequence is: Can Georgina's new-found love survive in Albert's brutal world?

135

Development Sequences

Friday's Menu

Slow track across the busy restaurant to find Georgina and Albert, who is mocking Mitchell for feeling sick. Mitchell throws up on the table. Albert's henchmen arrive with their latest acquisitions – silver cutlery for the restaurant and a pile of banknotes. Georgina quietly slips away for her assignation with Michael. Knowing that the toilets are too dangerous she leads him by the hand through the busy kitchen where she stops to appreciate the Cook's food. The Cook shows the lovers to the bakery area of the kitchen where he draws a curtain to give them privacy.

Albert struts into the kitchen to complain about the service. The Cook realizes the danger to the lovers and leads Albert away to show him the inferior quality of the new cutlery. Georgina and Michael quickly dress and are safely back in their seats when Albert throws open the huge restaurant doors and returns to his table to berate his men about the cutlery. Albert becomes maudlin when Mitchell asks why he hasn't got kids, but his mood quickly turns: he blames Georgina for not producing children and attacks Mitchell for asking questions. Georgina announces that she is leaving. Albert follows her, deliberately knocking Michael's book off the table as he passes. Georgina stoops to pick up the book but Albert snatches it from her and hands the despised book to the Cook, instructing him to cook it.

On their way out through the kitchen Albert is distracted by the kitchen boy's singing. He drunkenly attacks the boy and Georgina who tries to intervene. Albert drags them both out to where the dogs are barking in the parking lot and attempts to rape Georgina in front of the boy. He becomes enraged when he discovers that Georgina hasn't got her knickers on and drags both Georgina and the boy into the car. While Albert rapes Georgina the boy escapes.

– As we suspected might happen, the Cook becomes complicit in Georgina's love affair. It is he who shows the couple a place where they can make love, the bakery, which gives their lovemaking a deliciously wholesome eroticism, made even richer by intercutting with succulent images of cucumbers and red peppers being sliced. It is also the Cook who skilfully manipulates Albert in order to prevent their discovery. Greenaway is again working with colour: while the restaurant remains predominantly red and black, when Georgina enters the kitchen her dress becomes green, in harmony with the natural colours of the kitchen produce. With each camera track, from the restaurant to the kitchen and back to the restaurant, we are reminded of still lives from Dutch paintings and when Albert throws open the huge doors on his return to the restaurant, for a moment, the scene is reminiscent of a renaissance portrayal of the gates of hell.

The sequence proceeds to give us further insights into Albert's character: like an out of control child his mood swings rapidly from maudlin self-pity to violence, against his wife, Michael's books, the kitchen boy's innocence, anything which is beyond his control or reminds him of his insecurity or inadequacy. When Albert discovers that Georgina has forgotten to put her knickers on, we know the reason, we saw how quickly she dressed to escape discovery: this dramatic irony intensifies our sense of the lovers' vulnerability; we know how passionately the lovers desire each other and we have witnessed their narrow escape. We are afraid for them, despite the Cook's protection. How long will it be before Albert discovers the truth and what will he do then?

Saturday's Menu

Georgina and Michael are making love in the cheese pantry while the kitchen boy sings as if to celebrate their union. The Cook is again protecting them, this time against the curious eyes of his staff who can see the lovers' shadows moving behind a curtain. The restaurant is busy and Albert is as usual holding forth at his table when Georgina returns. He demands to know why Georgina has been gone so long and goes to the toilets to investigate. In the men's toilets he drunkenly attacks a guest, accusing him of homosexuality.

He returns to the restaurant and, almost as if he suspects something, insists that Michael comes to his table to meet his wife who, he tells Michael with heavy irony, spends hours reading. Georgina looks scared and we notice a large bruise on her jaw. On hearing Michael's name Albert scathingly accuses him of being Jewish and proceeds to dictate Georgina's conversation. At first she repeats after Albert, parrot fashion, but soon she demonstrates her independence by telling Michael about her gynaecologist and her three miscarriages which have 'ruined her insides'. Albert becomes furious and changes the subject by asking Michael what he does. 'I'm a gynaecologist,' Michael tells him and suggests that Georgina could always come to him with her gynaecological problems. This is too much for Albert and he instructs Mitchell to take Michael back to his table. Michael, dignified in the face of Albert's rudeness, thanks him for introducing him to his wife and leaves the restaurant.

Albert brutally drags Georgina into the kitchen where he accuses her of telling a complete stranger intimate personal details. Georgina fights back, mockingly telling him that not only is her gynaecologist a man, he is also Jewish and black and has been in prison in South Africa. Albert brutally punches her in the stomach and drags her out to the car. He drives off, leaving the dog he runs over yelping in pain as it dies.

– Georgina and Michael's lovemaking looks beautiful and their pleasure is emphasized by the delicious array of cheeses and by the kitchen boy's singing. But they are taking ever-increasing risks for their love; the huge shadow of their lovemaking dominates the kitchen (both literally and metaphorically) before the Cook draws the curtain to hide them. Again we wonder how long it can last until they are discovered. Albert is becoming suspicious by his wife's long absences and when he invites Michael to join his table we wonder if he suspects something. We see the fear on Georgina's face, her bruises remind us of her recent rape, and our sense of imminent danger increases.

Again Albert's fury is ignited by his wife talking about gynaecology – female things beyond his control. We also learn more about the harshness of her life with her bigoted, racist, homophobic husband – when Albert punches her in the stomach we realize the probable cause of her three miscarriages resulting in infertility. Although Georgina attempts to fight back with her wits she has no chance against Albert's brutality. The final pitiful image of the dying dog yelping in pain stands as a metaphor for Albert's psychopathic disregard for all living things. Georgina is truly Albert's victim, her love for Michael is her only hope. But can Michael's superior intelligence be a match for Albert's ignorant brutality?

Sunday's Menu

In the restaurant Albert presides over a banquet attended by his low-life associates. Georgina sits silently by his side with a scarf over her head in an attempt to conceal her bruises. Soon she slips away and we join her, sitting on a table of feathers in the area of the kitchen where the poultry and game are hung. Ironically, as a result of Albert's introduction, she and Michael are talking for the first time. Back in the restaurant Albert calls for dancing girls. Two of his guests, a crippled man and a prostitute, go to look at the kitchen – a pretext for the opportunity to have sex in the parking lot. While in the kitchen Georgina and Michael make love amongst the feathers, in the restaurant Albert's behaviour becomes increasingly rowdy. When the dancing girls arrive he insists the tables be moved to make room for them. When the restaurant guests complain he overturns tables and herds them all out into the street. The crippled man returns to the kitchen with the prostitute, whose boyfriend (one of Albert's henchmen) jealously demands to know where she's been. At that moment the prostitute sees Michael and Georgina emerge together from behind the curtain. She tells her boyfriend she has just been earning a little money and adds that she can make even more money out of what she has just seen.

– Georgina and Michael's love is growing – now they are talking as well as making love. There is a stark contrast between the loveless sordid sex in the parking lot and the growing intimacy between Georgina and Michael. But, as the lovers appear, oblivious to the danger they are in, our sense of their peril grows. All the kitchen staff know what is going on. Albert is becoming increasingly carried away by his own power and omnipotence – with the decadence reminiscent of a Roman emperor, he calls for dancing girls and when the restaurant guests complain he creates mayhem, demonstrating his disregard for all the rules of social behaviour. The prostitute, who naturally thinks of sex as a financial transaction, is the first of Albert's cronies to see the lovers together. She makes it clear that she is already contemplating ways she might exploit this knowledge financially. This is the penultimate scene which inevitably leads to the crisis.

The ending

Monday's Menu: The Crisis

A policeman with a dog is investigating an offensive smell in the parking lot. In the kitchen Michael pleads with Georgina to meet him somewhere else but Georgina insists that Albert will never believe that she 'does it under his nose, between courses'. Outside Albert arrives with his henchmen and the prostitute. As they walk through the kitchen to the restaurant Albert becomes abusive towards the prostitute. She retaliates by angrily informing him about Georgina's affair with Michael. Albert suddenly stabs a fork into her cheek. While she screams in pain Albert sits down alone to eat and think about what he has just heard. Suddenly wild with rage he goes on the rampage searching for Georgina in the toilets.

Outside in the parking lot the police open a van and find the source of the smell – inside, the meat rejected by the Cook for its poor quality in the opening sequence is rotting and maggot-ridden. The Cook comes to where Georgina and Michael are making love and hides them in a cold storage room. Albert arrives in the kitchen smashing everything in sight in his desperate search for his wife. He picks up a knife and fork and yells for everyone to hear, 'I'll kill him and then I'll eat him.' Georgina and Michael, naked and clinging to each other for warmth, listen to Albert's words. The Cook ushers them out to the parking lot where a second delivery van is still standing. The van is opened and, despite the overpowering smell, the Cook pushes the lovers in amongst the rotting carcasses and maggot-ridden pigs' heads. The naked couple are driven away to safety.

In a marble corridor one of the kitchen staff hoses the lovers clean. The music is gentle and harmonious. Still naked, Michael and Georgina walk through an impressive corridor of marble pillars and walls which are lined with books. Michael tells Georgina the place is a book depository; he is a book-keeper cataloguing French history. Georgina asks him how all these books can make you happy. Michael says he has '. . . always found them very reasonable – they don't change their minds when you are not looking'. They are now standing by a bed in front of an apse-shaped window with a stunning view of the city skyline. The lovers put on bathrobes and kiss.

– The police search of the parking lot opens the sequence with a renewed sense of danger. Michael feels this and wants to continue their love affair elsewhere. When Albert arrives with the prostitute in his entourage our fear that she might tell Albert about Georgina and Michael is immediately awakened. Informing on his wife is the only weapon the prostitute has against Albert's abuse, and she is soon forced to use it. The shocking image of Albert's fork stabbed into the prostitute's cheek is a forerunner to the later image, shocking but also absurd, of Albert clutching a knife and fork as he announces that when he has killed Michael he will eat him.

The Cook, true to form, rescues the lovers. Although their salvation transport, full of maggot-infested meat and pigs' heads, could hardly be more horrifying, there is also something poignant about the sight of the naked lovers' clinging to each other for comfort in such a terrifying place – a metaphor for the hellish conditions in which their love must survive.

With the cleansing of the lovers the atmosphere changes completely. The calm music adds to the sense of respite. As the lovers walk together through the book depository their nakedness is reminiscent of Adam and Eve before the fall. Michael's world is a sanctuary of marble pillars and books, a place of innocence which provides an air of tranquillity, culture and harmony – a vision of a possible future happiness for Georgina, made secure by the intellectual history of human civilization. The image of the naked lovers standing in front of the apse-shaped window with the cityscape beyond is again reminiscent of renaissance paintings. But at the end of the sequence they put on bathrobes – this covering of their sex reminds us of the next stage in the journey of Adam and Eve, the fall. Despite the fact that they are away from Albert's world, we are only too aware that the *crisis* has taken place – Albert has discovered their secret. The inevitable *climax* must follow.

Tuesday's Menu: The Climax

Georgina and Michael are in bed in the book depository. The kitchen boy sings as he serves them a meal the Cook has sent. While they eat the kitchen boy looks around at the books. Michael tells him he can borrow any he wants.

On his return to the restaurant, in an area of scaffolding with roaming barking dogs, the kitchen boy is set upon by Albert and his men. Albert tortures the boy for information of Georgina's whereabouts. Even Albert's men are sickened by the extent of Albert's cruelty but the boy refuses to tell. Eventually he falls unconscious. Albert then finds the borrowed books at the bottom of the boy's basket with the name and address of the book depository stamped inside the cover.

Late at night in the book depository the Cook comes himself with their meal. He tells Georgina the news that the kitchen boy is in hospital. He assures her that the boy did not tell Albert where she is. Georgina insists that she go immediately to the hospital. Michael walks with them to the front entrance and bolts the glass door after she has gone. In an old-fashioned hospital ward Georgina, carrying the Cook's meal as a gift, walks in procession with two nursing nuns to the kitchen boy's bedside.

Back at the book depository Albert and his men have broken in. Michael is lying half dead on the floor as Mitchell stuffs torn pages of books into his mouth with a wooden spoon. Albert wanders amongst the chaos of scattered books rambling about the killing: 'I didn't mean that you literally had to chew his bollocks off,' he tells Mitchell, 'I meant it metaphorically . . . It is what it is, a revenge killing, an affair of the heart . . . admire the style, he was stuffed and Albert liked good food, stuffed with the tools of his trade . . . ram the bloody books down his throat, suffocate the bastard.'

Late that night Georgina returns to the book depository to find Michael's body. She takes a torn page out of Michael's mouth, wipes away the blood and reads '*The French Revolution*'. She covers Michael's body, kisses him on the lips and curls up next to him. She talks all the time as if he were still alive and they were planning the breakfast they will have together in the morning. The sequence is intercut with scenes of Albert at the restaurant. His violence is out of control and he begins to turn on his own men. The Cook has had enough and instructs his kitchen staff to throw Albert out of the restaurant. Albert threatens the Cook reminding him that he is the owner and he will have the restaurant bulldozed into the ground.

– As soon as Michael suggests that the kitchen boy might like to borrow his books, we become alarmed – Michael's generous concern for the kitchen boy's interest in learning might also be his downfall. For a man like Michael there is nothing more important than a child's aspiration to learn. But this also might suggest that Michael does not understand what it means to have an enemy like Albert. Happiness and the fulfilment of their love is again giving the lovers a false sense of security.

The kitchen boy is tortured on the scaffolding, a setting reminiscent of the opening of the film where the scaffolding underpinning the stage area represented the primitive or lower 'id' level of human consciousness. Also the kitchen boy is very nearly strung up as if it were a scaffold – a place where many innocents have been sacrificed as a result of the unconscious need to find scapegoats for their projected ills. The design of the hospital ward where the kitchen boy is taken, the high ceilings and lighting, bring a timeless religious or mythic quality to the scene, further emphasized by Georgina and the nuns' ritualized procession to the boy's bedside.

What first attracted Georgina to Michael, his reading, now becomes the agent of his destruction. The borrowed books lead Albert and his men to the book depository and the climax of the film which is Michael's murder. As with all classic dramas the theme of the film becomes clear in this climax. When Georgina fishes the bloody front page of *The French Revolution* out of Michael's mouth we are invited to consider what Greenaway is saying. His portrait of Albert's world is one where extreme bigotry and unrestrained greed has enabled gangsters such as Albert to become rich and powerful. Psychopathologies such as Albert's have long been associated with hatred of intellectuals and destruction of books. The French Revolution was an attempt to overthrow the aristocrats – Albert's predecessors in exploitation, tyranny and gangsterism. The sense of timelessness, enhanced by the repetitious nature of Nyman's music, suggests history endlessly repeating itself – in the late-twentieth century Albert and his henchmen are the new aristocrats. But whereas the old aristocrats were often patrons of the arts and culture, if it served their self-image and interests (such as in the Franz Hals painting), the newly powerful, such as Albert, driven by ignorance and greed, are the new barbarians on an orgy of destruction threatening civilization itself.

But the sequence does not end with a vision of Albert as all powerful. While Georgina spends her last night with her lover, prompting us to wonder what she will do when she finally accepts that her lover is dead, Albert turns on his own men, and finally on the Cook – not realizing that, like all tyrants, his power is dependent on those around him.

The Resolution (part one)

In the morning Georgina wakes next to Michael's body. She talks quietly about Albert's abuse; the times she left him, the times he came after her, how he sometimes cried before abusing her, how she thinks he didn't really like sex, not with women. That evening Georgina goes to the restaurant where she finds the Cook sitting alone in his deserted kitchen. She tells the Cook Michael is dead, stuffed with his own books. 'Could you cook him for me?' she asks. The Cook refuses. He assumes Georgina's grief has made her unstable. They talk quietly, about the culinary art, about how the most expensive foods are black and the second most expensive are aphrodisiacs – even through people's eating tastes they are connecting with death and birth. Georgina wants to talk about Michael, she wants the Cook to tell her what he saw of their lovemaking. The Cook looks at her pityingly. 'How can I know it was real unless someone was watching?' Georgina pleads with him. The Cook tells her all he saw: Michael kissing her, undressing her, kissing her breasts, putting his hands between her legs, making love like all lovers, like his parents. The Cook talks until Georgina cries. He gently tells her that eating Michael won't make him a part of her. 'But I'm not going to eat him, Albert is,' Georgina explains. Now the Cook understands her plan he finally agrees to her proposition. This releases Georgina to grieve her love. The camera pans through the kitchen to the deserted parking lot to arrive on the painting of the Dutch burghers now standing outside battered by the rain.

– Although Georgina is devastated by her lover's death she also gains new insights into herself and Albert. She sees the pathetic sexual inadequacy at the heart of Albert's brutality. Her experience of loving Michael has changed her, she is no longer dominated by Albert, she has discovered her inner strength. When she and the Cook talk quietly about cooking and lovemaking they are also talking about art; how people need to explore the meaning of death and life through art – how our experience of life needs to be told and witnessed to penetrate the truth of it. At first we think, like the Cook, that Georgina, stricken by her grief, is motivated by some primitive urge to eat Michael as a way of making him a part of her. But her plan is even more bizarre – she wants to force Albert to eat Michael. Just as Albert wanted Michael's killing to be 'a revenge killing', Georgina now wants her own revenge, and just as Albert had Michael stuffed and claimed that he would eat him, she will now take him at his word.

The kitchen, which we saw as a hive of activity dedicated to boosting Albert's power in the opening of the film, is now bare and deserted. The vast reproduction of the Franz Hals painting, which in the opening adorned the stylish restaurant wall, has been dumped outside in the parking lot where the elemental forces of wind and rain have already begun to reclaim the painted images of the powerful Dutch burghers, just as they too have been claimed by death. As is common with classic narrative structure, we find in the resolution a repetition of visual motifs which have become familiar during the course of the film, and are now changed completely as a result of the climactic events.

The Resolution (part two)
Friday's Menu. The Restaurant is Closed for a Private Function

The restaurant has been completely cleared of all signs of its former opulence, leaving only a single table and two chairs. Albert arrives with just two of his usual entourage; Mitchell and a middle-aged woman. Albert demands to know what the special invitation he has received means? Georgina greets him, dressed exotically for the occasion. 'Happy anniversary,' she

Midnight Cowboy
The energy of Joe's preparations tells us that this will be a very special day.

The beauty salon is derelict which tells us we have entered Joe's memory of a time when, as a boy, he was somehow servicing an older woman's sexual needs – which relates directly to his aim.

We are getting increasingly worried that Ratso is going to rip Joe off. So our hopes for the potential in the relationship are pitted equally against our fears, exacerbated by our knowledge of Joe's naivety.

Midnight Cowboy
As we watch their
friendship growing
in the face of
adversity, we find
that a shift has
taken place in our
hearts.

Despite the onset of
winter and Ratso's
worsening health,
we share their
optimism as they
go to the party.

The motif that has stood for Joe's pride in himself as a hustler
throughout the film, now becomes a cheap amusement and object
for destruction.

Midnight Cowboy
Joe again attempts to boost his courage by confronting his reflection in the mirror, but this is now combined with his paternal words about having a sick boy on his hands.

Ratso asks the question we are asking ourselves: Was it murder? Joe doesn't reply. Instead he tenderly tucks the blanket around poor shivering Ratso.

Ratso's spirit seems to pass both into Joe's history and back into the city landscape.

A Short Film About Love

Top: By saying 'I am not good' she is also telling Tomek that she is not who he imagines her to be. Magda's project is to show Tomek the reality, not to nurture his illusions of reality.

Bottom: Magda's change is emphasised by her dishevelled hair and little make-up which makes her look younger, more open, less in control of her life.

The Cook, The Thief, His Wife and Her Lover
Top: (From left to right: Her Lover, The Cook, His Wife and The
Thief). Albert is becoming suspicious of his wife's long absences
and when he invites Michael to join his table we wonder if he
suspects something.

Bottom: Georgina and Michael's pleasure is emphasised by the
delicious array of cheeses and by the kitchen boy's singing… but
they are taking ever-increasing risks for their love and we feel
anxious for their vulnerability.

The Cook, The Thief, His Wife and Her Lover
Top: Albert's gun passes from the Cook to the kitchen boy and then
to Georgina; associating each of them with the revenge killing.

Bottom: Georgina punishes Albert with the fruits of his own greed.

Heaven's Gate
Through ritual communal events – a cock-fight, a roller-skating
dance, and finally meetings about what to do about the death list –
we are given remarkable, emblematic portraits of a newly formed
and somewhat anarchic community.

Mirror
The woman we see on screen is both his wife and his memory of
his mother. The boundaries that we usually use to define the self
and the other, time and present reality, memory and imagination,
have somehow dissolved.

Top: *American Beauty*
We are conscious of the variety of images, or ways of seeing:
reflections, mirror images, digital images, fantasy images,
characters seen through windows at night, all impacting on the
senses of both the characters and the audience.

Bottom: *Pulp Fiction*
The film is packed with references to other films; the cabaret club
Mia takes Vince to has Marilyn Monroe look-alike waitresses, Elvis
music plays and when the dance competition begins we are
immediately reminded of John Travolta's great dance routine in
Saturday Night Fever.

says but refuses to tell him what the anniversary represents, other than that it is an occasion which she will always celebrate and he won't. She has a special present for him, which the Cook has prepared. The huge doors to the kitchen open. The Cook leads the procession. Behind him his staff and all the people Albert has abused carry a stretcher-sized platter: the man beaten in the opening of the film, the prostitute with her cheek still bandaged, her boyfriend, the kitchen boy in a wheelchair. The platter is placed on the table in front of Albert. Georgina takes off the linen cover: '. . . you vowed you would eat him. Now eat him,' she instructs Albert, who stares incredulously at Michael's cooked body surrounded by vegetables. Albert looks ill and begins to tremble. He draws a gun from his jacket pocket but is quickly disarmed by the Cook's men. The gun is handed to the Cook, who gives it to the kitchen boy, who passes it to Georgina. She aims the gun at Albert, insisting that he eat. Humiliated and shaking with fear Albert takes a sickening mouthful. Georgina then shoots him dead. The red stage curtains close.

– As is central to the revenge tragedy, a violent act must itself be avenged to enable a proper catharsis or purging to take place. By having the Cook cook Michael, in a bizarre way Georgina has dignified his death. This is emphasized by the ultimate ritual, the ultimate procession, the ultimate food. The sight of Michael's cooked body drains away any modicum of power Albert may have left. By forcing Albert to eat Michael Georgina is punishing him with the fruits of his own greed before killing him. Again we are given a sense of unity by the inclusion of more familiar elements which made up the whole: the ritual processions for serving food, the presence of Albert's former victims. Albert's gun passes from the Cook to the kitchen boy and then to Georgina, associating each of them with the revenge killing. Finally the stage curtains which opened the film are closed. We are left to contemplate Georgina's new-found insight and strength and how she has overcome the crude masculine domination of her husband, the Thief.

Three

DEPARTURES FROM CLASSIC STORY STRUCTURE

Introduction
What is a Departure?

The vast majority of feature films originating from the western narrative tradition can be analysed according to the basic elements of the classic structure outlined earlier. It is in the image and sound texture of the unfolding story that the individual life view of the writer and director manifests itself, while the classic structure acts as a backbone for the overall story, giving it a unity, a sense of direction and a forward motion. But what happens when this 'remoulding' actually amounts to a disruption, or a significant departure, from the classic form, which has of course happened in notable cases throughout feature film history?

Although many of us may not, until now, have been so consciously aware of the basic principles underlying the form, it will have been very familiar because of our long relationship with stories, ranging from the fairy stories and adventure stories we first encountered as children right through to the feature films we now see. Indeed, our expectations of story have been so conditioned that as soon as a departure from the classic model takes place we react. Often we are not aware that such a departure has taken place: our reaction is simply a spontaneous response to our disrupted expectations. This reaction manifests itself in many different ways. We may find ourselves feeling confused, bored, alienated, angry, sad, amused by the unexpected or disturbed because we are feeling something we have never felt before. We may so dislike the experience that we decide that the film is bad; the film-maker obviously doesn't know how to put a film together. Or we may feel that something intriguing and new is taking place and, although it's more difficult than usual to understand our thoughts and feelings, it's worth the effort demanded because the film is taking us into territory we've never visited before.

Our need for a sense of structure is great because without structure there can be no unity. Consequently, if there is a radical departure from the classic form, the audience's passage is eased if the film provides a detectable alternative structure. Pasolini's *Theorem*, which he described as 'a little lay tract, constructed like an unresolved canon, around a religious visitation',* is a fine example of this.

The religious visitation Pasolini is referring to, if somewhat ironically, is the arrival of a young Englishman (Terence Stamp) into an Italian household. The household consists of father, mother, son and daughter (both teenagers) and a middle-aged maid. In the first part of the film each member of the household, in turn, forms a relationship with the new arrival and falls in love with him. The Englishman then leaves the household and we follow the reaction of each family member in turn. The son becomes an abstract artist and is reduced to pissing on his paintings in his attempt to find his true self. The mother drives round the streets seeking a replacement for her beloved in the young men who roam the streets. The daughter withdraws from the world, becoming catatonic. The maid returns to her village and refuses to eat anything except nettles the children bring her, which results in her becoming so light she rises into the air, as high as the church steeple. The father decides that his bourgeois life is inauthentic and, in the final scene in the film, takes off all his clothes in a crowded station concourse. We then enter his interior world and see that, although all the bystanders think he's having a nervous breakdown, in his imagination he is striding naked across a stony desert, proud and free.

*Quoted by Raymond Durgnat, *Sexual Alienation in the Cinema* (Studio Vista, 1972) p.209.

Reviews of this film normally describe the young Englishman as the protagonist, but this simply reflects the loose way the term is frequently used. The Englishman doesn't fulfil any of the requirements of a protagonist. His role is best described as a catalyst in that he remains unchanged while causing change to take place around him. He arouses the love of each household member almost by default, because of who he is, rather than this being his aim and it is the uncompromising nature of this love which, after his departure, confronts each of them with their inner selves and causes them to change.

The structure of *Theorem* would be better described as having one catalyst and five protagonists, although this stretches our definition of protagonist somewhat, because the film focuses far more on each character's change, which is rather like a chemical reaction to a catalyst, than on their pursuit of their common aim, which was to seduce the Englishman. According to the classic form there can only be more than one protagonist if they are united by the same aim. And it is the common nature of the aim, and the fact that it causes them each to change, which connects Pasolini's five characters and gives the film its structural unity. But the classic form also demands that the story reaches a climax in the fulfilment or failure of the aim, which is clearly not the case in *Theorem* – after all an 'unresolved canon' goes round and round. Sturges' *The Magnificent Seven* (based on Kurosawa's *Seven Samurai*), on the other hand, is an example of how the classic form works with more than one protagonist: although each of the seven protagonists has his own highly individual motive they are united by their single aim, which is to protect a village from bandits, and the aim is not resolved until the village is saved.

Our decision about whether films which depart from the classic structure without replacing it with a detectable and satisfactory alternative structure are bad or taking us into new and exciting territory depends, of course, both on the nature of the departure and on our personal predisposition. But the reaction itself is inevitable. One of the more famous cases of such a reaction was the furore caused in Cannes by the release of Antonioni's *L'Avventura* (1960). In the beginning of the film we are led to believe that Anna, a beautiful young heiress, is the probable protagonist, although her friend Claudia's presence is also significant. But when Anna and Claudia go on a yachting trip Anna mysteriously disappears. Claudia, and Anna's fiancé, Sandro, spend the rest of the film looking for her, but their search becomes increasingly half-hearted and by the end of the film we no longer care about Anna's disappearance and the mystery is never solved. Although many people love this film for its melancholy, existential beauty, many others scream with boredom and frustration because for them the film is obscure, alienating, hermetically sealed and doesn't fulfil any of their storytelling expectations.

But, whatever your opinion of the film, one thing is not in doubt; it's quite clear from Antonioni's other films that, although he always remoulds at the level of image and sound, he has a perfectly adequate understanding of classic narrative form. In *L'Avventura* he deliberately disrupted his audience's expectations because he wanted to draw our attention to aspects of human experience that he felt were concealed by a goal-orientated plot. Woody Allen also disrupted audience expectations when he made *Interiors* (his homage to Bergman's *Persona)*, which I believe to be one of his best films, but it is a serious drama and as such out of line with the usual 'Woody Allen genre' of comedy his audience has come to love and expect of him. The price of innovation is often a smaller audience.

There are so many examples of narrative departures from the classic form in cinema history that I've decided to focus in depth on just a few film examples, each of which shed light on a different aspect of the subject and a different set of problems to be solved.

7 A Departure from the Western Genre

Cimino's *Heaven's Gate*

HEAVEN'S GATE (1980)
Written and directed by Michael Cimino

Heaven's Gate caused a critical storm when it first opened in America in 1980. The critics damned it absolutely saying that Cimino had had a fit of self-indulgent megalomania and the film was an unqualified disaster. In Cannes the film was subsequently slow-handclapped (although this version had been drastically cut). But a few lone voices spoke out in favour of the film claiming it to be a masterpiece. I prefer to call it a flawed masterpiece.

The film is certainly a departure from classic narrative form, which usually causes confusion in an audience on first release. It's also likely that the anger caused by the film was, in American audiences at least, a reaction to Cimino's then radical portrait of American history. He based his story on a little-known incident called 'The Johnson County War'. But he made little attempt to portray the actual facts of the incident. Instead he used it as an imaginative stepping-stone to invent a story that communicated his own feelings about American history. There's nothing new in this. Shakespeare's *Macbeth* bears very little resemblance to the known facts about Macbeth's life. Aristotle commented on the uneasy relationship between art and history when he said 'poetry [referring to drama] . . . is concerned with universal truths, history treats particular facts'.*

*Classical Literary Criticism, Aristotle/Horace/Longinus, trans. T. S. Dorsch (Penguin, 1965) p.44.

Heaven's Gate, because it's about the conflicts encountered by immigrants settling in the West, fits loosely into the western genre. When we think that the film we are going to see fits into a particular genre our expectations are not only conditioned by the classic narrative form, but we also have expectations, rooted in our previous experience of the genre, about what the film's mythology should be. In the case of the western this means that we expect a certain kind of heroism, we expect to know who is good and who is bad, and we expect the outcome of the conflict to reinforce the genre's mythology about heroism, good and bad, and the nature of the West.

By the time Cimino made *Heaven's Gate* the western genre had already been disrupted, most notably by the spaghetti western. Leone's films conform absolutely to the classic narrative structure, but are distinguishable because of the way he has remoulded, and so carved out their special identity, at the image and sound level (see pp. 52–8). Also, although the films are markedly different from American westerns, they don't upset audience expectations of the parent genre because Leone has chosen to exaggerate a particular aspect of the western mythology rather than to fundamentally challenge the mythology itself. Spaghetti westerns are a fine example of how new innovations can cause a genre to mutate creating sub-genres. But in *Heaven's Gate* Cimino does challenge the fundamental mythologies underlying the western genre. To exacerbate things further Cimino also departs from our expectations of classic narrative. Although it's not always easy to decide whether some of his departures from classic story-telling conventions are based on conscious, deliberate decisions, because of the originality of what he wants to say, or are simply flaws, or mistakes, which make the film unnecessarily difficult to follow.

Story Outline and Points of Departure

In the opening sequence we are introduced to two young men, Averill (Kris Kristofferson) and his friend Irvine (John Hurt), who are graduating from Harvard in 1870. We see Averill first, which suggests that he might be the protagonist but, although the two young men have the usual youthful, romantic inclinations and there is a general feeling of optimism generated by the situation, there is no mention of what either Averill or Irvine is specifically aiming for. Instead of the specific narrative clues we expect from the beginning, our attention is drawn to the themes of two speeches made in the graduation ceremony. Irvine's speech, which is reactionary and complacent but clearly expresses the views of the new young generation, is in sharp contrast with that of his ageing professor, whose speech expresses a real fear for a future dominated by material values and a plea for the students to remember the importance of cultural idealism. The sequence then goes on to show how everyone is swept along by the emblematic rituals of graduation, and to establish visual motifs (which recur throughout the film) of large numbers of people moving in processions and in circles within circles, which are quite magically captivated by the cinematography. (The processions and the circle motif are reminiscent of Bondarchuk's *War and Peace.*)

We then cut to Averill dozing in a train compartment. A caption tells us that we are in Wyoming twenty years later. Long processions of newly arriving immigrants are trudging across the beautiful uncultivated landscape. An immigrant homesteader is murdered in cold blood. Irvine is at a wealthy club where the local cattle barons, threatened by the immigration from central Europe, are meeting to discuss a death list of 125 immigrants they have drawn up as part of their campaign to stop mass immigration into the county. Averill's train arrives in the town, which is packed to the brim with newly arrived immigrants. He goes to the cattle barons' club where he learns from Irvine about the death list and about its legality; it has been sanctioned by the US President. Averill angrily leaves the club.

In classic terms the beginning of the film clearly should be here, and it is, almost. The premise to the story, the drawing up of the death list, is established, as is the awful vulnerability of the immigrants and the fact that cold-blooded murders are already taking place. It's also now clear that Averill is the protagonist because he is the one most disturbed and affronted by the death list. But instead of giving us much needed information about his leading characters, Cimino has chosen to give us more emblematic scenes, contrasting the harsh and chaotic conditions encountered by the great processions of newly arriving immigrants with the old-world wealth and bigotry of the cattle barons' club.

The crucial information, that Averill is the marshal of Sweetwater, the settlement where most of the immigrants on the death list live, is not at all clear on a first viewing. We are told nothing about how he has led his life over the past twenty years nor are we given any clues to help us understand what's motivated him to become marshal. We're told that he's a wealthy man, so we assume that he has a wealthy family somewhere, which makes his reasons for becoming a marshal in a remote immigrant backwater even more intriguing, but we are told nothing about who, or where, his family are. We are given the important information that he turned his back on the cattle barons' club and its values some time ago, but with so little insight into his attitudes beyond that, other than a general sense of nostalgia for his student days and of defeatism in the face of present circumstances, his character remains elusive. Irvine's character remains equally elusive. We learn little about him other than that the defeatism he shares with Averill has led him to become a drunk and, although he also shares Averill's distaste for the powers that be, they now find themselves on opposing sides as Irvine is still a member of the cattle barons' club.

Some clear exposition at this stage in the story would have transformed our ability to identify with Averill's character and to fully understand what is going on. But instead, at the end of the beginning, when we return to Sweetwater with Averill, we are still trying to get our bearings in the story.

The development sequences are focused mainly around two

locations in Sweatwater: the brothel and the Heaven's Gate roller-skating rink which is also the bar and the community meeting hall. It's here that we get to know the people of Sweetwater. But again we learn little about individuals. Instead, through ritual communal events – a cock-fight, a roller-skating dance, and finally meetings about what to do about the death list – we are given remarkable, emblematic portraits of a newly formed and somewhat anarchic community; a leaderless mass of conflicting needs and desires rooted in many different cultures and languages and backgrounds. The events celebrating the joyful freedoms of their new life are in sharp contrast to their horrified reaction to what is in store for them.

Interwoven with these emblematic community sequences is the intimate, although equally anarchic, love triangle between the young brothel madame, Ella (Isabelle Huppert), and the two men she's in love with, Averill and Nate (Christopher Walken), a local uneducated man who, in order to get on in the world, works as a gunslinger for the cattle barons. Ella's name is on the cattle baron's death list because the brothel receives stolen cattle in payment for services. Averill wants Ella to save herself by leaving the county but she won't leave unless he marries her, and he can't bring himself to make such a commitment. Nate, on the other hand, wants to marry Ella, but she can't bring herself to make that choice.

On the surface it appears that these two elements, the story of the community and the story of the love triangle, could easily weave together, according to classic narrative conventions, culminating in the arrival of the cattle barons to put their death list into practice. But Cimino has chosen to be as unconventional about the development as he was about the beginning. Although he does provide us with the occasional plot point or dramatic question, he doesn't build his sequences around the developing plot, instead he continues to focus on the confused and anarchic aspects of the characters' lives and the ritualistic and emblematic nature of events.

In the final development sequence news comes that the cattle barons' army of mercenaries is just outside town. The people appeal to Averill, as their marshal, for help. But Averill doesn't know what to do and gets drunk rather than supplying them with the leadership they so desperately need. This scene epitomizes how Cimino departs from the attributes we normally expect of a conventional protagonist. At no time in the film does Averill have a clear aim, even his attempts to persuade Ella to leave the county lack the energy of heroic action. He's endearingly romantic with her but unable to give her what she wants, even to save her life, until it's too late. Averill's laid-back, confused, defeatist characterization is a crushing blow for those members of the audience who expect, and want, mythological behaviour from their western genre heroes.

The climax is, of course, the inevitable massacre when the cattle barons finally arrive. The people fight because they have no choice; most of the men are on the death list anyway. Averill becomes involved in the battle despite himself and finally tries to rescue Ella and take her away to marry her, but it's too late and she is killed. We cut from Ella's death to the resolution, which is twenty years later. Averill, now elderly and listless, is on a yacht with a woman who seems equally listless. Averill stands alone on deck looking out at the dark ocean.

So, in *Heaven's Gate* the will of the protagonist to achieve his aim does not provide the dramatic energy for the story. Averill, like everyone else, is simply a part of a chain of tragic events which take their natural course. Instead of 'the occasion, the means, and the reason' being illuminated by the climax we simply experience the horror of the massacre itself and (for those in the audience who were able to enter into the spirit of the story despite its narrative departures) an overwhelming feeling for the defeat of anarchic freedom, represented by the immigrants, in the face of power and corruption, represented by the cattle barons and the government which sanctioned their actions.

The resolution – the listless, ageing Averill, apparently adrift on his rich man's yacht – is the final emblem. Rather than telling us anything specific about Averill himself, it communicates a general feeling of loss of meaning which, if we connect the scene with the opening of the film, suggests Cimino is saying that this is the inevitable outcome for a generation who valued reactionary complacency and material acquisition above cultural idealism, an attitude which finally enabled the unscrupulous, fascistic elements in society to take power.

In some ways, this departure from the usual emphasis on plot liberates the theme of the film and makes what could have been a familiar western upholding all the usual myths of the development of the West, all the more powerful. Cimino's vision is fresh and new. He is concerned with the truth rather than a romantic portrait of the early pioneers' experience. But the lack of clear exposition and detailed characterization causes a degree of confusion and alienates some audiences on first viewing, when we are, after all, trying to work out what on earth is going on. On the other hand, such exposition may have shifted the emphasis of the film, turning it into a story about a specific incident involving specific individuals at a specific time in history, and thus may have weakened the emblematic universal quality which is clearly what Cimino was most interested in communicating.

8 A Post-modern Departure from the Gangster Genre

Tarantino's *Pulp Fiction*

PULP FICTION (1994)
Written and directed by Quentin Tarantino

Traditionally gangster films, like westerns, are about the conflict between the good forces of law and order and the bad forces of lawlessness and corruption, only rather than taking place on the wild frontier the stories are set in the underworlds of major metropolitan cities such as Chicago and New York. The genre was first established during the depression and prohibition of the 1930s when gangsters thrived off bootlegging alcohol, narcotics deals and protection rackets. Orson Welles' *Touch of Evil* (which we discussed in chapter one) is a classic example of the genre. Charlton Heston, the honest policeman, represents the force of good and Orson Welles, who plays the corrupt policeman, represents evil along with the gangster family who are dealing in narcotics. Finally good triumphs and corruption is vanquished.

The first clues to Tarantino's subversive intentions in *Pulp Fiction* lie in the title itself and the opening image which shows us the text of a dictionary definition of 'pulp': '*1. A soft moist shapeless mass of matter 2. A magazine or book containing lurid subject matter and being characteristically printed on rough unfinished paper.*' This might suggest that the film to follow is going to be a cinematic equivalent of this kind of book. But why draw our attention to the genre in this way unless Tarantino wants to plant in our minds the idea of the genre itself.

A Post-modern Departure from the Gangster Genre

The pre-credit sequence opens in a coffee shop where we join two young people, Ringo and Yolande. The shape of their conversation is casual, meandering, inconsistent and completely naturalistic – similar to that of any young couple taking a meal together while they discuss their work, their relationship and their future, except that unlike most couples Ringo and Yolande's work is crime. Ringo wants to give up robbing liquor stores, it's becoming too dangerous, but Yolande is appalled by the thought of a 'day job'. The pre-credit sequence ends with the two of them declaring their love for each other, drawing their guns and holding up the coffee shop.

So, it appears that we have met our two protagonists and we have been introduced to their conflict – whether or not to continue their life of crime. But after the credits, instead of returning to Ringo, Yolande and their hold-up, we meet two new characters, Vince (John Travolta) and Jules (Samuel L. Jackson), driving to a job. Vince and Jules are also involved in a casual, meandering naturalistic conversation about many things: trips to Europe, what the French call burgers, the drugs scene in Amsterdam. They pull up outside an apartment block, take guns out of the car boot and continue the conversation on their way into the block. They are talking about Mia, their boss Marcellus's wife. Recently Marcellus had a man thrown out of a window for giving Mia a foot massage. Vince is troubled by this information as Marcellus has asked him to take care of Mia while he is away on a trip. Vince and Jules finally arrive at the apartment of three young men who seem like pleasant middle-class students. Jules's casual conversation takes on an increasingly menacing tone and, like a demented preacher, he quotes from the bible as he shoots dead two of the young men. The third is reduced to a state of terror.

A caption appears: 'Vincent Vega and Marcellus Wallace's Wife'. Yolande and Ringo, the potential protagonists introduced to us in the pre-credit sequence, seem to have been forgotten. It now appears that Vince is the protagonist, and his problem or conflict is the worrying task of having to take out Marcellus's wife. We meet Marcellus, a formidable black gangland boss, who is doing a corrupt deal with a boxer, Butch (Bruce Willis). The deal is for Butch deliberately to lose a boxing match that Marcellus is planning to bet on. Vince is troubled because he doesn't understand the ethical rules of his coming encounter with Mia. (Although he doesn't appear in the least troubled by his having just been party to the murder of two young men on Marcellus's behalf.) He visits his drug dealer to score heroin – he needs to boost his confidence for his date. The use of image and music during the drug-taking sequence are reminiscent of the spaghetti western genre.

Vince goes to Marcellus's opulent house. Mia (Uma Thurman) tells him over an intercom to wait in the sitting room. While he waits she watches him on a CCTV monitor and snorts a line of coke. Like Vince, we don't actually see Mia's face in this sequence, although Tarantino shows us her back view, a big close-up of her lips and we focus on her bare feet as she goes to join Vince (which reminds us of her foot massage and the man who was thrown out of the window). In this way the tension is built as we share Vince's growing anticipation and his vulnerability in this situation.

Mia takes Vince to a cabaret club packed with 50s memorabilia, Elvis music and Marilyn Munroe lookalike waitresses. Mia is beautiful, sexy, feisty and flirtatious. Vince is both fascinated by her and afraid of finding her too attractive. A dance competition begins. When Mia insists that they enter we are reminded of John Travolta's great dance performance in *Saturday Night Fever* and our anticipation grows as we wait for him to perform brilliantly – as he does to begin with, but Tarantino subverts even this expectation by shooting much of the dance from the waist up. Vince takes Mia home and goes to the bathroom where he tries to boost his flagging confidence by talking to himself in the mirror. He is clearly falling for Mia and the dramatic question is: Can Vince save himself before he gets too involved with his boss's wife? But the story takes an unexpected turn: in the sitting room Mia finds Vince's heroin in his coat pocket and snorts the white powder assuming it to be cocaine. In order to save her life Vince rushes her to his drug dealer. There Vince's courage is tested to the limit as he is forced to stab a syringe of adrenalin directly into Mia's heart. Luckily the treatment works and Vince takes Mia home. They part outside Mia's house where Mia agrees to keep the events of the evening a secret from Marcellus. 'Now if you'll excuse me, I'm going home to have a heart attack,' Vince jokes endearingly.

So again we have scenes of high drama and near-death experiences being handled in a jokey casual way. The effect on the audience is that this is both real and not real at the same time. We believe it and don't believe it. This is storytelling playing with storytelling. We recognize the realism of our own lives in aspects of the encounters but at the same time we are in a storyland of gangsters, hitmen, murder, drugs deals and near-death experiences. We suspect that the real psychopathology of the people who inhabit this underworld is not being explored, at least not in depth, but we suspend our disbelief and enter the story on its own level.

But what happens next is a real surprise. Instead of staying with Vince and his fear of Marcellus we cut to a 1970s sitting room. A soldier (Christopher Walken) has come to give Butch, who is here a little boy, a gold watch. The soldier tells the little boy a long story about the watch; how it first belonged to the boy's great-grandfather in the first world war, it was then passed on to his grandfather who was killed in the second world war. Butch's father hid the watch in his ass while he was in a prison camp in Vietnam, where he eventually died. Now the soldier has come to pass the watch on to this 'little man'. The adult Butch wakes up as if he were dreaming the story – he is in the rest room just before he is due in the boxing ring. A caption, *The Gold Watch* appears on screen. Instead of losing the fight Butch kills his opponent – with a soldier's heritage like his how could he do other? Marcellus is furious and instructs his men, including Vince, to find Butch and kill him. This is the last we see of Vince for a while. Butch takes over as the new protagonist. His problem or conflict is how he and his charming French girlfriend can escape from Marcellus's revenge? Throughout Butch's story we are waiting for Vince to appear and kill him, which provides considerable suspense. But at the same time our feelings are confused. We have already identified Vince as our protagonist but because we haven't seen him for so long we are now beginning to identify with Butch. We like his relationship with his girlfriend and we don't want Vince to kill him. Our loyalties are split. This is a considerable disruption to the narrative – far greater than losing the young couple in the pre-credit sequence – we did not really have time to identify with them.

'The Gold Watch' caption serves both to introduce us to Butch's story (although somewhat late) as well as functioning as a 'plant'. (Another playful game with classic narrative – it is usually the job of the screenwriter to disguise plants to prevent them standing out like a sore thumb.) The problem is that Butch's girlfriend has forgotten to pack this most precious of Butch's possessions for their escape. Butch must risk his life by returning to his apartment for the forgotten heirloom. While Butch is reclaiming his watch he notices a gun lying on the kitchen counter. He hears the cistern flush, the toilet door opens and Vince appears with a book in his hand. Butch shoots and Vince falls back on to the toilet, dead.

The shock of this shooting is intense – it is always hard for an audience to accept their protagonist being killed unless it is the cathartic moment in the climax of the film. But the dramatic pace of *Pulp Fiction* is such that we have no time to grieve for Vince: instead we are caught up in a bloody, violent show-down between Butch and Marcellus. Again Tarantino subverts our narrative expectations – if we have any left. Just when we think that Butch and Marcellus have killed each other, a corrupt sheriff appears on the scene and captures them both for his personal sadistic sexual pleasure. This appears to be a comment on the gangster genre itself which almost always includes corrupt law-enforcers. When this gory story thread has finally played itself out we assume the story will end. After all our first protagonist, Vince, is dead, and our second protagonist, Butch, has survived to escape with his girlfriend. But again our narrative expectations are thwarted. This time the leap in the story is so great I found it difficult to comprehend or discover any explanation. Instead of ending the film Tarantino takes us back to near the beginning. The screen caption is *'The Bonnie Situation'*. (We have yet to discover who Bonnie is.) We cut to a reprise of the scene in which Jules and Vince terrorized and shot two of the three young men in the apartment. It is as if none of the ensuing story has taken place. Vince is not dead. Instead we embark upon an alternative story which begins when a fourth young man comes out of the toilet (reminding us that we have already seen Vince killed on the toilet), shoots Jules and Vince at point blank range but miraculously misses. Jules and Vince shoot him dead in retaliation. Jules then insists that the fact that he and Vince are not dead is 'divine intervention. God came down from heaven and stopped the bullets.'

The story meanders on. Vince and Jules escape, taking the remaining youth with them. In the car Vince's gun goes off by mistake killing the youth. They go to a friend of Jules's house to dispose of the body and clean up the mess of blood and brains which has splattered all over the car. We learn that the friend (played by Tarantino himself) has a wife called Bonnie who won't approve of her nice home being used in this way. This is 'the Bonnie Situation'. When the mess is cleaned up and the body and the car disposed of, Jules and Vince go to a coffee shop for a meal. Jules is contemplating a change in lifestyle as a result of the 'divine intervention'. Vince is shocked – if Jules gives up work he will just be another unemployed bum, there's nothing worse than that. At this moment we hear Ringo's voice and realize that this is the same coffee shop as the pre-credit sequence. We have gone back in time to the few moments before Ringo and Yolande began their hold-up. While Vince is again in the toilet the robbery proceeds with shocking intensity but, as a result of what Jules insists was 'divine intervention' and because he cannot allow the young couple to take Marcellus's attaché case, he pulls his gun on Ringo. Finally Vince and Jules follow Yolande and Ringo out of the coffee shop without anyone getting killed.

At first it seems as if Tarantino's narrative subversion is purely playful – he is a brilliant, talented child who, left alone in the film studio nursery surrounded by the film equivalent of paints, brushes, colours and canvases, discovers that instead of painting a conventional picture he can in fact do anything that he wants. On closer examination it becomes clear that the film has been very carefully constructed. It is packed with cross references, plants and references to other films including the gangster genre itself. Each individual sequence or 'story' is beautifully and stylishly constructed. The conversations are light, casual, amusing and often refer back to earlier conversations. The characterization, at a superficial level, is excellently observed, the performances brilliant, the dialogue sparkling. But what are we to make of the narrative subversion? What does it mean? Does it mean anything other than that Tarantino can be a Hollywood bad boy and do whatever he wants when he tells stories? The film reminds me of some of the 1960s New Wave French films, such as Godard's *Pierrot le Fou*, when the French directors were also discovering a new freedom with the form and playing with the Hollywood gangster genre. What was then called New Wave is now called post-modern. How can one answer the question what is the film about other than to reply that the film is about film itself?

But finally I am left with unsettling moral qualms about the film. As we have already noted there is an important moral dimension to gangster films. Whether the questions who is good?, who is bad?, who is corrupt and what corrupted them? are simplistic or complex depends on the quality of the film, but the questions are always present. Even in Francis Coppola's *The Godfather Trilogy*, where the protagonists are the godfathers themselves, we see how De Niro became inveigled into the gangster underworld and we see how his son, Al Pacino, inherits his legacy, becomes isolated by his own power and finally struggles with his guilt and the desire to become legitimate. The psychological character portraits of the gangsters are complex and believable and the moral questions, of what makes good men bad and whether it is possible for bad men to redeem themselves, are clear.

Does the fact that *Pulp Fiction* is a black comedy rather than a serious drama absolve it from moral responsibility? As we have already observed in classic story structure the moral position of the film and consequently what the film-maker is saying always becomes clear in the climax irrespective of whether the story is a serious drama or light entertainment. It is the absence of this moral dimension, or what the film is finally saying, that I find unsettling in *Pulp Fiction*. This is partly a result of the narrative disruption – there is no clear climax towards which all the events have been leading unless we take the final scene in the coffee shop to be the climax. Jules is contemplating giving up being a hitman, but the outcome of the film does not arise from the unity of events leading up to the climactic moment; instead the film is resolved by what Jules believes to be 'divine intervention'. Here Tarantino again breaks the rules by deliberately using a *deus ex machina* to resolve his story for comic effect.

But the absence of a moral position lies also in the characterization of the hitmen. We believe in and are entertained by Vince and Jules's banter, but do we really believe it when they kill people? Are these true portraits of psychopaths? A psychopath is by definition a person who can kill and feel nothing or even enjoy killing. There is certainly no sign that Tarantino's characters have any real feelings either way about killing people, they are basically just fun guys and killing happens to be what they do for a living. The fact that Jules likes to quote the bible when he kills people and that he quotes the same passage from the bible when he decides to give up being a hood, is amusing rather than edifying. The predominant feeling one is left with is that of an indifference to killing both by the characters in the film and by the film itself.

Tarantino has taken the trouble to remind us at the outset that *Pulp Fiction* is a comment on 'lurid subject matter' or cheap trash, although I remain unconvinced that this assertion of self-awareness solves the moral problem. Of course it is important to remember that there are numerous films which have huge body counts that nobody seems to mind that much about. They also frequently contain a simplistic, unquestioning moral philosophy which deems that most of the dead are bad and killing them is all part of a day's work in the triumph of good over evil. It is as important for film as it is with any other artistic medium to remain questioning of clichéd assumptions about what is right and wrong, good and evil. It is an important role for any new artist to question the form and over-familiar assumptions about morality. But does this mean that morality can be thrown out altogether?

The post-modernist would point out that all stories are an attempt to impose order in what may be an essentially meaningless universe and our notions of morality are not necessarily any closer to the truth than a story which portrays an absence of morality. This relativist position is essentially that of an observer who sees no reason to make value judgements. My position is with the existentialists who, while recognizing the essentially meaningless nature of the universe, believed that to live each of us must construct our own meaningful world which for most of us involves constructing a sense of order and value.

9 Multiple Protagonists with Conflicting or Separate Aims

Mendes' *American Beauty*

The dramatic form of employing multiple protagonists with conflicting or separate aims has become familiar to us because of its common use in television series. The form is also common in many nineteenth-century novels which were written in instalments for serialization in literary magazines – for instance, Charles Dickens and Henry James wrote many of their novels for publication in this way. Although the novels usually have a single protagonist whose story provides the backbone for the overall unity of the work, the authors are also concerned to engage us with a tapestry of characters whose stories interweave, sometimes conflicting with the aims of the main protagonist, sometimes coinciding, and sometimes taking us off on quite different journeys – each with its own aim, obstacles, climax and resolution. Often nineteenth-century novels adapt more successfully for television serialization than for film because a far longer screen time is required to do justice to the complex interweaving of stories.

Television soap operas also use multiple protagonists, employing fast and increasingly sophisticated intercutting between separate stories of characters whose lives are connected by family, friendship, neighbourhood or work place. Because these stories run over weeks, months and sometimes years there is no need for a single protagonist with a dominant aim to provide an overall sense of unity. Although, if you take the time to disentangle all the story threads from the overall tapestry, each strand will be seen to operate along the lines of classic narrative structure. The dramatic shape of each episode will be dictated by the dramatic questions raised by these story threads. The episode will end with a particularly poignant dramatic question, or 'cliff-hanger', to induce the viewer to turn on next week, and often the internal story structure will be arranged to present a more minor dramatic question before each commercial break to persuade the viewer not to switch channels. (The term 'cliff-hanger' was first coined in the early days of the cinema when films for children were serialized and episodes frequently ended, quite literally, with a character hanging from a cliff.)

Because of the problem of length it is more rare for feature films to have multiple protagonists with conflicting or separate aims. Two notable recent exceptions are Robert Altman's *Short Cuts* and Ang Lee's *The Ice Storm*. *Short Cuts*, based on a selection of Raymond Carver short stories, is episodic in structure, each story being tenuously linked by friendships or chance encounters. *The Ice Storm*, adapted from Rick Moody's novel, is more similar to *American Beauty* in that it focuses on two neighbouring families and two generations, the parents' and the children's. Although the story concentrates on the build-up to a single event, a key party, which happens to take place on the night of the ice storm, the effect of shifting from one protagonist to the next is quite distancing for an audience. This is because the structure of the storytelling is episodic rather than interweaving, each episode having its own protagonist with his or her point of view of the unfolding events. The effect of shifting from one protagonist to the next is more successful in the novel as the author is able to take the time necessary for us to identify with the new protagonist. *American Beauty*, as we shall see, engages us with all the protagonists and their separate conflicts in the beginning of the film and through a complex interweaving of the story strands maintains a strong sense of the dramatic development throughout.

AMERICAN BEAUTY (1999)
Written by Alan Ball, directed by Sam Mendes

The film opens with sixteen-year-old Jane talking straight to
camera criticizing her father. 'Do you want me to kill him for
you?' a male voice asks. Jane thinks for a moment before
replying, 'Yes.' Credits followed by a shot from the air of a
suburban neighbourhood in America. Lester Burnham (Kevin
Spacey) introduces himself to the audience in voice-over first-
person narration. He tells us that in less than a year he is going
to die, although he doesn't know that yet. Cut to scenes in the
neighbourhood below as Lester introduces us to his gay
neighbours, his wife Carolyn (Annette Bening) and his
daughter Jane. His marriage has become stultified in bourgeois
materialism and Jane is in rebellion against her parents. He
also has problems at the magazine where he works. The
management has hired an efficiency expert – Lester is given a
last chance to do what management says or lose his job.
Lester's portrait of his life is not a happy one. He describes his
life as 'sedated' and tells us that he used to be a loser although
it's never too late to get your life back.

Like the opening voice-over narration, which has a
storytelling prose style reminiscent of modern American
writers such as Raymond Carver, the visual style suggests that
the film is not concerned with an overly naturalistic portrayal
of the world. The sense that something unusual is happening
visually is intensified when, after an evening of conflict with
his wife and daughter, Lester is alone in the kitchen. The
images on screen take on a quite different quality – we realize
that we are seeing him from the point of view of a young man
who is filming him from outside the house with a digital movie
camera. The impact is intensified by music which underscores
the importance of the moment, causing us to question how it
connects with what the film might be about.

At the end of this opening sequence we assume that Lester is
the protagonist and the overriding dramatic question is his
impending death. The impact of this is powerful. How is he

going to die? We can't help but connect this with his daughter's words in the pre-credit scene and the young man who offered to kill him for her – although their conversation seemed more like an adolescent fantasy than a real death threat. The question of how Lester got his life back from being a loser is also arousing our curiosity.

The next sequence is devoted to Carolyn Burnham. Superficially Carolyn appears to have everything many average middle-class women want: she's attractive, she has a family, she lives in a reasonably well-off neighbourhood, she has a good job in real estate. But when she fails to sell a house she reveals another side to her character – she draws the curtains and alone in the darkened room she screams and cries. Like Lester, the psychological pressure is so great that she, too, is nearing crisis point.

Jane Burnham is performing in a cheerleaders' dance routine at her school basketball match. Carolyn insists that the reluctant Lester goes with her to this important event in their daughter's life. During the performance Lester becomes sexually aroused by Jane's friend, Angela. He fantasizes Angela opening her top and revealing her young breasts in a haze of floating red rose petals. After the performance Jane introduces Angela to her parents. She is embarrassed by her father's obvious attraction to her friend. After Jane's parents have left, Angela tells Jane that she thinks her father is sweet and that he and her mother obviously have not had sex for a long time. We cut to Lester and Carolyn in bed that night as Lester again fantasizes about Angela – she is lying naked in a sea of red rose petals (a seductive if somewhat kitsch image of American beauty). In the car as they drive home Jane and Angela's conversation is peppered with heavy irony, revealing their superficial sexual and psychological sophistication. But when Jane walks to her house the image quality and atmosphere changes – we are seeing her through the digital camera. 'Asshole,' Jane shouts when she realizes she is being filmed.

In the morning Jane disturbs Lester just as he has dialled

Angela's number. Lester quickly hangs up and leaves. Jane dials last number recall to find out whom her father was phoning. We cut to see her from the window of her neighbour's house where Ricky is again filming her. Ricky is called downstairs to where his mother is cooking breakfast – she's forgotten he doesn't eat bacon. The gay couple who live nearby call to welcome the Fitts family who have recently moved to the neighbourhood. In the car, while giving Ricky a lift to school, Colonel Fitts rails against homosexuals. 'Those fags make me want to puke my guts out,' Ricky answers him with such heavy irony that his father looks momentarily confused, not understanding his son's obvious mockery.

In terms of classic narrative structure this might be said to be the end of the beginning of the film. Lester's role as protagonist remains clear although his initial problem, the fact that he is going to die, seems to have been forgotten. Instead the whole of his life appears to be his problem; a middle-aged man facing a mid-life crisis, stressed at work, bored with his home life and his wife, convinced that his daughter hates her parents and now in the grips of a sexual obsession for his daughter's best friend. If we ask ourselves the question, what does Lester want?, the answer has to be Angela, or at least his idealized image of her. The obstacles are also clear: his age, his wife, his daughter. The character of Angela herself, flirtatious, sophisticated, sexually aware, suggests that she might not be so hard to seduce. But in terms of screen time as well as story structure, Carolyn and Jane are also emerging as protagonists of their own stories – rather than merely as obstacles to Lester's story.

When Carolyn cried in the empty unsold house we experienced her vulnerability and a sense of impending crisis in her life. She wants success desperately. Jane on the other hand is trying to carve out a life of her own, free from the stifling suburban model of unhappiness her parents exemplify. Rather than thinking of Jane as an obstacle to Lester's desires, when she discovers whom her father was phoning we feel for Jane, not Lester. Finally Ricky could also be emerging as a protagonist. Seeing what he sees through the digital camera invites us to identify with him because we are seeing the world through his eyes – although the opposite could be true, his voyeurism could become a problem unifying the whole Burnham family. It's too early to tell but we are also aware that Ricky, like Jane, has problems with his parents, particularly with his bigoted father.

So, at the end of the opening the story structure is already beginning to resemble the serial; we have four separate potential protagonists each with conflicting problems and possibly conflicting aims.

At school Ricky introduces himself to Jane as her new neighbour. Jane is angry with him for filming her and Angela accuses him of being a 'psycho' because he has been in a mental institution. Ricky ignores Angela's bitchy comments and makes it clear that it is Jane he fancies, not Angela. Jane appears both shy and embarrassed by his attention.

Ricky joins his parents on the couch in front of the television. The three sit stiffly in a row – the image epitomizing the deadness of their family life. Mrs Fitts is portrayed as a woman in the grips of a severe depression and a dominating husband.

At a glamorous business function in a local hotel, Carolyn, determined to 'live the image she sells' chats up Buddy, a star in local real estate. She is surprised by her success. Meanwhile Lester gets to know Ricky, who is working as a waiter at the function. Lester is impressed to discover that Ricky is also a drug dealer and while they are outside smoking dope he is even more impressed when Ricky quits his job. He envies Ricky's youthful freedom, a freedom he has lost. High on dope Lester again fantasizes about Angela – this time with red rose petals floating from her pouting mouth.

When Jane invites Angela to stay the night he becomes even more fixated and eavesdrops on the girls' crude sex talk through Jane's bedroom door. The two girls look out of the window to discover that Ricky has 'written' Jane's name in fire on the lawn below. They also notice that Ricky's bedroom window overlooks Jane's and he is at that very moment filming them watching him. Angela assumes that he is interested in her and poses sexily for him, but we can see on the digital monitor behind Ricky that he has focused his digicam not on Angela but on Jane's face reflected in her dressing-table mirror. Ricky moves the digicam down to where he can focus on the Burnhams' garage window – Lester is stripped and exercising, trying to get in shape for Angela. Colonel Fitts comes into his son's room to give him a jar for a urine sample. We are curious about what this sample could be for and even more curious when Ricky swaps the empty jar for a full one he keeps in a fridge in his room. In bed that night Lester imagines himself in a glamorous bathroom with Angela submerged in a bath of red rose petals. Carolyn wakes to discover Lester masturbating. She is horrified. A furious row develops with Lester confronting Carolyn with the truth of their empty sexless marriage.

We have clearly reached a turning point in the narrative development. The truth about the Burnhams' marriage is out of the closet – it has now been spoken. How will this affect their marriage and their separate stories, as we know they are both already struggling with a sense of their lives in crisis? In contrast a love story between Jane and Ricky is just beginning. The generation divide between the young people and their parents is palpable. Lester's envy of Ricky's freedom reflects his sense of loss of his own youth. Carolyn's desperate struggle for success reflects her inner emptiness. The young people view their parents' generation with a sophisticated knowing cynicism which, while we can see the truth in their perceptions, is also shocking because they are so young. We are learning about Ricky by seeing the world through his eyes, through his own digital images, but the shots through the digital camera lens also raise the theme of film itself – it is an alienation device that, along with the theatrical staging of some of the scenes, invites us to consider the fact that we are watching a film, an artefact, and to question the meaning of the images themselves. At the same time we are conscious of the variety of images, or ways of seeing: reflections, mirror images, digital images, fantasy images, characters seen through windows at night, all impacting on the senses of both the characters and the audience.

As if to mark the turning point in the story we now return to the opening shot from the air of the neighbourhood below and to Lester's voice-over narration. 'It's a great thing,' he says, 'when you realize that you still have the ability to surprise yourself.' Instantly we are reminded that this is Lester's story. Somewhere in the back of our minds we also recall his opening speech about the fact that he is going to die. The dramatic question now is: What more will he do to surprise himself and might there be any connection with his impending death?

To discover the answer we go back down to earth where Lester is jogging with his gay neighbours who are clearly much fitter. They meet Ricky and Colonel Fitts and Lester goes with Ricky up to his bedroom where he scores some dope. Those who haven't already guessed now also learn the answer to the riddle of the urine samples Ricky has to give his father – they are dope tests which is why he swaps the jars for a friend's clean urine. This is another example of youthful sophistication pulling the wool over the eyes of the older generation. Lester looks at Ricky's room which is a shrine to the digital age – TV monitor, editing equipment and walls lined with shelves of tapes. Lester again becomes nostalgic for his own youth when he worked at a hamburger joint and he had his whole life ahead of him.

The drugs have a powerful effect on Lester – he is sacked at work but rather than taking it quietly he blackmails his boss for a year's salary. Carolyn is outraged when she discovers Lester taking drugs in the garage. On the other hand she is soon on a date with Buddy, the real estate king she met at the hotel function. For the two of them success, power and sex are intimately connected and they swiftly go to a motel to consummate their affair. Buddy tells Carolyn that when he is stressed he likes to fire guns at a local firing range. He offers to teach her to shoot – 'Nothing makes you feel more powerful . . . well almost nothing,' he adds seductively. Carolyn is impressed. Could this be the ever-elusive success that she wants more than anything in the world and is convinced will fill the vacuum in her life?

The sequence is intercut with scenes of the newly unemployed Lester seeking a job as a sales assistant at a hamburger drive-in restaurant. As we have already learnt, Lester worked as a hamburger cook when he was young and free – so we know exactly what he is hoping for now. The sequence is also intercut with scenes of Ricky meeting Angela and Jane at school. Angela sticks to her conviction that he is a dangerous psycho. But Jane ignores her and accepts Ricky's invitation to walk home from school with him. This indicates that Jane may soon be able to break free from the pernicious influence of her 'more obviously attractive' best friend.

As Jane and Ricky walk home they talk about death. Neither of them has ever known anyone who has died. Ricky tells Jane about a time when he filmed a homeless woman who had frozen to death. Jane is shocked – why film that? Ricky tells her it was beautiful, like 'God is looking at you . . . and if you are careful you can look right back'. At home Ricky shows Jane his father's study, which is strictly off limits. He says his father would kill him if he knew but the Colonel is out. Jane looks in awe at the study walls which are lined with guns. But what Ricky really wants to show her is a special plate which he takes carefully out of a glass cabinet. She turns the plate over and sees a small swastika printed on the back. She is shocked and a little scared. Ricky asks her if she wants to see the most beautiful thing he ever filmed. Upstairs in his room he shows her his film of an empty parking lot on a cold autumn day with a white plastic bag rising and falling in the gusts of wind. He tells her about the experience of filming it, how it was as if the white bag were dancing with him. 'That's the day I realized . . . this incredibly benevolent force wanted me to know there was no reason to be afraid. Ever.' Jane takes his hand and they kiss.

By the end of this sequence the overriding feeling is that of anxiety for Ricky and Jane. Although they appear to be sophisticated, sexually aware, cynical, familiar with the latest psychological jargon, they have never actually experienced death first hand and their deep needs and desires are still imbued with an honesty untainted by the lives their parents lead. They are still capable of experiencing hope and beauty in a simple image of a plastic bag blowing in the wind. They are still young. We are uncomfortably aware of the proximity of Ricky's father's obsession with guns and Nazism and Jane's parents' individual life crises. The dramatic question now is: How will the messed-up lives of the parents impact on their children?

At home Jane is once more seated between her conflicting parents, only now the row has considerably intensified. Later that evening Carolyn comes to Jane's bedroom, ostensibly to apologize for the scene, but she is soon in tears. Jane is not impressed and tells her mother she doesn't feel like having 'a Kodak moment'. Her mother slaps her hard and leaves. Jane looks at her reflection in the mirror – as if searching for her own identity. She then goes to her window. Ricky is, as usual, filming her from his window. Jane slowly begins to undress for him. The images here are strikingly complex. We have Jane from Ricky's point of view framed by the window undressing for him, intercut with Ricky from Jane's point of view with her image as filmed by Ricky on the monitor behind him – two images of Jane, one real, one filmed through Ricky's eyes and both immediately following Jane's rejection of her mother's 'Kodak moment', in other words a sentimental or unreal snapshot of life.

The moment is interrupted by Colonel Fitts whose anger has been provoked by discovering that Ricky has been in his study, his private sanctum. After violently physically attacking his son the Colonel manages to control himself and talks pathetically about the need in life for rules and authority. The moment is almost tender, before the Colonel leaves in embarrassment. In the silence Ricky sits alone on the floor nursing his wounds.

These two scenes of violence, from parents towards their children, resonate with a shocking intensity. They are both scenes where the children have seen a truth in their parents, a truth neither of the parents can bear about themselves. Carolyn's and the Colonel's rejection of their own truth is so powerful that they lash out violently. At the end of this sequence the violence underlying these two families is at the forefront of our minds. The dramatic question is: How and when will this violence erupt again?

As if in answer to our question the next scene shows Buddy teaching Carolyn how to shoot. She's high on the experience and when she gets home, for the first time in years, Lester desires her. They begin to make love but the moment is spoiled because Carolyn suddenly becomes anxious that Lester might spill his beer on the four thousand dollar Italian silk couch. Here the issue between Lester and Carolyn is again shown to be how materialism, wealth and possessions have come between their ability to love each other and live an authentic life.

Ricky and Jane are in Ricky's room filming each other while they interview each other about their lives. Ricky tells Jane how he ended up in a mental hospital – he had a row with his father about drugs and his anger erupted in a fight at school when he almost killed a boy. Jane talks about how angry she is with her father, she cannot bear Lester desiring her best friend. Jane conjures up a vision of hiring Ricky to kill her father for her (a reprise of the pre-credit scene). At the end of the scene Jane insists that she was not serious.

The psychoanalytic subtext in this scene is clear – Ricky fights with his father and Jane is jealous of her father desiring another woman. On the other hand the film so far has shown us that both Ricky's and Jane's problems with their fathers have been caused as much by their fathers' behaviour as any underlying Oedipal fixation. The fact that both young people are able to confess the truth about their lives on film reminds us of popular television's taste for public confessions – it is as if the camera provides a distance between them which frees them to open up fully to each other. The camera brings an air of both reality and unreality to their situation and somehow makes what they are saying less threatening. The camera and the way they can watch each other on film at the same time as being filmed, also adds an element of glamour and eroticism. While Jane is exploring the idea of hiring Ricky to murder her father we are reminded of the pre-credit scene and very conscious that Ricky is recording the evidence of her proposition. Talk of Lester's death also reminds us of the opening of the film when Lester told us that he was going to die. The dramatic questions are now taking on a new urgency. Might Ricky prove to be so unstable that he takes up Jane's proposition? What if someone else attempted to murder Lester? Might Ricky's film incriminate himself and Jane?

As if to mark the importance of this scene as the final turning point before moving on to the ending, the next scene once more opens with the shot from the air of the neighbourhood below. Lester's voice-over now focuses on the theme of his death before we join him at ground level jogging – he is considerably fitter now than he was at the beginning of the film. At breakfast, Jane tells her parents that she's bringing Angela home to stay the night. She confronts Lester on the embarrassing way he behaves towards her friend. Lester responds angrily and Jane leaves the kitchen in tears. In the Fitts house, after Ricky has accepted a lift to school with Jane, Colonel Fitts goes into his son's room. He looks through Ricky's tapes and plays one – he sits mesmerized by the film of Lester exercising in his garage, naked. We are reminded of the homophobia the Colonel displayed when we first met him. Does the Colonel suspect his son of being gay or does the fascination with which he watches Lester hint at the Colonel's own sexual ambivalence?

Carolyn and Buddy call in at the drive-through hamburger restaurant. Carolyn is horrified and humiliated to find Lester serving them. Buddy immediately ends his relationship with her. Carolyn is convinced this is because her image of success has been ruined by Lester's lowly occupation. Left alone in the car she expresses her frustration with hysterical screaming and tears.

That evening Lester is exercising in his garage when he realizes he has run out of dope. He bleeps Ricky who goes over to the Burnham house, watched secretly through the window by his father. The Colonel sees Lester half naked handing his son money. The dramatic irony here is clear – because the full picture of what is going on between Lester and Ricky is partially blocked by the window frame, from the Colonel's point of view it appears as if Lester is sexually engaged with his son. The dramatic tension is heightened by the brewing storm.

Jane arrives home with Angela who flirts in the kitchen with Lester. Jane walks away in disgust. Back in the Fitts house the Colonel confronts Ricky in his room threatening to throw Ricky out of the house and telling him he would rather his son were dead than a faggot. Ricky responds with heavy irony telling his father he is right, 'I suck dick for money.' As we have already seen, his father doesn't understand irony. The violence of the fight between them is shocking. At one stage it looks as if the Colonel might really kill his son. 'What a sad old man you are,' Ricky tells his father before leaving. He passes his terrified mother, hugs her and asks her to take care of his dad. Outside it is pouring with rain. Carolyn is parked on the freeway listening to a 'self-improvement' tape on how not to be a victim. She takes a gun out of the glove compartment.

The sense that the film is now moving towards its climax is strong. We suspect that an attempt is going to be made on Lester's life, the Colonel has a motive, but now Carolyn has a gun and she is also wild with rage at Lester for ruining her life.

Ricky goes to Jane's room to ask her to go away to New York with him. Angela again accuses Ricky of being a 'psycho' and is furious when Jane agrees to go. While Lester exercises he becomes aware of the Colonel standing in the rain watching him through the garage window. Lester opens the door and invites him in. We suspect that the Colonel has come to kill Lester but as the scene develops the Colonel becomes increasingly emotional. He cries, reaches out to touch Lester's cheek and kisses him on the lips. Lester gently pushes the

Colonel away telling him he has got the wrong idea. Humiliated, the Colonel turns and walks out of the garage into the rain.

Carolyn starts up the car and pulls on to the freeway.

Lester goes into the house to find Angela sitting alone in the living room. At last it looks as if Lester is about to get what he has wanted since the beginning of the film, the chance to make love with Angela. Carolyn is driving hysterically on the freeway. Will she arrive home, find Lester making love to Angela and shoot him? But the consummation of the seduction doesn't happen. Much to Lester's surprise (and ours), Angela confesses that she is a virgin. Lester suddenly sees the truth, that she is just a young girl who has been putting on an act. He gives her a fatherly hug and takes her to the kitchen to get something to eat. He asks Angela how Jane is? She tells him Jane thinks she is in love. 'Good for her,' Lester smiles quietly. 'How are you?' Angela asks him. Lester tells her it is the first time anyone has asked him that for a long time, but he's great. Angela leaves to go to the bathroom. Lester laughs to himself and repeats, 'I'm great' as he looks at a photo of his family. We hear a gun shot and Lester slumps on to the counter. But who shot the gun?

Ricky and Jane come down to the kitchen alerted by the gun shot. Jane is shocked but Ricky is fascinated by the smile on Lester's face as his blood spills on to the counter. (Ricky's fascination reminds us of his words earlier in the film when he said looking at death was like 'God is looking at you . . .') Over blue sky and fluffy white clouds we hear Lester's voice-over. He talks about how he has heard that your whole life flashes before you in the second before you die. We see a montage of images from Lester's childhood and the early days of his marriage to Carolyn when Jane was a child, intercut with Angela in the bathroom terrified by the shot, Carolyn arriving home to find his body and Colonel Fitts returning to his house covered in Lester's blood. In a state of shock Carolyn hides her gun in the bedroom closet, grabs hold of Lester's clothes and cries. The montage ends with Ricky's film of the white plastic bag blowing in the parking lot and a shot of the sky as Lester's narration ends.

In our exploration of classic narrative structure we saw how the theme, or the author's point of view, becomes clear in the crisis which inevitably leads to the climax of the story. Aristotle's dictum – that in order to decide whether a deed is morally good or bad we should take into account 'the person by whom and to whom it was said and done and the occasion, the means and the reason' – assumes that everything that has taken place in the preceding story has inevitably led us to the climax or cathartic moment. Because *American Beauty* has four or even five protagonists, the discussion about the themes of the film becomes more complex.

In retrospect we can see that the crisis leading to the climax, Lester's death, was a combination of factors; the moment when the Colonel saw his son with Lester in the garage, the fight leading to the loss of his son, and finally the moment when he kissed Lester in the garage which led inevitably to Lester's murder. We understand that as an extreme right-wing homophobe the fact that the Colonel's secret homosexual feelings were now exposed was too much for him to bear. We can see that the tragedy in the Colonel's life lies in his denial of the truth about himself. But his action does not provide us with any sense of moral dilemma arising out of our deep understanding of his behaviour (in the way that in *Midnight Cowboy* Joe Buck's action did when he killed Towny in the hotel room). This is because, although the Colonel appears to become one of the protagonists in the final part of the film, all the events of the preceding story have not been devoted to giving us deeper insight into his climactic moment.

As we have observed, *American Beauty* has invited us to look at a tapestry of interweaving stories, and we can now see how each story has arrived at its own crisis, climax and resolution and how the protagonists have changed as a result, enabling us to contemplate the themes of the film.

The crisis of Carolyn's story was when Lester saw her in the car with Buddy. This led inevitably to the climax, which was

Buddy leaving her, and with his departure the loss, in Carolyn's terms, of her dream of success. The resolution to her story was her hysterical breakdown and finally her mourning Lester's death. Carolyn's neurotic pursuit of success has destroyed her life.

The crisis and climax for Jane and Ricky's love story was reached in the fight between Ricky and his father. By standing up to his father and leaving, Ricky was free of him. Similarly for Jane, she confronted her father with the truth about his behaviour towards Angela and how it was hurting her and she stood up to Angela by telling her she no longer wanted her friendship. In that way she freed herself to love Ricky. Their youthful need for love, truth and beauty has sustained them. It is interesting how Ricky's film of the white plastic bag blowing in the wind is included in the final montage of images reflecting the most beautiful moments in Lester's life, not the kitsch images of beauty in Lester's fantasies of Angela.

Lester's story was driven by his need to recapture his lost youth, epitomized by his obsession with Angela. When finally he had the opportunity to have what he thought he wanted more than anything, sex with Angela, which was in a sense the climax to his story, he realized that he no longer needed this to be happy – he no longer needed to recapture his youth, he had changed, he had grown up, he felt 'great'. He dies at the very moment when he is seeing the happiness in the photograph of his family; the moment when he finally accepts his life is also the moment when he dies. We can see how he needed to go on his journey, to dismantle himself, to crack up, in order to put himself back together again, to achieve this new maturity. If Lester's character represents liberal America's concern with personal growth, the Colonel represents the repressive, puritanical attitudes of the far right. While Lester blindly pursues his own pleasure and self-fulfilment he remains oblivious to the very real danger he is in. The Colonel's character is so severely disturbed that when he opens the Pandora's box of his own repressed fears and desires he is quite unable to face what he finds and the consequences are disastrous.

Lester's voice-over narration opens and closes the film as well as punctuating it at key turning points in the development. One of the questions raised in the opening was how Lester came back from being a loser – which is intrinsic to his unfolding story and is answered by the ending. The other question, how Lester is going to die, overlays a sense of drama that is not intrinsic to the narrative development of the story itself, until the dramatic events of the final act, but it provides the overall film with a sense of unity and again the film ends with the answer. Finally we can see how, by exploring these various interweaving story strands, *American Beauty* is a brilliant portrayal of a microcosm of a whole society in turmoil.

10 The Question of the Woman Protagonist

Gorris's *Antonia's Line*

We have seen how the key concept in classic story structure is the conflict generated by a protagonist who has an overriding desire to achieve an aim that is very difficult to achieve. It is this which gives us the linear, forward motion towards the inevitable climax and resolution. Therefore an effective protagonist is a character with an actively striving will. This brings me to the tricky question, is there a conflict between the role of the protagonist in classic form and the role of women? Many women writers and film-makers have experienced a conflict, although the root cause of this conflict remains open to debate. On the one hand some argue that the conflict is embodied in the form itself: the role of the protagonist is essentially masculine in concept and favours the male protagonist or the woman who takes on masculine attributes. Others suggest that the restrictions commonly placed on the woman protagonist merely reflect the restrictions of her traditional role in society – the women's movement in the 1970s and 1980s and the current era of so-called post-feminism have changed all that.

There is little doubt that in the history of drama, literature and film, women have more often been portrayed as the object of desire, or fear, or both unless they are beautiful and their object of desire is a man. The exceptions are the larger than life women protagonists: mythological characters like Medea or Clytemnestra, the great historical figures such as Cleopatra or the first Queen Elizabeth, or more recently the pioneer women who have struggled to break through the barriers that have restricted the lives of the majority of their sex.

In the history of drama and literature two distinct female types are recognizable. The first Freud described as 'the ministering Angel to the needs and comforts of man'. She is the good woman who is receptive, passive and nurturing: the wife, the mother, the nurse, the saint. Virginia Woolf said of 'the angel': 'It was she who used to come between me and my paper ... who bothered me and wasted my time and so tormented me that at last I killed her.'* The second type is the bad, or dark woman. She has a mysterious and dangerous power, is sexually active, threatening and even demonic; the witch, the whore, the hysteric or mad woman. Both types have presented severe limitations for the role of the woman protagonist. The 'good' woman can actively strive to achieve her aim just so long as her aim is to love or to administer to the needs and comforts of others, which means her aim can be either marriage or good works. In much of nineteenth-century literature, stories with woman protagonists, such as *Jane Eyre*, *Sense and Sensibility*, *Little Women* (all made into films in the 1990s) and numerous others, ended with marriage, or despair, or both, depending on whether the woman finally got, or finally lost, her man. The great tragic heroines, such as in Tolstoy's *Anna Karenina* or Hardy's *Tess of the D'Urbervilles*, are victims of hostile repressive social attitudes towards 'fallen' women who stray and are consequently punished. Even Isabel Archer, heroine of *The Portrait of a Lady*, finally succumbs to the requirement to be 'good' and returns to live out her life in a bad marriage – at least this is how Henry James's novel ends. In the film version Jane Campion, as a late twentieth-century woman director, clearly cannot bear to have her heroine make such a sacrifice in the name of goodness, and so she fudges the ending of her version of the story with an ambiguous kiss which suggests that her heroine just might not go back to her loveless marriage.

*Virginia Woolf, *Women and Writing* (The Women's Press) p.58.

The enormous popularity of Margaret Mitchell's *Gone With the Wind,* first the novel and then the 1939 film version, showed how women who behave 'badly' (i.e. selfishly) can make very popular protagonists – although Scarlett certainly gets her comeuppance in the end when she finally realizes she loves Rhett, but too late, he doesn't 'give a damn'. On the other hand, she got Tara, her childhood home, which was perhaps her greatest need and her greatest love. Similarly Thackeray's Becky Sharp in *Vanity Fair* selfishly uses her feminine wiles to pursue the wealth which she wants far more than love. It is interesting how in both of these stories Scarlett O'Hara and Becky Sharp, the 'bad' protagonists, have best friends who are typical selfless 'angels' whom they envy for their goodness. It is no coincidence that in both stories it is only the 'good' best friends who get their man.

This splitting of women into good and bad archetypes is as common in writing by women as it is in men's writing. Even in the nineteenth and early twentieth century the constraints presented by the 'good' heroine were somehow suffocating and a counterbalance was needed. While good Jane Eyre tended to Mr Rochester's needs in the parlour the mad woman, who represents the unacceptable face of woman's rage, threatens to escape from the confines of the attic and wreak havoc and destruction. In 1966 Jean Rhys published *Wide Sargasso Sea* (made into a film directed by John Duigan in 1993), in which she makes Charlotte Brontë's mad woman her protagonist – hers is a story of social and sexual repression leading to her heroine's retreat into madness as a form of escape. In Daphne du Maurier's *Rebecca* (made into a film directed by Hitchcock in 1941) the good heroine is similarly haunted by the ghostly presence of the ex-wife; a demonic out-of-control woman who threatens to destroy her.

The heroines of film noir, a 1940s genre characterized by ambitious women protagonists attempting to compete in a man's world, were usually punished for their selfishness or came to see the error of their ways in the end. *Mildred Pierce* is probably the most well-known and the most complex example of this phenomenon. The film is also a departure from the classic form. Strictly speaking, the male detective is the protagonist: we begin with his aim, to solve the crime, and end with his achieving his aim. Mildred, as the accused woman, is his major obstacle. But, because most of the story, told in flashbacks, is concerned with Mildred's life leading up to the crime, she becomes the protagonist as the dynamics of the drama centre on her aim and the obstacles confronting her. Her punishment also lay in her seeing the error of her ways too late, as a single mother who tried to make her way in the world without the support of a man.

In *Ways of Seeing* John Berger says, 'A man's presence is dependent on the promise of power which he embodies. The promise of power may be moral, physical, temperamental, economic, social, sexual – but its object is always exterior to man. It suggests what he is capable of doing to you or for you. By contrast a woman's presence expresses her own attitude to herself and defines what can and cannot be done to her . . . And so she comes to consider the surveyor and the surveyed within her as the two constituent yet always distinct elements of her identity as a woman . . . in other words men act and women appear.'* If you agree with John Berger here it's not difficult to see how men, with their external object orientation, lend themselves more naturally to the traditional interpretation of the role of protagonist than do women. But Berger is also making the more controversial point that the splitting between 'surveyor and surveyed' is a psychological prerequisite of the feminine condition.

John Berger wrote *Ways of Seeing* in the 1960s. Since then western civilization has experienced the women's movement of the 1970s and more recently post-feminism. It has undoubtedly become more acceptable in society for women to strive to achieve similar goals as men and this should be reflected by both a proliferation of women directors as well as

*John Berger, *Ways of Seeing* (BBC and Penguin, 1972) p.45.

women protagonists, although at the time of writing there are still not many of either.

ANTONIA'S LINE (1996)
Written and directed by Marlene Gorris

Marlene Gorris takes a distinctly feminine perspective in *Antonia's Line*, her epic portrayal of the changes in women's lives through following the stories of four generations of women in a small Dutch village.

In the pre-credit sequence we meet Antonia as an old woman. She wakes in bed in the morning and decides that today is the day she will die. After the credits the story takes us back in time to soon after the end of the second world war when Antonia, accompanied by her teenage daughter Danielle, returns home after an absence of twenty years for the death of her elderly mother. Apart from Farmer Bas, a local widower, and Crooked Finger, an old friend and philosopher, the village is depicted as a harsh environment dominated by men who have very little time or respect for women. Nevertheless Antonia, a beautiful, formidable and indomitable woman, decides to take up residence in the village with her daughter. Very soon Farmer Bas proposes to her, telling her his five sons need a mother. Antonia turns him down. Although she likes him she neither wants to be married nor does she need five sons but she tells him that he may visit her with his sons and help with the jobs it is difficult for women to do. Antonia wants freedom and independence for herself and her daughter above all else. The dramatic question is: How will single, independent women like Antonia and her daughter survive in a place that, with a few exceptions, is so clearly hostile to women?

On her way home from school one day, Danielle rescues Deedee, a local retarded girl, from being raped by her brother Pitte. Danielle hurls a pitchfork into Pitte's hands and takes Deedee home to be looked after by Antonia. Pitte leaves the village. We realize that despite the sexist climate in the village

Danielle, like her mother, is determined to follow her own spirit.

Danielle goes to art school leaving her mother to work the farm. Years pass. Deedee falls in love with Loony Lips, the village idiot. After her graduation Danielle comes home. She tells her mother she wants a baby but not a husband to go with it. The two women go to the city to find a father for the baby. They arrive at a home for unmarried pregnant women. One of the pregnant women, Letta, offers her cousin's services to Danielle. While Danielle and the cousin have sex in a luxurious chateau hotel, Antonia sits in the garden chatting with Letta.

Back in the village Antonia and Danielle, now obviously pregnant, go to church. The parishioners are shocked by Danielle's condition and the priest preaches against 'the sins of Jezebel and her accursed daughter'. Antonia and Danielle hold their heads up high and walk out of the church, followed by Farmer Bas and all his sons. Despite Antonia's refusal to marry him, Farmer Bas loves her and wants to give her his support. He goes to the church at night where he catches the priest abusing a young girl. Farmer Bas uses this incident to blackmail the priest. The following Sunday the priest's sermon begins with 'Let he who is without sin cast the first stone . . .' and goes on to praise women and celebrate their forgiving natures.

Danielle gives birth to Therese. When Therese is still a little girl she shows a remarkable interest in learning. Danielle takes her to Crooked Finger, the learned philosopher, who agrees to take Therese under his wing. The seasons pass. Antonia still refuses to give Farmer Bas her hand in marriage but she tells him he can 'have the rest, once a week'. Farmer Bas builds a little house in a copse by the river specifically for lovemaking and once a week he takes Antonia there in his tractor. Antonia presides over meals in the garden for her growing 'extended family': Farmer Bas, his five sons, Danielle, little Therese who is always reading, Deedee and Loony Lips, and the curate and Crooked Finger. When Letta arrives, pregnant again and with two children but no father, she is welcomed to join Antonia's 'family'. Letta immediately falls in love with the curate and the narrator tells us 'they lived long and happily'.

Therese's intellectual brilliance continues to develop, particularly in the area of mathematics. Danielle, who has converted a barn into a studio for her work as a sculptor, decides that her daughter needs extra tuition. She engages Lena, a teacher who gives private lessons. Danielle falls in love with Lena and has a fantasy of her as Botticelli's Venus. 'And then love burst out everywhere . . .' the narrator tells us as the sequence intercuts between the lovemaking of Danielle and Lena, Antonia and Farmer Bas, Deedee and Loony Lips and Letta and the curate. It's all too much for poor little Therese; the noise of lovemaking everywhere keeps her awake.

After fifteen years Pitte, the rapist, now wearing military uniform, returns to the village for his father's funeral. Danielle is shocked to see him in the village square and tells Lena he is 'the devil'. Pitte's own family is afraid of him and his sister Deedee screams when he finds her in the haymaking field. And then one night Pitte rapes Therese. While Danielle and Deedee look after Therese, Antonia takes a shotgun and goes to find Pitte in the village café. She aims the gun at Pitte, curses him with a stream of invectives and tells him to leave the village for ever. As she walks away Farmer Bas's five sons beat Pitte up. Pitte staggers home for help but there he is finally murdered by his own brother who fears that Pitte is after his inheritance. The narrator tells us that the village was buzzing with rumours about Pitte's death but they were all glad to be rid of him.

Therese leaves the village to study music and mathematics at university. She experiments sexually with various student colleagues but finally she realizes that she cares only for Simon, Letta's son and her childhood friend. Like her mother and grandmother Therese has no desire to get married. At a communal meal in the garden she announces her pregnancy. Everyone begins arguing about whether she should have the baby or not. Her intellectual mentor, Crooked Finger, whose philosophical position is that 'the best thing is not to be born', is particularly against his protégé, with her brilliant career ahead of her, having a child. Therese has her baby, Sarah, but soon goes back to her musical studies, leaving the women in her extended family to look after her child.

Time passes, baby Sarah grows to be a little girl whose greatest interest is in simply observing all the people in the world around her. Suddenly there is a glut of deaths in the village including Letta, Loony Lips and Crooked Finger, whose final act is to write a dark pessimistic letter to Therese before he hangs himself. Therese is devastated by his death and goes into a deep depression. Little Sarah wants to know where Crooked Finger has gone. Antonia tries to explain the cycles of life and death to her great-granddaughter. Sarah sits high up in a barn and watches all the people she thinks of as her family having a meal in the garden below. Antonia and Farmer Bas begin dancing. Through Sarah's eyes we see the people who have died, now mingling amongst the living. We also see the old people, such as Antonia and Farmer Bas, as they were when they were young.

Finally we arrive at the day when the film opened, when Antonia awoke to the realization this was the day she was going to die. She explains that she is going to die to Sarah and asks the little girl to fetch everybody to the house. Antonia dies surrounded by her family and loved ones.

Although Antonia is clearly the protagonist – the story opens and closes with Antonia and her presence dominates the film – the progress of the story is also shaped by, as the title suggests, Antonia's line. The protagonist's baton is passed down through the generations from Antonia to Danielle to Therese and finally to Antonia's great-granddaughter, Sarah, who, we realize in the final scene, has been the story's narrator throughout. The aim of each of the women is to live a free and fulfilled life which means standing up against the dark forces of misogyny in society, loving men who love women on an equal footing and not falling into the traps that have traditionally befallen women. Even though Sarah is still a child at the end of the film, we can see how, as the narrator, she has also taken up this baton – by telling the story of the women in her family she has given them a voice.

Each woman's struggle to find her own path to fulfilment is only part of Marlene Gorris's story. She is equally concerned to show us an epic portrait of the life cycles of the village; people are born, seasons pass, people fall in love, people make love, festive occasions come and go, terrible events take place such as rape, murder and suicide, people leave the village, people die. The cyclical rhythm and flow of her story, which is at the same time full of love, humour and tragedy, offers a particularly feminine insight into the nature of life itself.

11 A Feminine Disruption
Tarkovsky's *Mirror*

Earlier I connected Aristotle's writings on drama to the beginnings of a new epoch and a shift in man's view of himself. The nature of the shift, which had slowly evolved over the centuries preceding Aristotle, involved the decline in belief in external, mythical and magical forces and the ascent of a view of the world controlled primarily by the rationality, logic and reason of man. It is only relatively recently that a few signs have begun to emerge that suggest a possible radical shift in the pendulum which leads some people to believe that we are on the verge of a new epoch.

The relatively new science of chaos dramatically questions our assumptions about linear, rational determinism with its discovery that order can breed its own kind of chaos. Some theories of psychoanalysis also challenge our ideas about rational determinism. Jung's concept of a collective unconscious not only suggests that we have archetypal images within our innate psyche but also throws into question our concept of ourselves as individuals and the seemingly insurmountable boundaries between us.

The new epoch Aristotle heralded marked the end of the long changeover from the matriarchy (the dominant aspect being the feminine archetype) to the patriarchy (the dominant aspect being the masculine archetype). I have qualified the concepts of matriarchy and patriarchy deliberately because it is both simplistic and dangerous to think of this shift as being a changeover of power from women to men. Edward Whitmont, a Jungian analyst and writer of the fascinating *Return of the Goddess,* puts it this way: 'Maleness and femaleness are archetypal forces. They constitute different ways of relating to life, to the world and to the opposite sex. The repression of femininity, therefore, affects mankind's relation to the cosmos no less than the relation of individual men and women to each other.'*

In other words Whitmont is saying that because all of us, irrespective of whether we are men or women, contain aspects of both masculine and feminine archetypes in our psyches, the 'repression of the feminine' isn't just a women's issue (which isn't to undermine its special importance for women), it raises fundamental questions for all of us about our identity and our view of life. Whitmont tells us that the 'opposition and complementariness of male and female belong among the most basic representations of the experience of dualism. They underlie the polarities of solar and lunar, light and dark, active and passive, spirit and matter, energy and substance, initiative and receptiveness, heaven and earth.'† This is not a question of one set of archetypes being good and the other bad, it is about acknowledging the natural law of duality and the creative energy which arises from these oppositions. It is also about the danger when either the masculine or the feminine archetype becomes so powerful it tries to exterminate the other.

Feminine archetypes, and consequently women, have been devalued during the patriarchal epoch. Whitmont suggests that this is a result of the separation of the 'masculine' ego, with its pursuit of a rational understanding and control of all things, from the encompassing awareness of the magical, mythological and unconscious world which can neither be totally controlled nor fully understood and is consequently deeply threatening to the ego. Whitmont, and Jungian psychology generally, suggest that although the descent into the

*Edward Whitmont, *The Return of the Goddess* (Routledge & Kegan Paul, 1983) p.123.
†Ibid. p.128.

underworld, or the unconscious, can be frightening, and destructive, the magical and mythological is also an essential part of the transformative experience and as such crucial to the process of change in the 'feminine' creative cycle of growth.

Transformation, or change, is also crucial to the classic narrative form, but the structure dictates that it can only be achieved through the climax resulting from a journey caused by the will and obedience to man's rational laws. This suggests that the Aristotelian form is a 'masculine form'. However, the aggressively striving protagonist is just one interpretation of the classic form. The protagonist who is on a quest for life and meaning is a softer interpretation, but equally valid, as we have seen in some of the film examples we have explored. In other words some film-makers, who are in touch with their feminine aspect, whether they are male or female, find working loosely within the classic structure helps to liberate their work – the masculine helps to liberate the feminine – while others have clearly found that they need to depart more radically from the classic structure in order to express themselves fully.

One of these film-makers is the Russian director, Andrei Tarkovsky. His film *Mirror* seems to me to be one of the most complete disruptions of the classic form.

MIRROR (*Zerkalo*, 1974)
Written and directed by Andrei Tarkovsky

The first time I saw *Mirror*, soon after its release, I was both utterly bewitched and totally bewildered by the film. Tarkovsky's use of image and sound is amongst the most beautiful I have ever seen; it is tactile, deeply sensual and profoundly spiritual. But he doesn't lead you by the hand into 'the third dimension', he plunges you into it, and holds you captive there, defying not only the rules of film grammar and logic, but also what we have come to believe to be cosmic laws of space, time and gravity. Consequently the feeling is like falling into a magically beautiful, yet profoundly disturbing, very familiar yet totally unfamiliar place where, if you try to grasp hold of some bearings, and fix the film in terms of linear narrative development, those bearings quickly begin to feel fragile and even spurious.

It was only on the second and then repeated viewings that some of these bearings began to consolidate in my mind as crucial links feeding my need to piece together a sense of unity for the whole. For me the film then became far richer because I was not only awash with strange feelings, but intellectually the film had now begun to teach me its own way of understanding it.

Because *Mirror* has so completely disrupted the classic form – it doesn't have a traditional order of sequences that make up the story development – it is very difficult to give a summary of the film; one could only do it justice by attempting to describe the entire film and I am not going to attempt such an awesome task. But there is another crucial point of departure which I can talk about and that is the role of the protagonist. We never actually see the protagonist in *Mirror*. It is only a while after the film has begun that we begin to realize that the protagonist is not the woman we are watching on screen but a man, whose voice we hear and whose presence permeates the entire film, although we never see him. We realize that everything in the film is exploring the subjective experience of this man whose marriage has broken up and whose life is in crisis. We never see him on screen because we have been transported into his mind, his thoughts and his memories. The woman we see so much of on screen is both his wife and his memory of his mother. The two characters are played by the same actress and, instead of trying to clarify or create order out of the confusion between memory and time present, Tarkovsky seems happy for us to fully experience the confusion, to be unsure of the difference between his wife and his mother just as we are unsure of the precise borders between the past and the present.

Also the protagonist's memories are not only confined to events that actually happened to him, his experience of life includes other people's experience of life, his mother's and his wife's, his son's, his father's, his nation's, other nations'. All the boundaries that we usually use to define the self and the other, time and present reality, memory and imagination, have somehow become dissolved. Instead the film flows with disorientating ease from one experience to another and is concerned not so much with defining experience in terms of time, place and linear connection, as with reaching the essence of experience itself. This demands that we make connections between microcosmic and macrocosmic events according to our intuitive intelligence rather than according to the process of rational deduction which is our familiar mode.

This is why I feel that to understand the film we have to give ourselves over completely to 'the feminine aspect'.

Four

THE CREATIVE PROCESS AND TELLING YOUR OWN STORIES

Introduction

In my profession I meet many aspiring screenwriters but when it comes to actually putting their ideas on paper something is stopping them. They have lots of ideas but haven't got the time to write. They are living in the wrong house or the wrong country. They can't write because of their job, their family commitments, their financial problems. They have an idea they began five years ago but haven't managed to complete it. They once wrote a script but became discouraged after the first rejection. They know they are really screenwriters at heart but are still waiting for inspiration. When they've got the right idea they will take the world by storm. It's easy to think up numerous reasons to explain why you are not writing, as all professional writers know, but they also know that these rarely have anything to do with the truth of why you are not writing.

The real reason is usually a psychological attitude they have about exposing themselves. Deep down they simply can't believe that their experiences and ideas are worthy of their attention and would also, if valued enough, be worthy of sharing with others. It's more socially acceptable to be cool, sophisticated, objective, cynical, ironical; in other words to keep their true feelings to themselves and to remain hidden. This protects them from social disapproval and it also protects them from one of their greatest fears: rejection. But as a result, when it comes to writing they feel crippled by a sense of embarrassment, an acute lack of confidence and even shame about exposing feelings, ideas and images that have a special meaning for them.

Becoming a writer is finally a decision you make about yourself and your attitude to life. You have to decide that you, as an individual, are prepared to be open, which means to be vulnerable, to take risks, to say what you have to say and to live with your fear of rejection and to trust your own instincts and intuitions. Making such a decision is the single most important factor in any creative person's life. Beyond that there is, of course, much you can learn to assist yourself on your journey. Developing a thorough understanding of film language, structure and the craft skills involved is obviously a major part of this journey. But screenwriting is essentially a personal, not an academic, activity. A major factor which hinders many new writers in their progress is their lack of knowledge of some of the methods and techniques which can assist in liberating their own imaginations.

The creative process involves using two very different parts of yourself: the unconscious and the conscious. The unconscious is where your imagination and originality reside, and the conscious is the home of your intellect, your developing craft skills and your inner critic. When developing yourself as a screenwriter it is of equal importance to train both of these aspects of yourself. The unconscious may produce wonderful, imaginative and original material, but without the process of sifting and crafting and shaping, the material will remain largely esoteric and unusable. Conversely, the conscious may have a thorough grasp of structure, complex intellectual ideas about the nature of film and know all the tricks of the trade, but unless your unconscious is feeding it original, imaginative material the conscious will produce work that is merely soulless imitations of what has gone before. So the question is how you can fully train and use both your unconscious and your conscious selves, so they both become a natural and harmonious part of your working process.

Great films are not great because of the idea but because of the realization of the idea. When you attend to the process the product looks after itself. Attending to the process means accepting that the creative cycle, like any form of growth, has its own stages and rhythms. These stages involve periods of gestation, as well as periods of activity and making things happen. It also means acknowledging the interconnected dual nature of process; on the one hand we have to attend to a sequence of activities with a natural order and on the other hand we ourselves are living organisms with our own rhythms and cycles which need attention. In other words we are not just talking about getting to know the process as if it's a separate entity, like a plant that we are growing in our garden; we are at the same time getting to know ourselves and our individual relationship with the process.

In the following chapters we first look at the preconditions for creativity itself and the early stages of generating and gathering material. I also suggest some methods for working with both your unconscious and your conscious mind and ways of bringing into being ideas, images, characters and sequences. We then move on to look at some methods for getting in touch with the stories you have to tell, including developing a writing routine, writing the first-draft screenplay, the question of evaluation and the giving and receiving of feedback. We go on to consider the film-making team and the variety of collaborative models facing screenwriters. For those readers who want to be film-makers I have suggested a short film-making exercise. Finally, in order to stimulate our imaginations and remind ourselves why it is that we want to tell stories, I have returned to the age-old question of the role stories play in our lives.

12 Eight Preconditions for Creativity

The first question we have to ask ourselves is whether we are in a creative state of being to begin with. And if not, what changes can we make practically, in our lives and our ways of thinking, to bring about a creative state of being? Silvano Arieti, in his book *Creativity: The Magic Synthesis,** suggests that there are eight key preconditions for creativity. Although his research relates to all forms of creativity in the arts and sciences, as a starting point for us I have decided to borrow his eight headings and consider what each of them means to the specifics of writing for film.

1. *Aloneness*
Although most creative people need intense and fertile periods of contact, it is equally important to enjoy being alone and have the space for contemplation and time with your own thoughts.

2. *Inactivity*
Time off for doing nothing except thinking and feeling about things. This isn't as easy as it sounds. We have been brought up to believe that if we are not involved in an obvious activity, whether it is one of the many mechanical tasks that fill our lives or actual productive work, we are being lazy, for which we feel guilty. Conversely there are times when it can be beneficial to engage in seemingly mindless mechanical activity. These are

*Silvano Arieti, *Creativity: The Magic Synthesis* (Basic Books, 1976) p.373.

times when you need to stop consciously thinking about things and allow the unconscious its period of gestation. It's often during these periods that answers to difficult problems rise to the surface.

3. *Daydreaming*
This is a kind of fantasy thinking that involves a fair degree of inwardness and introspection as well as immersing yourself in your imagination. It also relates directly to the roles that dream, memory, fantasy, metaphor and archetype have to play in film which we explored in Part One.

4. *Free-thinking*
This means allowing the mind to wander in any direction it chooses to go in with no constraints. It is not the same as free-association, which is a psychoanalytical process for generating material specifically about yourself. In free-thinking your thoughts may be wholly imaginative or intellectual, concerned with philosophical, political, or spiritual matters, or they may be about people you know, people in the news, overheard conversations, etc.

5. *Being in a State of Readiness for Recognizing Similarities*
This is about making connections between apparently disparate and random thoughts. Arieti uses the examples of Kekule who 'identified himself in a dream as a snake swallowing its tail, and saw an analogy to the benzene molecule as a ring rather than a chain of carbon atoms', and of Bell 'who compared the human ear to a machine (which became the telephone)'.*

Similarity is, of course, the essence of metaphor (a subject we looked at in some depth in Part One). 'Being in a state of readiness' seems to be the key here. It's a natural part of the process to consciously invent metaphors but we also need to be receptive to those which are already a part of our life, in our

*Ibid. p.376.

memory and our daily encounters. For screenwriters and film-makers this activity is a way of seeing and thinking about seeing.

6. *Openness*

Openness is a willingness to explore everything, to become attuned to what seem to you, in the moment, to be truths, and the ability to rule out the negative effect of untimely criticism and the suspension of untimely judgement. The important word here is untimely: there is, of course, a time for making discerning and critical judgements, but remember, we are talking about the preconditions for creativity. If the judge in you is allowed too strong a hand too early in the process you will simply feel stifled and as a result become blocked.

7. *The Remembrance and Inner Replaying of Past Conflicts*

We have already noted, in the section on dramatic structure, that conflict and the need for resolution are the central elements of dramatic energy; it is what motivates the protagonist and moves him or her forward. So it is not surprising that conflict, and the drive towards resolution, now also arises in relation to what is motivating our own creative energy and moving us forward. The importance of this concept is that it acknowledges that we all have, and will continue to have, key conflicts in our lives. There is not only an intimate link between our motivation to create and these unresolved conflicts, but they also draw us towards our particular creative explorations, or what stories it is important for us to tell.

Numerous films, as different as Bergman's *Fanny and Alexander*, Terence Davis's *Distant Voices, Still Lives* and Sylvester Stallone's *Rocky*, have been rooted in their author's personal history, as was *That'll be the Day*, written by Ray Connolly, one of David Puttnam's first productions and among his best films. In Puttnam's biography *Fast Fade* we learn that the film, which is about a school dropout trying to make his way in the world, is a result of a remarkable writer-producer collaboration when 'both men shaped key characters from their own younger images and events in the story were largely autobiographical'. *

The telling of an autobiographical or semi-autobiographical story can have an important part to play in helping you find and liberate your creative voice, so enabling you to move on to new pastures at a later stage. If you feel this is the case, it would be foolish to fight against it simply because of some puritan notion that personal conflicts should be hidden away like dirty linen. Many a good film would not have been made if this were true. Although most writers acknowledge that a period of transformation is necessary. This refers to how the process of crafting the often shapeless and chaotic autobiographical material into a story transforms the material into an artefact with universal meaning.

Even the 'new pastures' I referred to earlier are linked to our own conflicts. We may find ourselves wanting to tell the story of a character who lived in another period of history or in another country, but it is our understanding and awareness of our own conflicts which both draws us to the story and enables us to tell it with empathy. Also, conflicts which are important to us, or what Arieti calls our 'psychological leitmotifs', tend to recur during daydreaming and free-thinking, which means that if we learn to listen to our unconscious it naturally provides us with the source of our creative impetus.

8. *Discipline, or the Will to Put What Has Been Discovered into Action*

This is obviously essential. But for the writer, who for much of the time works alone, it's really a question of self-discipline as there is usually nobody to tell you to get on with it except yourself. And without the discipline to get down to the work at hand the other seven preconditions become redundant. In some cases, because the fear of getting on with the work can be great, the self-discipline needs to be quite brutal. You can't stand shivering on the edge of the swimming pool for ever,

*Andrew Yule, *Fast Fade* (Delacorte Press, 1989)

worrying about whether you've forgotten how to swim or not, there comes a time when you have simply to push yourself in. The first hours, days, or even weeks may be painful, but the flow of work will not come through thinking too much, it will only come through doing because getting what is inside of you outside, and on to paper, generates its own energy and momentum, and finally it's the activity itself which sustains you.

13 Generating and Gathering Material

If you were developing yourself as an athlete you wouldn't enter for a race straight away, you would first undergo a period of training involving routine, discipline and exercises. This is similar to the process of developing yourself as a writer, our equivalent to the race being the first-draft screenplay. This early stage of the process makes all the difference when you are just beginning to get to know yourself as a writer, but many well-established, professional writers also see this as an important stage in the work-in-progress of each new project, especially in regard to generating and gathering fresh material. Only recently, a writer friend told me that he had just spent six months gathering his material and only expected to spend a few weeks actually writing the first draft, but he wasn't yet ready to begin because the shape of the whole still hadn't quite fallen into place and he hadn't yet 'found his metaphor'.

The following are some suggestions for ways of generating and gathering material. These are exercises that I have used both in developing myself as a writer and in the work I have done with my screenwriting students over the years. You may find that some of the methods are more suited to your particular temperament than others, but beware, we are full of prejudices about when and how we work best and sometimes these prejudices, if they remain unquestioned, can be real hindrances rather than the assets we've always assumed them to be.

First try letting go of all the assumptions you normally

make about yourself and starting afresh. Tell yourself you know nothing about what working method is best for you; you don't know whether you like to begin work in long-hand or straight on to a computer; you don't know whether you work best in the early morning or the middle of the night; you don't know whether your best quality is thinking in images but you can't write dialogue, or whether you're good at writing imagery and dialogue but as far as your intellect is concerned you need to read the entire contents of your local library before you are fit to put pen to paper. It's amazing how tenaciously people will cling on to these fixed notions about themselves, notions very often originating way back in their history in reaction to a few judgemental words from a thoughtless parent, teacher or professor.

Now think of yourself as a stranger you've just met. You are so intrigued with this person you want to know every aspect of them intimately. You want to know your deep inner life, your history and background, what makes you laugh, what makes you cry, your philosophy, your spiritual pursuits, the kind of other characters who populate both your inner and outer worlds, your ideas about the nature of life, your ideas about other people's ideas about life, what makes you angry, what excites you intellectually, what brings you to despair, what turns you on. This stranger is also something of an actor and a magician: he or she isn't restricted to telling you about the characters that populate your life and imagination, the stranger can speak like these characters, think like them, feel their feelings and know their aspirations, in short the stranger can perform the most extraordinary feats of metamorphosis if given half a chance.

These exercises are about giving yourself that chance by approaching yourself with an attitude of fresh discovery, finding out what you can and want to say and so getting to know the writer in you.

1. Free-Writing

This is a technique known to novelists as a way of getting in touch with their creative flow, but for some reason it's virtually unheard of in the screenwriting community. This is perhaps because novelists are aware of the important role their unconscious has to play in informing their writing, whereas many screenwriters tend to assume their work is more conscious and craft based, which is certainly true, but applies more to the later stages of the process.

Free-writing is essentially a method for discovering who the writer in you is and what the writer in you wants to say. You don't have to sit for hours torturing yourself by trying to force great ideas out of thin air. What you want to write about is already deep inside you. The question is how to get in touch with this material and how to get it on to paper.

The Free-writing Method

When you are asleep you give yourself over to your un-conscious; you are literally in the dreamtime. Very soon after you wake your conscious takes over and all your usual preoccupations and inhibitions come flooding in. So the first stage in the process is to get as close to your unconscious as possible and to find out what's going on in your imagination before your super-ego, or inner critic, has woken up and begun to take control.

Stage One, Early Morning Writing

1. Choose a specific day in the near future and make an appointment with yourself for what will be a sort of pre-breakfast meeting. Make this appointment for an hour before you normally wake up and set a time limit for the encounter of exactly one hour. Once you've decided on the date and the time of the appointment you must treat it as sacrosanct, nothing barring the most severe crisis will persuade you to break it.

2. When you go to bed the night before the appointment make yourself a thermos flask of tea or coffee (or whatever you

normally drink first thing in the morning) and set the alarm for the appointed time.

3. When the alarm goes off force yourself into action immediately. Either go straight to your writing desk, or (if you sleep alone and find it works better for you) pick up the pen and paper you have ready by your bed, and start writing.

4. Begin writing straight away and don't stop. You may at first find yourself writing about how cross and tired you are because your sleep has been interrupted or you may have woken during a dream and find yourself writing down the dream. Never mind what it is, write it down, even if you feel that what you are writing is repetitive nonsense – what matters is that you are pushing that pen across the page and not sitting in blank inactivity. You will soon tire of writing nonsense and more specific thoughts will occur to you, a memory might suddenly appear, or a fragment of a story, or a place just asking to be described, and then maybe some characters who are acting out some kind of drama in that place. Whatever it is, whether it seems ordinary or quite fantastic, don't censor or criticize it, simply explore it through writing, going wherever it wants to take you.

It doesn't matter if you find yourself writing in prose. During free-writing it can be unnecessarily restricting to attempt to stick strictly to screenplay form, but do remember that your ultimate goal is to be a screenwriter, not a novelist or short-story writer, so encourage your mind to work as if you are describing a film you are watching in your imagination by noting down all the details, the images and sounds, observations about characters and actions, everything and anything that helps bring your writing to life on the page and that would also be manifest on film.

You may find that you spend most of the hour exploring one specific thing, or that you alight on two or three apparently unconnected fragments, or that your writing remains fairly abstract, wandering around an internal domain of feelings and present or past dilemmas. Don't worry, there is no single right or wrong way to do this exercise. And at this early stage be open to everything as you have no idea what will prove to be useful to you later.

5. When your hour is up *stop writing*. Head what you have done with the date, appointment time and the length of the session and put the work away in a folder. Then either go back to sleep for another hour or begin your day as you normally would.

6. *Don't* read through what you've written, however tempted you may be. Instead schedule in your diary three or four such appointments a week for the next two weeks.

Stage Two, Appointments with Yourself at Other Times

Once you have tried a few early morning writing sessions, begin to make appointments with yourself at different times of day or night: mid-morning, late afternoon, mid-evening, just before bed, etc. Once again make these appointments in advance, give the appointment a time limit, anything from half an hour to an hour (but not longer, you want to work at your optimum energy level, not drain yourself) and each time remember to treat the appointment as sacrosanct. And most important, when the appointment begins *write, and write anything that comes into your head*.

Although it is important to begin to associate your writing table as the place where your creative flow functions well, for some of these sessions you can also start to experiment with place: meet yourself on a park bench for half an hour, or in a café, or the reading room of a library. But wherever you are be sure to put all your energy into the encounter with yourself and write for the specified time, whatever comes into your head.

Stage Three, Your First Read-through and Process Sessions

I suggest you put aside a weekend for this task, two weeks after you first began the exercise, and schedule two sessions over the weekend.

Session One: Read-through

Read through all you've written (hopefully about ten or twelve sessions of writing). Remember, don't censor or criticize for writing style or content, that is not what this exercise is about. Your purpose is to discover what is going on deep inside your writer's mind, not to judge yourself. And this first read-through can be an extraordinarily rewarding experience, partly because you have forgotten much of what you have written, especially the early morning writing which tends, like dreams, to slip back into the unconscious, but also because you will find there is a marked difference between the kind of work you are used to producing and the writing confronting you now. You might at first find this difference very strange and confusing and not be at all sure how to react to it. But remember to be open to it, enjoy it and value it for what it is.

Now read it all through again, but this time take a coloured pen and give the sections which seem to have a thematic unity a title or heading in large capital letters – this is so you can glance at the section from a distance of five or six feet and know what it's about, which will be important for your second session. Now put all the material away and forget about it until the next day.

SessionTwo: Process

Clear a large space on the floor of your workroom. Lay all the sections of writing out on the floor so you can see the headings clearly from a distance. (If a single writing session has broken down into a number of different headings simply take a pair of scissors and cut it up.) Your floor will now be covered with piles of paper. Find a place to sit where you can see all the headings and spend a while meditating on what you have in front of you.

You will soon begin to see that certain patterns and specific preoccupations are emerging and some 'umbrella headings' will suggest themselves as you begin to want to define the patterns and similarities. There will be some obvious headings like the disgruntled 'I don't know what I'm doing or why I want to be a writer', and 'dreams'. There will probably be a whole variety of memories: 'childhood', 'adolescence', 'relationships', etc., and a whole variety of incidents, both memories and imaginary, which may be connected by theme or place. Whatever these new headings are, write them down on separate sheets of paper as they occur to you, lay them out on the floor and reposition the sections of writing under the new headings.

You will now find that you have a strange and endlessly moveable jigsaw in front of you. Some pieces of writing will want to be positioned under more than one heading. Some pieces will seem more important to you than others. Some headings will intrigue you more than others. You may want to position those which are of most interest nearest you and those of little or no interest on the periphery.

So simply play with the various permutations for a while. Then begin a period of selection. Put on one side the pieces that are of least interest to you, that you really wouldn't mind throwing away. Place by them the pieces that are of second-least interest to you and so on until all you have remaining on the floor are those pieces, maybe four or five, which intrigue you most. You don't have to consciously know why they are apparently insisting, of their own accord, that they remain in the arena. All you need to know is that you still want them on the floor in the most important position. Sometimes you might discard something and then find that you feel unhappy without it, in which case bring it back, even if it doesn't fit under any of your existing headings, give it a heading of its own and place it on the floor in a position that feels right to you in relation to the other pieces which remain in the arena.

Finally, put the whole lot away in two separate folders, one for those of lesser interest, and the other for those of most interest to you. But don't throw anything away. You may find that a piece of writing you at first wanted to discard takes on a special importance later.

Stage Four: More Free-writing

Schedule another two weeks of writing appointments, both in the early morning and taking into account what proved to be the optimum times for you during the day or night. Approach these free-writing sessions in the same way as you approached the earlier sessions. You may feel that you want to focus on some of the incidents, themes or characters that have already begun to emerge, but let your unconscious decide. If it wants to develop some of the earlier material it will, or it may want to bring some completely new things into the arena; if so it's important to be receptive to this. Also, if you start forcing your work or pushing it in a specific direction too soon you will be in danger of losing some of the spontaneity.

If you now find that you suddenly want to spend time writing that hasn't been scheduled, go with it. But apply the same discipline as the scheduled sessions, writing whatever comes into your head. Your unconscious will by now be learning that it's being taken into account and you will find the flow of your work will be that much easier.

This period of free-writing and fortnightly read-throughs and selections may go on for four, six, eight weeks depending on what you find emerging on your workroom floor. The material itself will eventually tell you when you are ready to develop it into a screenplay outline and move into the craft period of working. There will almost certainly be many possible stories in your folders, but one story will be rising to the surface as the story you want to explore now. (It may well be that you will return to some of the other material at a later stage.) You will recognize the moment of transition because the key elements of a story will finally be in your arena. You will be able to see the rough shape, know who the main characters are, and most important, the conflict will be clear. Until this moment arises you may want to return to the free-writing, because something is still missing.

2. Image Gathering

'The primary factor in film is the image . . .' was the opening of the Bergman quote I used in my introduction to this book and much of Part One was devoted to an exploration of how image is fundamental to film language. The purpose of this exercise is to raise your awareness of your personal relationship with images so that they become a natural part of your working process. It is similar to free-writing in that it is another way of getting in touch with your imagination and the stories you will find there.

The exercise is primarily for those of you who, because you've come from a literary or academic background, may feel insecure when it comes to working spontaneously with images. (Although, if you are from a visual or fine art background, you may find it a helpful way of overcoming any insecurity you may have about expressing yourself verbally by incorporating your love of images into the scripting process.)

The method is very simple. Your objective is to gather images to which you feel personally drawn, in order to write a short film script. Set aside a few hours a day for a week as the time when you gather images. Start by looking at images that you have already gathered – in that they are in your home; pictures, old photographs, mementos, newspaper cuttings, postcards, pictures in books – and select just six images. Remember that your only criterion for the selection is whether the image absorbs you in such a way that you want to gather it. Next go to a different place each day: specific places that have a personal meaning for you, places that intrigue you visually, places that make you want to watch what's going on, and places designed to stimulate visually like museums and art galleries. For these trips you may want to take a drawing pad or camera, but don't get sidetracked into trying to make perfect images, remember you are simply gathering records of the images for a larger purpose.

The stages in the process now become similar to those in the free-writing method. You begin by placing your images in a chaotic mass all over your floor. You then address each image by asking: 'How important is it to me?' and 'Why is it important to me? (bearing in mind that you are thinking in terms of film and finding your own identity in relation to film). You then make your initial selections and groupings.

After a few weeks of gathering and processing material in this way you will find that your relationship with your chosen images will have developed considerably. In your imagination they will be suggesting ideas for characters, relationships between characters, metaphors, archetypes, locations, film moments, scenes and sequences. Some images may also be demanding to be in written form. Don't resist. Simply write the image or scene down and include it with the rest of your material. The final step is to arrange the material in what will be a moveable linear sequence. You can then work with the juxtaposition of images, the sequence order, decide whether you want to add or subtract images, and consider the whole in terms of beginning, middle and end. This is your basis for writing what will probably be a short film.

3. Developing a Sense of Place

In film, as the microcosm sequences we explored earlier show, place is not merely the location of the unfolding story, it is integral to the expression of ideas and emotions. This is what distinguishes film from theatre and this is why it is especially important for screenwriters and film-makers to develop a sense of place.

Many film-makers form intense and passionate relation-ships with specific places. The Taviani brothers' love of the simple and often harsh rural landscapes in their native Italy has been fundamental to their development as film-makers. Leone was equally enamoured with the mythic elements of

222

the frontier desert landscape, although this was a place which existed in his imagination and the world of stories rather than having had an actual part to play in his personal history. Wim Wenders, through exploring the landscapes of his own life and times in films like *Kings of the Road, Alice in the Cities* and *Wings of Desire*, has developed a now familiar iconography of the northern European and north American industrial and urban wastelands, expressing the sadness and alienation he feels about modern man. For each of these film-makers the story and the place are indivisible from each other.

The same is true for Wenders' contemporary Werner Herzog, only Herzog's quest for metaphor, through identification with a place, has led him far away from his European roots in search of places which express the conflicts and needs of the more primitive aspects of our psyche. Herzog's two South American films, *Aguirre, Wrath of God* and *Fitzcarraldo* are fine examples of this. The following extract from the screenplay of *Aguirre* (which is about a group of Conquistadores searching for El Dorado in the Amazon jungle) gives some insight into how Herzog's creativity was inspired and fuelled by his relationship with the place. It also shows how for him the script is far more than merely a blueprint or schematic plan. He needs to express himself emotionally and poetically in the script just as he does in the finished film.

Slowly the canoe penetrates into the dusk of the jungle. The oars dip quietly, and the long slender canoe proceeds slowly among the huge tree trunks. Lianas are dangling down touching the boat. Far away a jaguar roars. Leaves the size of wagon wheels are floating on the water with turned up edges, huge water lilies amongst them. Brooding dusk in the woodland. All around, the staring flowers, the ardor of orchids. The men in the canoe are very quiet. Monkeys begin to chatter above them, single leaves are fluttering down and start to float. The men are crouching in

223

terror and only row lightly. The water stretches out
through the jungle endlessly.*

But Herzog did not begin making films in exotic jungles, he
began in his native Germany, although some of the places he
shows in his German films, such as *The Enigma of Kaspar Hauser*,
appear equally strange through Herzog's eyes.

The purpose of the following exercise is to help you
develop an individual sense of place in such a way that,
irrespective of whether you finally want to work from
places you know or whether you prefer to invent places in
your imagination, it will become a natural part of your use
of film language and an intrinsic part of the stories you have
to tell.

The Sense-of-Place Method

In the world of fine art there is a well-known story about how
the Eskimos make sculpture. The story is basically this: the
Eskimo takes a lump of stone, sits in front of it and waits. When
asked what he is doing he replies that he is waiting for the
stone to speak to him, to send him feelings, to tell him what it
wants to become. A while later the Eskimo begins to make
some marks on the stone. Then he waits again. And so on until
finally the stone has been transformed into a work of art, a
sculpture. This is the basis of the sense-of-place method, only
your objective is to write a single film sequence, not make a
piece of sculpture.

Stage One, Finding the Place

Your choice of place matters less than what happens to you in
the place. This is because the stance you take in the place will
be meditative, the principle being that any stone will speak to
you if you are receptive enough.

I do, however, have a few guidelines for your choice. Try
to find a place that is away from a populated area. You want

Werner Herzog Screenplays (Tanam Press, 1980) p.85.

to be alone there, not find yourself watching lots of people. And look for a place which has a distinctive landmark: a disused gravel pit, a derelict factory or mine, a railway tunnel or level crossing, deserted buildings, abandoned vehicles, a cave, a small wood, a pond or lake, a ruin. When you have found your place decide on the boundaries of the territory, say a hundred yards across.

Stage Two, Spending Time in the Place

Try to choose a time to do this exercise when you can go to the place for a few hours every day for a week.

Go there with no preconceptions, no ideas that you might want to work on. Instead *empty your mind*, move about the place slowly and quietly, look and listen and become a part of the place. Don't impose anything on the place, just allow it to speak to you. After a while you will probably find yourself drawn to specific spots in the location. You will find spots where you like to sit and specific images that you like to look at. You will begin to notice sounds. You will begin to make choices between the images and sounds that interest you and hold your attention and those that don't particularly affect you. You will begin to make connections between specific images and between images and sounds. The place, or aspects of the place, will begin to suggest a sense of meaning, mood, atmosphere, and maybe metaphor. Characters may begin to appear in your imagination and events that might have or could have taken place there that connect with the feelings you find growing inside you. In your imagination the place might become a part of another country or another time in history, past, or future (remember film is based on illusion: a small wood, a pond, a quarry or a sand-pit can give the illusion of being anywhere in the world at any time).

After spending a few hours in the place go home and spend a short time, maybe just half an hour, making notes about your experience. These notes will at first appear like chaotic or confused notations of images, feelings, incidents, possible relationships or encounters, or even sometimes appear as little drawings of images you've been looking at. But be careful not to force these notes to go beyond a simple record of what you actually experienced in the place itself. In other words don't start thinking up narratives to fit the place. Many of us, because of the speedy lives we live, have forgotten how to be open and receptive to a place. So it is important simply to record your experiences at this early stage in the process and not to anxiously force stories to come before they are ready.

Try to visit the place at different times – dawn, midday, evening – and if the weather varies a great deal so much the better. The experience you have there at dawn may well be quite different from how it affects you in the middle of the day or at dusk, and the grey, gloomy day or the rain-storm will almost certainly affect your imagination quite differently from a hot sunny day. And this is all a part of your exploration.

After four or five visits to the place you will probably find that your notes are naturally beginning to focus themselves. Specific images, thoughts and ideas will have begun to recur and may have already developed in some way or other. Some characters and a situation may have appeared in your imagination, or several different scenarios may be evolving. If you have more than one idea now is the time to choose just one to focus on. (Remember you are only focusing on an idea for a five-minute sequence not an entire feature film.)

Stage Three, Preparing for the First Draft

This session should last for a few hours and take place in your writing room. Ask of the material you are focusing on who is or are the main characters and what is happening to them. Give them names and spend the time free-writing in prose about them. Where have they come from? Where are they going? What do they want? What's going on in them now? How do they feel in the place they are in? Write down anything that occurs to you that helps you get to know them better.

Stage Four, Writing the First-Draft Film Sequence

Again this should be done in your writing room and take no more than a couple of hours. You have your idea, you know your characters, you know the location intimately, simply write the sequence paying special attention to how you are using film language to communicate what is happening.

Although the description of this exercise may sound a little mystical the basic idea is similar to the early morning free-writing. In the early morning exercise your unconscious flows to the surface because you are still close to the dreamtime and your conscious censor and critic is warded off by the uninterrupted flow of your writing. Being in a place and 'listening to it' is another way of encouraging your unconscious to flow to the surface, but this time with the associative process being guided by the specific atmospheres, images and sounds you are encountering in 'your place'.

By asking you to empty your mind and to 'listen to' the place I am not suggesting that you have to negate who you are for the place to speak to you, but rather that *the place speaks to who you are*. When you are most receptive to the space around you, you will at the same time be most receptive to what is deepest within you. This is because, as we saw earlier, the unconscious prefers to manifest itself through stories, metaphors and archetypes than to speak directly to you. Also, paradoxically, the deeper you go into your unconscious, although you may feel as if you are getting closer to the specifics of who you are, you are also getting closer to the archetypes – which is very important if you want to touch that place in other people, your audience, which is universal.

4. Research

Your subject matter or source material does not always have to be inspired by images and incidents lying dormant in your own unconscious. Most writers, at some time in their lives, feel a positive need to get out of themselves and immerse themselves in characters and situations which at first they may know little about, whether these be characters from an historical incident or something read about in the newspapers.

But the maxim, *write what you care about and know about*, applies just as much if you are working from research as it does if you are writing about something rooted in your personal or community experience. After all, what is it that draws you to one historical character or incident rather than another, or causes one newspaper story to fascinate you more than all the others? It has to be a special sense of contact, which means there is something about the material which connects with your own experience, even if this connection at first seems oblique.

The prospect of going on a journey of discovery outwards is exciting. It gives the secret detective, explorer and archaeologist within us a chance to stretch their legs. It's fun burrowing around in libraries, newspaper archives, museums, making contact with strangers, visiting places that have played a special part in your subject's life, gathering together the pieces of the jigsaw, piecing together the clues as your story takes shape.

In a sense this process of gathering is not unlike the process of generating material in free-writing. It's just that you are collecting your images, scenes, important incidents, character portraits, places, etc., from out and about in the world, rather than excavating them from your own unconscious. And there will come a time, just as with the free-writing process, when the floor of your writing room is covered with the material you have gathered and you will be shaping and ordering and making choices about what to include and what to leave out.

There are obviously a number of different approaches to research. Some writers prefer to know the rough shape of the story they want to tell before they begin, then they know precisely what they're looking for when they go on their gathering expeditions. Other writers prefer to begin with an image or incident (which is usually a metaphor), or the bare bones of the character who has inspired them, and find the shape of the story they want to tell only when it begins to emerge from the material gathered.

But every method has its dangers. The danger of the second method is that you can over-research, or simply get bogged down in so much material that you begin to feel overwhelmed by it. The danger of the first is the risk of going into a research period with a kind of tunnel-vision, looking only for facts which will fit your preconceived storyline – this leads to superficial films. The genuine quest after truth means a spirit of enquiry and an attempt to disprove hypotheses as well as to try out theories. The rewards of this method lie in the surprises as you discover and piece together the complex network of interconnected hidden ingredients which make up the story. Surprise and discovery are, of course, the two major elements which enrich the texture of all storytelling forms. Also you will find that material about the unique nature of characters is as important and revealing as the incidents which make up the plot-line and invaluable if you want your audience to become emotionally involved with your story.

Costa-Gavras's film *Missing* investigates the 'disappearance' of a young American when the junta seized power in Chile. *Missing* is a fine example of a true story that goes way beyond an accurate record of events to communicate what those events actually felt like for the characters who were caught up in them. The film does this though the remarkable characterization of its two protagonists, the father and wife of the young American. It's through their quest for the truth that we encounter the horror and carnage inflicted by the junta and the controversial political question of American complicity. But it's the complexity of their characterization, their relationship with each other and the way their shared experience changes them, that make the reality of the coup and the political issues not merely available to us, but meaningful. The lesson here is that characters are not just cyphers to serve a story, they're there to live and it is through their living that the story lives.

So, although it may at first appear as if you are going on a journey outwards, if you are really to bring the story alive you have to take the material gathered inside of you, and then bring it out again with the same kind of insight you would bring to bear if you were writing from your personal experience. This is why your choice of source material is so important. It is not just a matter of choosing a character or incident that you think would make a good story that would sell, it's a matter of choosing a character or incident that intrigues you in such a way that you want and need to tell it. And your need to tell someone else's story is usually rooted in exactly the same place as your need to tell your own stories. That root is located in the heart of the conflict, which relates to our seventh precondition for creativity – the remembering and inner replaying of past conflicts. Even if the life and times of your chosen character seem a thousand miles away from your own, and their conflict is of such dramatic proportions that your own life experience seems insignificant in comparison, your identification and empathy with their conflict is, nevertheless, your way in and your motivation for telling. It is also the key to the shape and direction, not of their story (there's no such thing as an objective story), but of the story you have to tell about them.

14 Characterization and Dialogue

Characterization and story are interdependent. Characterization is all the information, both visual and verbal, which communicates to an audience the totality of who a character is and what he or she wants and needs and, especially in the case of the protagonist, it is these wants and needs which determine the backbone or structure of the story.

In films the most important visual information about characters tends to be communicated through their actions, what they do. All actions give us some insight into the nature of a character and who they are, whether these actions are highly dramatic, like placing a bomb in the boot of a car, or very minimal, like looking out of a window when someone is speaking to them. Characterization is also communicated through physical appearance, dress, gesture, and mannerisms, seeing a character from the point of view of another character, and most of all seeing the world through the character's eyes, experiencing their imagination and sometimes even sharing their fantasies, their memories and their dreams. It's this intimacy which enables us to identify with them. (Remember the beginning of *Midnight Cowboy*.)

We also learn about characterization through words, dialogue; the things the characters say and the things other characters say about them. Almost all major characters and many minor characters in films speak, unless they happen to be deaf and dumb, in which case they would almost certainly find some equivalent of speaking to communicate their wants and needs. But dialogue writing is one of the great bugbears for many aspiring screenwriters. How often I have heard the refrain 'But I can't write dialogue', or 'I don't know how to write dialogue', or 'Of course my dialogue isn't any good'. Why is this fear of writing dialogue so common when we all use dialogue, we all talk to each other, in our daily lives?

I think there are two main reasons for this fear: the first reason isn't ostensibly to do with dialogue writing as such, it's more to do with the way we relate to the characters we create, and the second reason is to do with the craft of screenwriting and the lack of understanding many new writers have about the role the dialogue has to play in the overall scheme of things.

The Importance of Empathy

It's one thing to know a character from the outside, to know how they look, how they dress, how they move, what they do and the kind of things they say. But to create convincing characters, and to write convincing dialogue for your characters, you have to take a crucial step, and that step is from being outside of them, from seeing them in your imagination, to fully entering them, becoming them in your imagination.

Empathy literally means the power of understanding and imaginatively entering into another person's feelings. An empathic person is usually a caring person because they can imagine what it's like to be in another's shoes. And it's the same with your characters: it is only when you are inside of them, thinking their thoughts, feeling their feelings, experiencing the world through their eyes, that you really begin to understand who they are and know not just the kind of things they would say but what they do say and how and why they say it.

Inside every dramatist there is a secret actor trying to get out. When it comes to actually being an actor, on stage or in front of a camera, you might be the most appalling bag of nerves and entirely unconvincing. But when you are alone at your writing desk, inside your imagination, you come into your own, you become the most brilliant and versatile of actors, you have the ability to move in and out of all of your characters at will, you play all the parts, you become each of them and experience each of them from the other characters' point of view. You know what they are thinking, what they are feeling, what they want and what they don't want, what they do and what they would never do in a million years, and you know what they say, how and why they say it, what they wish they had said and what they regret having said.

This necessity to empathize with your characters applies equally to those who are bad or evil as well as to those who are good. And the prospect may well appal you. How can you possibly empathize with a torturer, a concentration camp commandant, a child molester, a psychopath. But empathize with them you must, because you will only be able to create a whole character for them, rather than a familiar stereotype, when you can see the world from their point of view, and not just know but feel their wants and needs. This is one of the most difficult tasks for any writer and could be what distinguishes the great writers from the good. Macbeth and Lady Macbeth are bad characters. The reason they have so fascinated mankind, and film-makers (Polanski and Kurosawa to name just two), since Shakespeare first created them is because, through Shakespeare's empathy with them, we not only understand their badness, we recognize in it ourselves. Empathy is the only route to insight, both for you and for your audience.

The question for us is how you can further train your ability to empathize so that creating characters and writing dialogue becomes a natural and organic part of your writing process.

Portraits

A good way to begin this exercise is to incorporate it into your

233

free-writing programme. In other words to devote some of your hour-long writing sessions to focusing on specific character portraits.

Also, at first, it's best not to try and create fictional characters but to focus on portraits of people from your own past life. This is because people you have known have revealed themselves to you in special, unique and intimate ways through actions, words and gestures which are sometimes very direct and at other times full of complexity and contradictions. And it's these special characteristics, the small and intimate details of the ways characters manifest themselves, which bring them alive on the written page and on screen.

I suggest you begin writing about characters from your past, even though you may still know them in your present, because your memory will already have begun the process, first by deciding what to remember and what to forget, so the scenes that come into your mind are those that have some special meaning for you, and second by sifting out irrelevant details and retaining only those images, actions, feelings and words spoken which give special insight into the character in the scene or sequence remembered.

Another useful way of getting to know a character is to write a brief life history, writing down all you know about them in note form, where and when they were born, where they grew up, what their relationships with their parents and brothers and sisters were like, special friendships, important incidents that helped to form their personality, important adult relationships, important choices they made in their lives and why. Again begin with characters you know or have known well enough to piece together a network of connections which gives insight into who the character is.

Both these exercises will have a very important part to play when you begin to work with fictional characters, or even if you decide to research into an historical character. Through the little scenes and sequences you write, you will learn the kinds of particular details that illuminate character and event, as well as getting you used to focusing on the heart of the matter. And the brief life histories will tell you the kinds of things you need to know about a character's past in order for you to empathize fully with their present actions. It will also tell you if you are creating a fictional character who is acting or behaving in a totally implausible manner.

It is often the case that you, as the writer, know a great deal more about all of your characters than ever appears in the text of your scripts. But this is no bad thing. In my experience many of the first conversations you will find yourself having with your director and the actors will be concerned with much of this background information because this is their way of getting into the script and so an important part of the beginning of their creative process.

When you are well used to empathizing with and writing about characters you know, their dialogue will begin to flow quite naturally because it is an intrinsic part of their self-expression. And a natural outcome of this approach is that you will find yourself writing, with the same degree of inner knowledge and complexity, about characters you have invented or researched, and their dialogue will also flow, as they express or pursue what they want or need, and cardboard characters and stereotypes will become a thing of your past.

The Craft of Writing Dialogue

Speech can tell you more about character than any other manifestation of personality. The way a person talks reflects their communality – their country, their region, their city (or even a specific district in a city, like the East End of London or the Bronx in New York), their education, their class. At the same time their speech is, like their fingerprints, unique. Their tone of voice, their speech rhythms and their use of language makes a person as easy to identify on the telephone as if we had met them in the street and tells us not only about the particular mood they happen to be in, but also about major aspects of their personality.

Apart from empathy, the single most important attribute for a writer is to be fascinated by the way people talk. Listening must be as important a part of your personal training programme as looking. And the best way to begin is to get into the habit of noting down what you hear, whether it's short snatches of dialogue overheard in the street, the philosophical or political debate you had over dinner last night, or the confused feelings your friend or lover confessed to you recently.

One of the first things you will notice, when you start recording dialogue in this way, is how difficult real communication is and how much of conversation is spent avoiding rather than striving for communication. Dialogue is all too frequently not so much listening and responding as watching eagerly for the next opportunity to grab a space in the conversation and continue with your own train of thought. This kind of conversation can best be described as interrupted monologues. You will also notice how rarely people talk directly about anything, instead their dialogue is full of subtext, postponement of the question, avoidance of the question, manipulation, play, jokes, wit, sudden unexpected outbursts, contradictions, non-sequiturs.

One of the reasons for using memory when you do this 'listening exercise' is because your memory is a natural editor, it retains only those moments which have meaning for you and naturally provides you with an illusion, rather than an imitation, of real life. The same applies to most good film dialogue. If you compare a transcript of a taped conversation with a page of screenplay dialogue, even if the taped conversation is interesting, more often than not it will have a flat, rambling quality about it, whereas good screenplay dialogue will be performing so many different functions, in both the text and the subtext, that it appears more lifelike than real life. This is because it is about life as it is subjectively experienced rather than objectively recorded. Even documentary film-makers spend a great deal of time in the editing room cutting dialogue scenes in an attempt to communicate the essence of what was said, rather than what was actually said. But in fiction the dialogue is performing many more functions than just communicating the essence of what was said. The first of these functions lies in implying the psychological subtext.

Every screenwriter is also a psychologist, constantly questioning the complex inner workings of their characters' minds. To illustrate how this works we can take just one simple situation – a person wants somebody to do something for them – and consider just a few of the many possible permutations arising from the situation.

1. I want you to do something for me, so I ask you and you say yes.
2. I want you to do something for me but you might say no, so I remind you of something I did for you, so you will feel indebted to me.
3. I want you to do something for me but you might say no, so I try and persuade you with logic, reason, passionate argument, pleading for the cause, etc.
4. I want you to do something for me but you might say no, so I pull rank, reminding of you of my superior status, hinting that I can make your life difficult if you refuse.
5. I want you to do something for me so I threaten you physically.
6. I want you to do something for me but I'm so shy, or ashamed, that I can't find the courage to ask you.

Each of these propositions tells us, even in its abstract form, something about the character of the wanter, or the character of the recipient of the want, or both, and a little about the nature of their relationship. Each of them, that is, except for the first, 'I ask you for what I want and you say yes', which is also the least interesting because the transaction is perfectly straightforward, it contains no conflict. But characters in real life, and in films, are rarely that straightforward, unless what is wanted is relatively unimportant. If what is wanted really matters most of us are capable of behaving in the most extraordinary, contorted, creative, imaginative, misguided, funny, conniving, scheming, calculating, machiavellian, destructive or self-destructive ways to get it.

Just think of the implications of all this, and all the other possible life situations and resulting permutations, for what we, and even more so, what our characters say to each other.

Conveying the psychological subtext is just one of the many functions that fiction dialogue has to perform. Below I have listed some more functions and taken an extract from the original screenplay of *Midnight Cowboy* by Waldo Salt so that, by considering the effects of the text, you will be able to see how these functions actually manifest themselves.

Some More Functions of Dialogue

1. To reveal something about the character of the speaker.
2. To reveal something about the character of the recipient.
3. To reveal something about the nature of the relationship between the character and the recipient.
4. To give the audience information relevant to the developing story.
5. To connect with the previous scene and to set up the next scene.
6. To foreshadow what is to come, or to 'plant' some information which will have a part to play later in the story.
7. To carry exposition, or tell us something which has happened off-screen which we need to know to have insight into the developing story.
8. To make the scene believable or lifelike.
9. To reflect the speaker's mood or emotional state.
10. To be economical, which means the dialogue is there for one of the above reasons and there's not too much of it.

Midnight Cowboy: Joe Buck's first meeting with Ratso

TEXT	EFFECT

INT. BAR. DAY

JOE sits at the bar, staring morosely at his image in the mirror, oblivious to the assorted types hiding from daylight in the barn-like saloon, waiting for night to fall.

The set-up: Joe, upset after his first defeat, is vulnerable.

> RATSO'S VOICE
> Excuse me, I'm just admiring that colossal shirt . . .

Does Ratso really like Joe's shirt? Or is he after something?

RATSO studies JOE across the corner of the bar – a sickly, child-sized old man of 21 – hopefully nursing an empty beer glass, contemplating the money on the bar in front of JOE.

Sizing Joe up? An empty beer glass plus his interest in Joe's money on the bar – so he's after Joe's money.

> RATSO
> That is one hell of a shirt. I bet you paid a pretty price for it. Am I right?

Beginning the con, flattery, trying to find out how wealthy Joe is.

> JOE
> Oh, it ain't cheap. I mean, yeah, I'd say this was an all right shirt. Don't like to, uh, you know, have a lot of cheap stuff on my back.

Joe's falling for the bait! Ratso's touched his weak spot, his pride in his clothes. What's more, he's pretending to be wealthy!

RATSO spits as JACKIE leans on the bar next to JOE – a feminine young person, heavily made up, hair teased, wearing earrings and a lace-trimmed blouse over shocking pink Levis.

So Ratso's not the only one who sees that Joe's easy bait.

> JACKIE
> Got a cigarette, cowboy?

In this New York bar Joe's outfit stands like a Christmas tree.

TEXT	EFFECT
RATSO (*a stage whisper*) More goddam faggots in this town.	Fighting to get his pitch back.
Reaching for a cigarette, JOE glances at JACKIE, startled as JACKIE twitches his pink Levis angrily and turns away.	Joe heeds Ratso's warning.
JOE Shee-it . . . (*shakes his head*) Kee-rist, you really know the ropes. Wish to hell I bumped into you before. I'm Joe Buck from Texas and I'm gonna buy you a drink, what do you say to that?	Further revealing his naivety and vulnerability. Realizing what he needs is to 'know the ropes'. What's more, he also needs a friend and thinks he's found one.
RATSO Enrico Rizzo from the Bronx. Don't mind if I do.	Building up his own image to match Joe's.
JOE (*slaps the bar*) Same all around! For my friend, too!	Showing off, spending his meagre resources. We know he's in danger, but he's oblivious to it.
In a booth now. JOE is refilling RATSO's beer glass as he speaks.	Brief time-cut – their new position in the bar increases the intimacy.
JOE . . . you see what I'm getting at here? She got a penthouse up there with colour TV and more goddam diamonds than an archbishop and she bursts out bawling when I ask for money!	Joe's telling his new friend his problems – looking for advice. He certainly needs it but is Ratso the right man for the job?
RATSO For what?	
JOE For money.	Ratso plays innocent

Characterization and Dialogue

TEXT	EFFECT

RATSO
For money for what?

JOE
I'm a hustler, hell, didn't you know that?

Joe's aim confidently reasserted.

RATSO
How would I know? You gotta tell a person these things.
(*shakes his head*)
A hustler? Picking up trade on the street like that – baby, believe me – you need management.

A moment of hope, maybe the streetwise Ratso is not so bad, after all Joe does need help.

JOE
I think you just put your finger on it, I do.

Joe also sees the sense in what Ratso is telling him.

RATSO
My friend O'Daniel. That's who you need. Operates the biggest stable in town. In the whole goddam metropolitan area. A stud like you – paying! – not that I blame you – a dame starts crying, I cut my heart out for her.

O'Daniel? a memorable name. Sounds very convincing although maybe a little over the top, is it real or part of the con?

JACKIE
I'd call that a very minor operation . . .

Jackie gives us the answer.

RATSO grabs the neck of a bottle, sliding back in the booth. JOE scowls as JACKIE appears with a tall farm boy.

Ratso's vulnerable now.

JACKIE
. . . in fact you just sit comfy and I'll cut it out with my fingernail file, Ratso.

Increasing our awareness of Ratso's physical vulnerability.

TEXT	EFFECT
RATSO The name is Rizzo.	So he's sensitive about his name.
JACKIE That's what I said, Ratso.	Now we see Ratso's vulnerabilities we begin to care about him.
JOE (*suddenly*) Hey now, you heard him.	So does Joe, he leaps to his defence.
RATSO That's okay, Joe. I'm used to these types that like to pick on cripples. Sewers're full of 'em.	Ratso is strengthened by Joe's trust and brawn. Also tells us his predicament – a cripple trying to survive in New York's 'sewers'.
JACKIE May I ask one thing, cowboy? If you sit over there and he sits way over there, how's he gonna get his hand in your pocket? But I'm sure he has that all figured out . . . (*to Ratso*) Good night, sweets.	'Cowboy' – reminds us of Joe's predicament. Jackie shops Ratso in revenge for when Ratso shopped him earlier and we learn that Ratso's a pickpocket.
JACKIE swings his handbag over their heads and walks away.	Jackie's convinced his warning will pay off, but are we?
RATSO (*calls after him*) Faggot.	Ratso's trying to win Joe's confidence back by slurring Jackie.

Although all the functions I mentioned earlier are at work in this scene they don't, of course, all have to be operating in every scene. But it is a rule of thumb that if you come across a section of dialogue and you can't think of a single good reason for it being there, although it might, in itself, be wonderful, the script will usually benefit from cutting it out. Another thing you have to take into account is the overall rhythm of the screenplay. A dialogue scene may be beautifully written, you feel proud of it and it performs all of the above functions as well, but at the same time the scene may be so long that it breaks the rhythm of the developing film. It is as if you have slipped into a theatre play by mistake. This is also a good, although sometimes painful, reason for cutting it, or failing that, for moving some of the important dialogue to another scene.

Another rule of thumb is to ask yourself if what is being said in the dialogue could possibly be communicated in a more filmic way through image or action. Your medium is, after all, film, not theatre, and what a character does often tells us more about them than what they say.

It's also worth remembering that silence, in films, can be as powerful, if not more powerful, than long speeches or explanations. Characters, like people in real life, are not only interesting because of what they reveal; their mystery, or what they choose to keep hidden, can be even more tantalizing. In real life, if someone tells us too much about themselves too early in a relationship they can rapidly become as boring as someone who refuses to open up at all, so we begin to wonder if there's really anybody in there worth knowing. The presence of an actor or actress can contribute enormously to this mystery. And in film the huge size of the cinema screen and the potential of the close-up means that a single look or gesture, or in Robert Mitchum's case a slight twitch of his eyebrow, can tell us as much as a speech, and in a far more captivating way.

The text-effect method I used for the *Midnight Cowboy* scene is a very good way of finding out about the craft of dialogue writing as a part of your personal training programme. If you apply the method to a variety of different screenplays (which are increasingly appearing in published form) you will soon learn, not only a variety of craft skills which will help your own work, but also how many widely differing approaches there are to writing dialogue, according to who the writer is and what the writer is trying to say.

If, for instance, you look at Harold Pinter's dialogue in *The Servant* you will see how his primary concern is to explore the complexity of his characters' manipulative power struggles, whereas Marguerite Duras's dialogue in *Hiroshima Mon Amour* has a different mood, rhythm and emphasis altogether, as her two protagonists, motivated by their new-found love for each other and their need to exorcize past traumas (his in Hiroshima, hers in war-torn France), struggle to reach each other fully. For Duras there is conflict enough to be overcome in the mere fact of her characters' separateness.

I think this difference demonstrates how the most important function of dialogue is that it serves your characters and what you, as a new and highly individual writer, are trying to say through your characters. Which takes us back to the two aspects of your self-training as a writer, the conscious and the unconscious, and another warning: try not to get the two aspects of your training mixed up. When you are working on the first drafts of your 'portraits' or free-writing *don't* analyse the dialogue or test it for text-effect, or consciously apply structural principles to what you are writing, or you will inhibit your flow and never find your own voice as a writer.

The conscious analytical judge or critic in you should always be restrained until the time is right, which is when you decide you are ready to move from the unconscious free-flowing stage to the conscious crafting stage. It's always better to have a scene that is pages too long, but truly original and expressive, to mould and craft and make economical at a later stage, than to have a technically competent scene that fulfils all the functions of dialogue but is somehow dead on the page. In other words trust the process and what you are learning from the craft side of your training will automatically feed into your unconscious.

15 Make Your Own One-Minute Film

Campion's *Passionless Moments*

PASSIONLESS MOMENTS (1984)
Written and directed by Jane Campion

Actually making films – writing the script, casting, choosing your locations, planning the art direction in order to get the 'look' of the film you want, organizing the shoot, shooting, putting your shots together in the editing suit and finally adding any post-synch' sound effects or a music track – is altogether a complicated business. It is also worth remembering that professional directors work with crews made up of people who each know their area of expertise and how to work together as a team. Most aspiring film-makers, when they are first starting out, don't have this pool of expertise. They are on their own with a group of friends or fellow students to help them achieve their aims. Some have access to equipment and editing suits at their universities, others have a digital camera and digital editing package on their home computers. But we all have to start somewhere and I have seen some exciting and original short films produced in the most adverse conditions. The most important thing to remember, for those of you who are just starting out on your film-making career, is to set yourself a small, clear, achievable aim. The *Passionless Moments* one-minute film exercise is an excellent way to begin.

I first had the idea for this exercise when I saw the published video of Jane Campion's *Passionless Moments*. Jane Campion, who later went on to make such major feature films as *An Angel at My Table, The Piano* and *Portrait of a Lady*, made *Passionless Moments* in 1984 when she was a student at the Australian National Film and TV School. The film later won Best Experimental Film at the Australian Film Awards. *Passionless Moments* is a twelve-minute black and white film made up of ten segments, each roughly one minute in length. The idea behind the film was to take a single Sunday in a Sydney neighbourhood and for each film to focus on a single thought process of a person living in the neighbourhood on that day. Each one-minute film opens with a title and a male voice-over narrator tells us who the character is and anything we need to know about their thoughts. I will describe just three of the ten films to give you some idea of how they work.

No Woodpeckers in Australia

Title over a black screen. On the soundtrack we hear a clear rhythmic knocking on wood. Cut to a middle-aged woman kneeling on the floor of her living room arranging a bunch of gladiolas in a vase. The rhythmic knocking continues as the voice-over narration begins: 'Mrs Gwen Gilbert, hearing this sound, at first thinks it is a Japanese woodblock being played in Mrs Witerczyk's backyard.' We move into a close-up of Mrs Gilbert's face as she thinks. 'This seems very unlikely. It's just a woodpecker, she tells herself.' Cut to a cartoon image of a cheerful woodpecker pecking a tree. Cut back to Mrs Gilbert, who is now peering out of her kitchen window. Outside she sees Mrs Witerczyk in the garden next door banging a stick against a carpet which she has hung on the washing line. We notice that the sound is a dull thud rather than the clear knocking of wood Mrs Gilbert has been hearing. We cut back to Mrs Gilbert as she returns to her sitting room, tips the flowers on the floor and begins to arrange them again. The knocking on the soundtrack is again clear. Close-up of Mrs Gilbert's face as she once more puzzles over the sound. 'Mrs Gilbert can not understand how Mrs Witerczyk can make that noise by beating a clothes-line with a stick. She reminds herself that we don't have woodpeckers in Australia.' Cut to the

246

cheerful cartoon woodpecker again. Cut to black.

– The title introduces us to the subject 'No Woodpeckers in Australia'. Our curiosity is roused by its oddness; why is it an issue whether or not there are woodpeckers in Australia? We assume the clear knocking sound to be that of a woodpecker. The opening image, a middle-aged woman kneeling on the floor arranging flowers, is quite ordinary but the voice-over narration gives the image a layer of complexity. The character is named – as we have already learnt, naming a character is an important first step in getting to know them – and we learn that Mrs Gilbert thinks she may be hearing the sound of a Japanese woodblock being played in her neighbour's backyard. If her neighbour were Japanese this might not be so odd but Witerczyk is clearly a Polish name. In chapter three, discussing dreams, memories and fantasies, we saw how important it is to show a close-up of the character's face if you want the audience to enter their thoughts. Jane Campion uses this device here: we cut to Mrs Gilbert's face as she puzzles over the theory that the sound is a Japanese woodblock and then switches her thoughts to the equally unlikely, according to the title, woodpecker theory. The insert of a cartoon woodpecker here is amusing. It also serves as a useful editing device, as when we cut back Mrs Gilbert is peering out of her kitchen window. (It would have been difficult to cut directly from Mrs Gilbert's thoughtful face as she arranges the flowers, to her peering out of the window without us thinking that the image we cut to was in her thoughts rather than actually happening.) We see Mrs Witerczyk from Mrs Gilbert's point of view and the cause of the sound is clearly Mrs Witerczyk's carpet cleaning – or is it? The sound we hear over this shot is a dull thudding, quite different from the sound we know Mrs Gilbert hears. When we cut back to Mrs Gilbert, as she returns to her flower arranging, we learn that she is also puzzling over this question. Furthermore we are told that there are no woodpeckers in Australia. Finally we see once more the playful image of the cartoon woodpecker.

So, both the Japanese woodblock theory and the woodpecker theory are equally implausible, but sometimes thoughts are like that – absurd and playful and quite lateral in their associative connections. We may not recognize ourselves in the superficial aspects of Mrs Gilbert's character – she is a rather ordinary middle-aged woman, the kind of woman who uses surnames rather than the less formal Christian names and appears to live an ordered tidy life with time for flower-arranging – but many of us will definitely recognize our own experience in the oddly anarchic nature of these thought patterns.

Focal Lengths

Two young gay men are in bed together. In the foreground Shawn lies naked with his head propped up by one hand and his back to Arnold who is behind him leaning against the wall in his pyjamas. The scene is lit by a low angle lamp. Voice-over narration: 'Shawn and Arnold aren't speaking.' Cut to a shot of Arnold; the lamp casts a dramatic dark shadow on to the wall behind him. 'Arnold's mad because Shawn has been playing around.' Cut back to the first shot with Shawn in the foreground. 'Shawn just can't seem to care.' Shawn shuts one eye and focuses on his thumb. The camera pulls focus between his thumb and a studded belt lying on the floor. 'He's wondering why he can't keep two things in focus at the same time.' Cut back to Arnold, staring angrily at Shawn, still dominated by the dark glowering shadows. 'Arnold's not going to warn him again.' Shawn turns restlessly on to his stomach. 'Shawn knows that one of these times it will be all over. But all he can think of now is vague diagrams from school containing focal lengths, umbras and penumbras.' A light flickers across the two young men as a car passes by in the street outside. Cut to black.

– As with Mrs Gilbert, we may not immediately see ourselves in Arnold and Shawn, but this microcosmic portrayal of a conflict in a relationship is probably familiar. Jane Campion uses both staging and lighting to demonstrate the difference between the two young men. Arnold is the angry one stuck with the problem – he wants to be able to control Shawn but he can't. By placing him in the background leaning against the wall and lighting him from below, Campion literally fixes him in a single position which expresses the uncompromising and all-consuming nature of his anger. Shawn is mentally removing himself from the situation by playing with the idea of focal lengths (as in the title). 'Focal lengths' also serves as a metaphor for a problem in a relationship: if you focus on one the other goes out of focus and vice-versa – how can you keep both in focus at the same time? Umbras and penumbras, or shadows and half shadows, takes the idea a stage further as shadow play is also metaphorically a part of their relationship.

What His Mother Said

A middle-aged man wearing a silk dressing-gown is lying flat on his back on the carpet in his living room with his head on a cushion. Voice-over narration: 'Gavin Metcalf, bachelor, has been trying to get his life together for three or four years. At this moment he is listening to the beat of his own eardrum.' The camera slowly circles around Gavin. We move into a close-up of his face as he stares up in space. 'As this fades from his attention he notices particles of lint drifting through the air in front of his eyes.' Shot of the tiny white lint particles drifting through the air to the accompaniment of 'cosmic' music on the soundtrack. 'He watches the lint for a moment...' Gavin blows and the lint swirls as if in a small wind. '... remembering his mother used to tell him they were angels.' Cut to black.

– The details we are given here are brief, but each is crucial to our understanding of the film. Gavin's silk dressing-gown suggests a certain fastidiousness, he is a bachelor, and he has been trying to get his life together for three or four years. Why, what happened three or four years ago? The overriding feeling we get from this film is one of loneliness – emphasized by the way the camera circles around Gavin's isolated figure. The experience of his seeing the universe in the particles of lint is transportingly beautiful. When we hear the final phrase of the voice-over everything seems to fall into place – his mother used to tell him they were angels – Gavin wasn't always alone, he once shared experiences like this with his mother. Is that what happened three or four years ago when his life fell apart? His mother, perhaps his only intimate relationship, died and he was left alone. If the particles of lint are angels might his mother now be one of those floating particles? When he recalls his mother he is also, for just a moment, bringing her back to life again in his imagination.

Jane Campion ends her film with the words: 'There are one million moments in your neighbourhood. But as the film-makers discovered each has a fragile presence which fades almost as it forms.'

For your one-minute film exercise I suggest that you write a few 'passionless moments' of your own, set in your own neighbourhood based on characters you know, yourself maybe, or your neighbours, family or friends. Then put on your producer/director's hat, choose the script you like best and take it into production. When I have given this exercise to my students the results have sometimes been stunning, although the length has proved a problem, the films have a habit of growing in the edit to two or even three minutes. But try to stick to the one-minute brief, the economy of saying something quite profound in such a short time is part of the magic of the exercise.

16 Story Outline, First Draft and After

There is no 'right' way of writing a first draft. Some writers like an office hours routine, writing from nine to five with strict lunch and tea breaks; others will write an entire first draft in frenzied sittings, working day and night, with the minimum of breaks for food and sleep. The same variation of approach can be found when it comes to writing methods. The two main approaches can be described as 'holistic' – working over the whole story in outline form before beginning the first draft – and 'linear' – after an intense period of gestation or research plunging in on page one and discovering where the story takes you.

The 'linear' method is really free-writing in first-draft form. The danger, as in life, is that if you don't know where you're going or why, you will probably get hopelessly lost. On the other hand, if you come to writing the first draft after a fruitful period of gestation, when you've got to know your story well in your imagination, you've got a clear idea of the conflict facing your protagonist – you know his or her aim, or where he or she is trying to get to, and why – and your creativity is stimulated by the challenge and the risk of plunging straight into the first draft to see whether you sink or swim, then this may be a way forward for you. And if you get lost you can always try making an outline.

The Outline

An outline is a précis of the entire story of the film. My

descriptions of the three films in Part Two will give you some idea of what an outline looks like (but remember these were written from the screen after all the storytelling problems had been solved, rather than being a part of the process of bringing a story into being). The purpose of the outline is to help you work out what your story is about and to enable you to find and remedy any structural flaws before you begin writing the first draft. The outline should therefore be a malleable thing so that you can easily change the order of scenes and sequences, insert new ones, delete old ones, try out new beginnings or endings, thread in new characters or new storylines and take out old ones. You will probably find that you are continually returning to the drawing board because you can see that the story you had in mind is not yet pulling together as a whole. The drafting and redrafting may take some time, but in the long run it will save you the time and unnecessary heartache of writing scenes and sequences which eventually have to be cut because they don't fit into the unity of the whole story.

You are ready to write your outline when you have generated or researched your subject and the story is beginning to take shape in your mind. Take about ten pages of paper – each page to represent the major segments of your film; the beginning, the six or eight development sequences, and the ending. On each page write the locations and rough descriptions of the contents of the scenes and sequences that make up each film segment. Then stick the eight or ten pages up on the wall so you can see your protagonist's entire journey, the structural patterns and unity of the whole film in front of you.

Some writers prefer to write their scene descriptions on index cards because of the need for plasticity. They can then pin the index cards to the wall to see the shape of the entire film and alter the order, insert or remove cards with ease. Other writers feel that the neat, orderly nature of index cards blocks their imagination and prefer to use the traditional cut and paste method. Other writers choose to write their outline in prose form, like a short story.

In the film industry the outline has a dual purpose; as well as being an important stage in the creative process it is also a sales document – film producers decide whether or not to commission writers on the basis of the outline. For this reason it is essential for professional writers and writer-directors to be able to write outlines that communicate the essence of the whole film; not just the introduction of characters and the dramatic development but also the emotional undercurrents, the atmosphere, the visual quality and the themes being explored. An outline should be as easy, enjoyable and gripping to read as a good short story. (The outline is sometimes called a treatment. But there is some inconsistency here as some production companies consider a treatment to be a one- or two-page document which is effectively a very brief description of the outline with an additional couple of paragraphs summing up the screenwriter's or film-maker's intentions.)

Many screenwriters find that having a document that is a part of the early stages of a creative process, and as such being constantly revised according to the discoveries made as the work progresses, while also being used as a sales pitch, can be dangerous, because of the tendency to assume that a story which has been sold, even if only in outline form, is somehow carved in stone. They are afraid that, once sold, the outline might 'die' on them. It's not an unreasonable fear. Once an idea becomes carved in stone creative energy can die: the story is no longer a question, instead it has become an answer, it has lost its mystery and so its hold over its creator. To avoid this happening it is important that both the writer and the producer treat the outline as work-in-progress and as such a malleable document which will continue to grow and may undergo quite radical change during the realization of the project.

The First Draft

Whether you've plunged straight in or you're working from an outline, once you've begun your first draft what matters most is that you keep your concentration, rhythm and flow of writing going until you've completed the screenplay. A routine and writing discipline are enormously helpful at this stage. It doesn't matter so much what your hours are, but that you have regular hours which you associate with writing the draft, and you treat that time as sacrosanct. Again this is a way of letting your unconscious know that you are working so it will contribute to the process, because the most important thing at this stage is that your concentration is focused in such a way that you are expressing fully your feelings, thoughts and ideas. The critical judge in you must still be kept at bay, or your writing flow may become blocked. At this stage it really doesn't matter if each individual scene is not perfectly crafted, if the dialogue scenes are too long or too short, or if some of your scenes seem to have gone 'over the top' in order to express your point. All these problems can easily be rectified when you come to write the second draft.

The First Read-through and Feedback

The first read-through is an important event. This is the first time you will be able to get a real sense of how your story is working as a film. So you must beware of reading it too soon after finishing the draft. You may feel so euphoric – you've finally got the script down on paper – that you've no real sense of how it will affect an audience. Or conversely, you may find that you are in the grips of a kind of post-natal depression and, oblivious to what is working well, you are able only to focus on the problems or failings. This inability to be able to value or love your own work can be as damaging as overestimating it. So make sure you read your work only when you feel distanced enough to be both appreciative and critical. Now is also the time to give the script to a few carefully chosen people for feedback.

The ability to give feedback is a highly developed skill in its own right and developing skills takes time and practice. Many people mistakenly think that feedback means either generalized praise of the 'I really loved it' variety, or negative criticism of the 'I didn't like it at all' kind, without being specific about what was or wasn't liked. The objective of feedback is for the writer to experience how what they have written affects an audience, what it is that holds your audience's attention, what moves them, what makes them laugh, what makes them sit up and take note, what confuses them, what bores them, what makes them lose their belief and interest in the story – in short what each scene and sequence makes them feel and think.

Only in the light of the answers to the above questions will writers be able to judge whether they are succeeding in communicating what they intended. Also, if the person giving the feedback 'didn't like the script at all' the writer will be able to make the very important distinction between whether the reader's dislike is based on a misunderstanding due to some confusion in the text, which can be rectified, or is an actual rejection of what the script is about at either a political, philosophical or emotional level. If this is the case you may need to find a reader who shares your beliefs and values before you can evaluate the script.

To give the kind of detailed feedback that I have described above, for an entire screenplay, is obviously a big job and of the kind that only an experienced writer, script editor or writing teacher will be able to perform easily. You may not know such a person who is willing to spare you the time. If this is the case try finding a writing partner or forming a writing group. This will enable you to swap your work and to take turns giving and receiving feedback with people who have an interest and investment in doing so. This will also give you a chance to develop your critical skills in relation to your own work as well as that of your colleagues. You will find that it can take half an hour to read through and carefully analyse a single five- or six-page sequence so I suggest that, in your first few sessions together, you swap single sequences, not entire screenplays. You will find that the learning gained from the in-depth feedback of a single sequence will quickly inform the rest of your writing. And when the time comes to swap your whole screenplay you can then focus mainly on questions of structure, character development and theme.

For all writers (new or old), receiving feedback on a new

work is a complex experience. You are emotionally raw; this is the first time your work has been read and you desperately want it to be felt and understood. You feel naked, stripped of all your defences and so wholly identified with your script that each word of criticism can be felt as a personal attack. Yet you have to fight against these feelings and remain open to criticism if you are to develop as a writer, because feedback sessions can be as beneficial to your creative process as all the stages of learning you have been through so far. When the feedback process is working well it can generate highly stimulating and creative discussions about your script. A fresh mind on your work can help you probe more deeply into your subject and give you insights that might not have occurred to you while you were working alone. Also, as in any good therapy session, an apparently irresolvable problem, once shared, can throw up some possible solutions and give you the renewed energy you need for writing the next draft. Finally it is important to remember that you have written a film in order to affect an audience; your feedback session is an initial taste of how successful you have been in your aims.

Whether to be writer, writer-director or collaborator?

In the theatre it's normal for the writer to initiate and develop the play, working largely alone until, satisfied that the play is finished, he or she finds a director for the project. The theatre director's job is then quite clear; his task is to realize the writer's play. The writer is traditionally present at the first read-through and main rehearsals of the first production of a new play and the final refinements to the text are made as a result of seeing how the play is working in performance.

Such clearly defined norms for the roles of writer and director don't exist in the film industry. This is mainly due to the hybrid nature of the film medium. It is the director who draws together all the different artistic contributions: writing, directing, acting, art-direction, camera, sound, editing and music, which in combination, as we discovered in Part One of this book, go to making up screen language. Also it is a truism in the film industry that the final film is made in the editing suit. This is why authorship is usually deemed to lie with the director unless the work is already celebrated in another medium, such as the films made of Tennessee Williams' stage plays or of any other great theatre writer's work.

It is not difficult to see why the writer-director is an ideal model – the self-expression that has gone into making the screenplay can be realized in screen language without the discontinuity of handing the script over to another for interpretation. Many of the films I have written about in this book have been made by writer-directors. Bergman and Tarantino began their career in films as screenwriters. Bergman's published screenplays are far from merely being blueprints for his films, particularly *Wild Strawberries* and *Fanny and Alexander,* which are both as complex and absorbing to read as any good novel. If you read *Wild Strawberries* carefully you will find that the text indicates a greater complexity than Bergman was able to realize in the finished film, because film requires a certain simplicity so that it can put its point across without losing the audience. Pasolini, another writer-director, was already an established novelist before he entered films as a screenwriter and later began to direct his own work. Bertolucci, who believes that 'cinema is the true poetic language' * began his artistic career as a poet. Tarkovsky was certainly influenced by his father who was a celebrated Russian poet. And Greenaway has been so influenced by his fine art background that it is difficult to see how anyone else could direct his screenplays.

But anyone who has either written a screenplay or directed a film will know what a gruelling prospect combining both tasks can be. The writer-director must have an enormous amount of creative energy to sustain a project from the birth of the idea through the writing, directing and editing processes. Also, having talent and skills in both writing and directing remains a relatively rare combination.

*Ephraim Katz, *The International Film Encyclopedia* (Macmillan, 1980) p.116.

This is why many directors choose collaboration, which they also find more creatively stimulating than working alone. It enables them to be fully integrated into the writing process, so that they can realize their own vision, while benefiting from the talent and craft skills of their writer collaborator. Buñuel chose to work in this way. His films, though inimitably his, also show the distinctly different inputs of his three major writing collaborators, as demonstrated by the difference and similarity in both style and theme in *The Exterminating Angel*, which he scripted with Luis Alcoriza, *Viridiana*, which he scripted with Julio Alejandro, and his later works, such as *Belle de Jour* and *The Discreet Charm of the Bourgeoisie*, which he scripted with Jean-Claude Carrière. We can see the same kind of change in Billy Wilder's films. His first major collaborator was Charles Brackett, with whom he wrote most of his early work, including *Sunset Boulevard* and *Double Indemnity*, and his later work, which included *The Apartment* and *Some Like it Hot*, was written with I. A. L. Diamond. Forming such collaborations, so that both parties can maximize their creative potential, demands a remarkable compatibility. If this is achieved, as in Buñuel's and Wilder's case, it can give stunning results.

But such collaboration is not for everyone and some writers prefer to write the screenplay in close consultation with the director, but for the boundaries between their two roles to remain clearly defined. In this model the initial idea may be the writer's or the director's, and there will be regular meetings between the two throughout the scripting process. Sometimes the producer is also part of this process.

One director who has been successful using this model is Alain Resnais. His highly personal style is apparent in all of his films. This may be because many of the writers he has worked with (such as Robbe-Grillet on *Last Year at Marienbad* and Marguerite Duras on *Hiroshima Mon Amour*, both top French novelists, and David Mercer on *Providence*, a leading British television writer), have shared his preoccupation with the somewhat blurred boundaries between our experience of the present, the past and memory. Resnais minimizes the discontinuity between writer and director by realizing their work faithfully, but with the additional benefit of having been a party to their creative process. On the writing of *Hiroshima Mon Amour* Duras writes: 'Their [Resnais's and Jarlot's] advice was always precious, and I was never able to begin work on any episode without submitting the preceding one to them and listening to their comments, which were always lucid, demanding, and productive.' *

Finally, the most common model in the film industry at present is for the writer to develop the screenplay in consultation with the producer – the idea being either the writer's or the producer's. (This was David Puttnam's preferred method of working.) The director is then found when the screenplay is ready to go into production and the final rewrites will be done in consultation with the director. The system is more similar to the theatre model, in the sense that the director works on the final rewrites of a screenplay rather than being a party to its conception and development, and his or her task is to interpret the text and translate it into film.

There are obvious financial reasons for this approach. The producer, with the backing of a production company, can afford to pay the writer. Although it may make artistic sense, it is not often considered economically sensible to bring the director into the picture until the production company has finally decided to make the film. Most production companies commission a great many more projects than they actually make, on the basis that it is only when they have the finished screenplay that they can really judge whether it's worth making into a film. Although there are some producers who prefer to back the director's choice of project and who see the artistic responsibility for the script development as an intrinsic part of the director's role. This approach applied especially to those who adhered to the auteur theory, such as French producer Anatol Dauman. He played an important part in

*Marguerite Duras, *Hiroshima Mon Amour and Une Aussi Longue Absence* (Calder and Boyars Ltd, 1966) p.7.

enabling many of the world's top directors, such as Alain Resnais, Jean-Luc Godard, Robert Bresson, Walerian Borowczyk, Wim Wenders, Volker Schlöndorff, Andrei Tarkovsky and many more, to make the films of their choice according to their own artistic judgement. In other words he always put the director first and backed whatever project they wanted to make next irrespective of the script.

If your screenplay survives the course and finally goes into production, the excitement of being a part of a team putting on a show for an audience is one of the reasons, apart from a love of film, that many writers choose the screenwriting profession. The process of making the film, like that of putting on a play, can give you the opportunity to get away from the isolation of being alone in a room day after day, creating an imaginary world which is entirely subject to your control but with only your imaginary characters for company. Whereas engaging with the film-making team, at first the producer and director and later the actors and crew, can, despite the power struggles and manipulation games, be great fun and can also bring fresh stimulation, new energy and new ideas to your development as a writer. Discussing your characters with the actors, and hearing your dialogue spoken aloud for the first time, is an invaluable learning experience as is the process of cutting your scenes and images together, either in the film editing room or on your computer screen. It is here that the magic of the film editor's craft becomes all-important. Entire sequences may be cut together in ways the screenwriter never thought of. Scenes which appeared important in the script may be dropped altogether or rearranged as the overall structure of the story is once more considered, this time in the light of the practical reality of the shot material. Finally, for a screenwriter, there is nothing more rewarding than seeing your work on screen, in front of an audience, for the first time.

17 'And they all lived . . .'

If we hear the words 'Once upon a time' or 'Once in an old castle in the midst of a large and dense forest . . .' many of us still feel a familiar tingling of excitement – we are about to be transported into the strange and magical world of the fairy story. These stories, which have been handed down from generation to generation, first by word-of-mouth, then written down, and most recently through film and television, are instantly recognizable and at the same time most extra-ordinary. A wicked queen transforms herself into a witch in order to give her daughter a poisoned apple; a beautiful princess is imprisoned by her jealous father in a tiny room at the top of a tall tower where she must wait until a handsome prince rescues her; a boy climbs to the top of a huge beanstalk, which he discovers growing outside his bedroom window, and finds himself in a strange and dangerous new world; in punishment for a sin a handsome prince is imprisoned in a castle and condemned to inhabit a beast's body – only the kiss of unconditional love can free him from this evil spell.

Fairy stories are always optimistic, although lasting happiness is never gained without a long and difficult journey and many challenging incidents along the way. The heroes and heroines the child identifies with always live '. . . happily ever after' because they have learnt from the many moral dilemmas and tests of character they have encountered on their journey. These are the rites of passage which assist children in those most difficult questions of childhood, which Bruno Bettelheim in *The Uses of Enchantment* defines as: 'Who am I? How ought I deal with life's problems? And what might I become?'* These are all questions which many of us remain bound up with for much of our adult lives, which is one of the reasons why fairy stories continue to be so compelling; not just because they are exciting and magical and remind us of our childhood but because they deal with the ageless and timeless archetypal conflicts at the root of all our hopes and fears and they tell us what we want to hear – that as long as we are good people and act wisely all will be well in the end.

But optimism is not a characteristic of the grown-up's fairy story, the myth, which is more usually tragic. Myths are also archetypal stories and in their traditional form they also tell of fantastic events taking place in fantastic worlds. But, unlike fairy stories, the characters in myths are always larger than life, superhuman, and their conflicts, which represent the full range of human conflicts caused by the aspirations and frailties deep within our individual and collective psyche, also have a larger than life, timeless quality. This is why, for instance, the plights of Oedipus, or Jason and Medea, or Orpheus and Eurydice are as relevant to us now as they were to the ancient Greeks. This is also why we like to see the essence of the stories acted out, over and over again, in the guise of new characters and new periods in history.

Aristotle said that 'the friend of wisdom is the friend of myth'. A mythic story is a story that has its roots in the universal experience, which is why all great stories are, almost by definition, mythic stories. But it is no good for a writer to set out with the primary intention of writing a mythic story. The writer's job is to delve into the truth, which, as we have seen, can only be found in the particular and, if Apollo looks kindly on you, the truth that you find might turn out to be mythic.

Ingmar Bergman, in Oscar's speech from the opening scene of *Fanny and Alexander*,* put it this way:

*Bruno Bettelheim, *The Uses of Enchantment* (Thames & Hudson, 1976) p.47.
*Ingmar Bergman, *Fanny and Alexander* (Pantheon Books, 1983) p.26.

'My only talent, if you can call it talent in my case, is that I love this little world inside the thick walls of this playhouse. And I'm fond of the people who work in this little world. Outside is the big world, and sometimes the little world succeeds for a moment in reflecting the big world, so that we understand it better. Or is it perhaps that we give the people who come here the chance of forgetting for a while . . . ?'

Acknowledgements

First I should like to thank my parents, Mary and Percy Potter, to whom this book is dedicated, and my husband, Brian Clark, for our many stimulating discussions about every aspect of this book, and for his detailed feedback on the manuscript.

I should also like to thank: Professor Brian Huberman of Rice University Media Centre, for our many enjoyable conversations about mythology and the Western genre; my former colleagues at the National Film and Television School, Beaconsfield, in particular Steve Gough, Shane Connaughton and Roger Crittenden, and all my former students who over the years contributed, through many stimulating workshop discussions, to the contents of this book, in particular Kim Flitcroft, Beeban Kidron, Gillies Mackinnon, Michael Caton Jones, Jean Stewart, Ashley Pharaoh, Shawn Slovo, Lena Voudouri, Gary Sinyor, Sal Anderson and many more. I would also like to thank Norman Jewison for inviting me to run the first screenwriting programme at the Canadian Centre for Advanced Film Studies, Ann Petrie for her encouragement and Lord David Puttnam for his support.

I should like to thank the directors, producers and production companies who have responded so positively to the book and who have personally sent me their best wishes with their permission to use stills from their films including: Paolo and Vittorio Taviani, Bernardo Bertolucci, Peter Greenaway, Jerome Hellman of Jerome Hellman Productions Inc, John Schlesinger who gave me stills from *Midnight Cowboy* from his

Acknowledgements

personal stills collection, and Artificial Eye Film Company. Janet Tovey helped me select the stills, and the Surrey Institute of Art and Design gave me technical support. Thanks to my agent Laura Morris and my editors Michael Earley and David Salmo, for making this new revised edition possible. Finally I thank the British Film Institute for use of their facilities and stills library, MGM, Miramax, DreamWorks Pictures and Svensk Filmindustri. I am sorry I am unable to thank Universal Studios as they refused permission to use stills from *Touch of Evil*. Best efforts have been made to contact the copyright holders for all the stills in this book before publication. If notified I undertake to rectify errors or omissions at the earliest opportunity.

Index